THE VANTAGE OF LAW

T0347933

The Vantage of Law
Its Role in Thinking about
Law, Judging and Bills of Rights

JAMES ALLAN
University of Queensland, Australia

Routledge
Taylor & Francis Group

LONDON AND NEW YORK

First published 2011 by Ashgate Publishing

2 Park Square, Milton Park, Abingdon, Oxon OX14 4RN
711 Third Avenue, New York, NY 10017, USA

Routledge is an imprint of the Taylor & Francis Group, an informa business

First issued in paperback 2016

Copyright © 2011 James Allan

James Allan has asserted his right under the Copyright, Designs and Patents Act, 1988, to be identified as the author of this work.

All rights reserved. No part of this book may be reprinted or reproduced or utilised in any form or by any electronic, mechanical, or other means, now known or hereafter invented, including photocopying and recording, or in any information storage or retrieval system, without permission in writing from the publishers.

Notice:
Product or corporate names may be trademarks or registered trademarks, and are used only for identification and explanation without intent to infringe.

British Library Cataloguing in Publication Data
The vantage of law : its role in thinking about law,
judging and bills of rights. -- (Applied legal philosophy)
1. Law and ethics. 2. Law--Interpretation and
construction. 3. Judicial process. 4. Human rights.
I. Title II. Series
340.1'12-dc22

Library of Congress Cataloging-in-Publication Data
Allan, James, 1960-
The vantage of law : its role in thinking about law, judging, and bills of rights / by James Allan.
   p. cm. -- (Applied legal philosophy)
Includes bibliographical references and index.
ISBN 978-1-4094-3060-5 (hardback)
1. Jurisprudence--Philosophy. 2. Law and ethics. I. Title.

K230.A45A34 2011
340'.112--dc22

                                                                    2011013142

ISBN 978-1-4094-3060-5 (hbk)
ISBN 978-1-138-26148-8 (pbk)

Contents

Preface

This book attempts to combine bits of legal philosophy and bits of constitutional law, wrapping them up together by stressing the importance of vantage in thinking about certain of the key issues they raise. It attempts that very tricky task of trying to say something at least partially new, and preferably in an interesting and enjoyable way.

The bulk of this book is brand new and started from scratch, though some of the ideas I have had for some time and have expressed in various ways in various publications over the years. In Chapters 3, 4 and 5, however, I reworked in small part bits of recent articles and chapters of mine and combined this with the general flow of my argument. So in Chapter 3 I made use of my 'The Travails of Justice Waldron' from (G. Huscroft, ed.) *Expounding the Constitution: Essays in Constitutional Theory* (CUP, New York, 2008); in Chapter 4 'Thin Beats Fat Yet Again – Conceptions of Democracy' (2006) 25 *Law & Philosophy* 533 and 'Jeremy Waldron and the Philosopher's Stone' (2008) 45 *San Diego Law Review* 133; and in Chapter 5 'Rights, Paternalism, Constitutions and Judges' from (G. Huscroft and P. Rishworth) *Litigating Rights: Perspectives from Domestic and International Law* (Hart, 2002) and 'Portia, Bassanio or Dick the Butcher? Constraining Judges in the Twenty-First Century?' (2006) 17 *King's College Law Journal* 1.

I owe thanks to my friends and colleagues in Australia and overseas who read earlier versions of this book and offered comments, criticisms and suggestions. Thank you. And I owe a debt of gratitude, as always, to my wife, Heather, and our children, Cameron and Bronwyn.

James Allan
December, 2010

Introduction

This is not a book that aims to construct an all-elucidating, philosophically sophisticated theory of law. Nor will it urge some particular, grand, unifying concept of law. Frankly, I am sceptical that there is any such all-encompassing theory or concept of law – one preceded by the definite article 'the' – that can be persuasively generated by analytical or conceptual argument or by empirical data, or by some combination of the two. The one, single, general theory of law for the modern age that was the subject of William Twining's satire back in 1978[1] is no less a mirage or dream three decades on. That, at any rate, is my view.

That having been made clear, the astute reader may already have noted that the title of this book intentionally alludes to H.L.A. Hart's *The Concept of Law*, to my mind (and many others') the best book available to introduce the reader to the central and persistent questions and problems of legal theory. Indeed, it is a *tour de force*, focusing as it does on three questions: *1)* How do legal obligations (and law) differ from, and seem similar to, orders backed by threats (or law as the gunman writ large)? *2)* How do legal obligations and legal rules relate to, and differ from, moral obligations and moral rules? *3)* What are rules and to what extent is law a matter of rules? In giving his answers to those three recurrent issues or questions Hart spawned a voluminous literature and provided many major insights, stretching from the distinction between core and fringe applications of a rule, to the notion of a rule of recognition, to an argument for why law (and legal obligations) should be kept separate from morality (and moral obligations).

Yet while it is true that Hart at one point claims that his 'analysis in these terms of primary and secondary rules has this explanatory power',[2] and even that the 'union of primary and secondary rules is at the centre of a legal system',[3] he goes on explicitly to say that his analysis 'is not the whole',[4] and earlier on says that the book's 'purpose is not to provide a definition of law … [but to] provid[e] an improved analysis of the distinctive structure of a municipal legal system'.[5] Frederick Schauer goes further. In the course of claiming that Hart's *Concept of Law* is his signal work, a lasting achievement, Schauer argues, convincingly to my mind, that '[i]t is not at all apparent that *The Concept of Law* was very much

---

1   See William Twining, 'The Great Juristic Bazaar' (1978) 14 *Journal of the Society of Public Teachers of Law* 185.

2   H.L.A. Hart, *Concept of Law* (Oxford: Oxford University Press, 1961), p. 95.

3   *Ibid.*, p. 96.

4   *Ibid.*, p. 96.

5   *Ibid.*, pp. 16–17.

focused on actually delineating the concept of law. It is not even clear that its goal was to provide any concept of law at all.'[6]

So while Hart can be read as offering a series of highly perceptive, discerning and thought-provoking insights into *the* concept of law, he can also be read as offering these powerful, useful insights without staking his all on there actually being any such single, grand, 'definite article' variety concept or theory or conception of law.

Whether that outlook, of being sceptical of unifying, all-explaining concepts and theories, is the most convincing way to read Hart or not, it will most definitely be the basis on which this book proceeds.

I will also follow Hart's *Concept of Law* practice of keeping footnotes to a minimum, reserving the noting of related readings and references to a section at the end of the book. I think the absence of numerous footnotes and their tangential arguments and digressions and appeals to authority can make a book better, and certainly make it more readable. Those who disagree or disapprove will, I hope, bear with this practice.

Lastly, as regards any further parallels to *The Concept of Law*, I note that Hart there shunned adopting the appeal court judge's vantage or perspective – one which is so often the implicit vantage or viewpoint in legal writing today (and more so even in legal education today where students often are fed little more than a steady diet of highest appeal court cases). Recall that up to chapter nine of *The Concept of Law* Hart wrote from the vantage of the outside observer, the visiting Martian. In these chapters, as I indicated above, Hart described how legal rules differ from, and are similar to, orders backed by threats. He described the extent to which legal obligations can be understood as flowing from and comprised of a system of social rules of a particular recognized or validated sort. He even pointed out the ways in which legal rules can differ from, and be similar to, moral rules.

His interest thus far was to describe aspects of any legal system. It was broadly descriptive, on the plane of the copula 'is'. Nothing thus far involved Hart or his readers adopting the judge's vantage. Indeed, even in the little bits of chapter seven where Hart did discuss adjudication – where he noted that the vast preponderance of disputes simply do not end up before a court let alone an appeal court, that the core applications of legal rules generally do not admit of the sort of uncertainty needed to lead people to spend the vast amounts of money required to take those disputes to court, and that in those extremely rare instances where the application of a legal rule does fall into what he termed 'the penumbra of doubt' so that a dispute might end up in court and a point-of-application judge might have discretion – even in that discussion of adjudication, Hart did not adopt the vantage or perspective of the judge.

This forswearing of the judge's perspective did not end when, part way into chapter nine of *The Concept of Law*, Hart no longer wrote from the vantage of the

---

6   Frederick Schauer, '(Re)Taking Hart' (2006) 119 *Harvard Law Review* 852, at p. 880.

visiting Martian. Hart certainly shifted perspective in chapter nine. He nowhere there argued that people do – as a matter of widespread fact – separate law and morality. Instead, he argued that people *should* separate them. He shifted to the plane of the copula 'ought'. But even here he did not adopt the judge's vantage. Rather, he adopted the vantage of a citizen within a legal system, someone who has a Benthamite concern for the gradual, piecemeal reform of his or her legal system. From that participant's vantage – *not* some appeal court judge's vantage overlooking the few unusual disputes passing that way where the legal rules regularly leave the outcome uncertain and unresolved by settled expectations – Hart argued that it is good to keep separate law and morality, 'law as it is' and 'law as it ought to be'.

I will return in Chapter 1 to the arguments for that 'should' claim. Here, I simply wish to emphasize the extent to which Hart shunned the judge's vantage, and so relatedly left largely unexamined the sort of issues involved in any theory of adjudication, in favour of first the visiting Martian's vantage and latterly the concerned citizen's.

This book, too, is concerned with vantages. Unlike Hart in *The Concept of Law* it will not wholly shun the judge's vantage. But neither will it make that vantage pre-eminent, explicitly or implicitly, as seems so often the case these days. In fact, the centrality and importance of vantage in understanding law, and in assessing bills of rights, and in deciding on how one wants judges to interpret and resolve cases, and much else besides, will be the cornerstone claim of this book. It will be the basis for any interesting insights that follow.

One final preliminary point or warning. As far as possible I will avoid labels, and arguments over whether or when or how labels do or do not fit. My goal is not to argue for the merits of some single, all-elucidating understanding of law. But neither is it to argue that some label or other is best understood as comprising positions A through E rather than positions C through H or B through G.

Take the various ongoing debates about the merits and deficiencies of legal positivism. My view on this is one I imagine might be shared by Ronald Dworkin, whose substantive views otherwise generally leave me cold. It is that too much of the debate within and about legal positivism has become almost scholastic. One reads about Kramer on Raz on Perry on Hart or about Dyzenhaus on Dworkin on Fuller on Hobbes or about Waluchow on Coleman on, well, whatever. Of course, this is a caricature. But not one that is unrecognizably related to reality. At the same time, more and more effort is expended on labels and categorizations. To the non-aficionado, even to the rather well-informed jurisprude, the important issues at stake can often seem obscured by the insularity of the terms of debate. One is reminded of substantive debate conducted between American (or for that matter Canadian) constitutional law scholars – there is so much dispute about texts and terms and authorities and the meaning of those authorities that the reader can easily lose sight of the substance of the disagreement. By then, of course, any interest the reader had has long since dissipated.

If we can see some of the strengths and weaknesses of particular ways of understanding how law relates to morality or whether a bill of rights is desirable or how a judge ought to decide cases (and more) then what tag to attach to any particular understanding is, at most, of secondary concern, and one I leave for others. The problem is not simply that labels for virtually all abstract, complex notions (think of 'Christianity' or 'feminism' or 'jazz music') will be for essentially contested concepts[7] – concepts where what falls within their proper ambit or aegis is open to reasonable disagreement amongst smart, well-informed, reasonable, even nice people – or, put differently and in more Hartian terms, will have 'a core of settled meaning'[8] and a 'penumbra of doubt'[9] or 'uncertainty'[10] (where there would be good grounds for saying that the label did apply and good grounds for saying it did not). No, a further problem with over-great concern about classification and labels and the attendant contrast and critique of competing positions is that it is prone to distorting simplification. Go back to Twining's satire on teaching and learning legal philosophy (or perhaps 'jurisprudence', to make the same point about labels):

> The first lesson was entitled Cocktail Party. Each student was provided with a list of 100 jurists and, associated with each name, a single word or phrase – for example, Kelsen – basic norm; Savigny – *volksgeist*; Hart – union of primary and secondary rules. As the title suggested, students were required to circulate and engage in interchanges which took the form of student A dropping the name of a famous jurist and student B responding with a key word, or *vice versa*. There was a strict system of scoring. For a correct reply, according to the list, a student would be awarded one mark. But if, for example, a student in response to the key word 'principles' were to say Pound, Llewellyn, or Bentham, instead of the correct answer, Dworkin, he would be fined 3 marks.[11]

With those preliminaries out of the way, let me say something more about the structure of this book. To begin, and as I noted above, it is concerned with vantages. What effect does one's vantage or perspective or standpoint have on how one understands, say, the desirability of a bill of rights or the best way for judges to decide cases or whether law is – and whether it should be – separate from morality? Of course pointing out the importance of vantage is by no means novel. Here, though, if not always the central focus it will certainly be the motivating consideration throughout this entire book.

---

7   See W.B. Gallie, 'Essentially Contested Concepts' (1965) 56 *Proceedings of the Aristotelian Society* 167.

8   Hart, *Concept of Law*, p. 140, *inter alia*.

9   *Ibid.*, p. 119, *inter alia*.

10 *Ibid.*, p. 131, *inter alia*.

11 'The Great Juristic Bazaar', *op. cit.*, p. 190.

More importantly, I will make explicit the various vantages I ask the reader to adopt or imagine as we consider a number of different legal topics or issues in turn. The first vantage I propose to use is that of the concerned citizen. This is the person who has a stake in the legal system in which he or she lives; this concerned citizen is neither morally perfect nor immorally wicked nor even amorally indifferent. He or she is the average citizen, of limited (but by no means insignificant) altruism and sympathy, who in the vast preponderance of circumstances is law abiding.

And then there will be the judge's vantage. Normally we can take this as a judge on an appeal court, if not on the highest court of the jurisdiction. This judge will be one of a very small handful of point-of-application interpreters of the country's statutes and constitutional provisions. When in the majority in deciding a case over the meaning of some disputed provision or section, or indeed how to understand some case law precedent, what this judge says the law or Constitution is, it is. Put more brusquely, but only from one other than that judge's vantage, the Constitution or statute is what the judge says it is. And where that decision or determination involves the judge having to make – or being free to make – more or less unconstrained moral evaluations or judgments, then one can go even further. In such circumstances one might say that 'the Constitution (or statute) is what the judge thinks it should be'. In marked contrast to the concerned citizen, the judge's opinion on what should be the case can become what is the case.

And then the Holmesian Bad Man gives us a third vantage. This is the person made well known by the Legal Realists, the amoral actor whose decisions, choices and motivations are unaffected by morality. He is not immoral, just indifferent to the claims of morality *per se*. Law, though, and legal rules, constraints and obligations are decisive factors in what he does and how he acts.

In Oliver Wendell Holmes' 'The Path of the Law',[12] the Bad Man appears as a thinly veiled stand-in for the office lawyer. Lawyers are not paid to give moral advice. They are paid to give legal advice. They tell their clients what the law demands of them (not what morality demands) and what the expected legal outcome is likely to be.

Now the vantages and perspectives of the amoral Bad Man and the client-advising lawyer do not align perfectly; there is not a 1:1 correlation. Lawyers have some constraints imposed on them by professional ethics, by obligations to the court, and by their own consciences (that is, by morality). The average lawyer is not himself or herself a Bad Man and so, at the margins at least, the advice that a lawyer gives to a client will not be wholly, solely and completely a function of what the law allows, forbids or makes possible – at least not in every possible situation.

That point conceded, the overlap between the client-advising lawyer's vantage and the Bad Man's vantage is nevertheless exceedingly large indeed. Both are overwhelmingly focused on what 'the courts will do in fact'.[13] It is law that

---

12   O.W. Holmes, 'The Path of the Law' (1897) 10 *Harvard Law Review* 457.
13   *Ibid.*, p. 461.

concerns them. Morality is only of interest when made so by the law. Hence, except where I explicitly distinguish between them, the Bad Man's vantage will subsume that of the average client-advising lawyer in what follows.

Those are the three primary vantages I will use, the ones I will be dealing with for the most part.

There will, though, be others that will be worth considering at various times. One such ancillary vantage is that of the Visiting Martian. This is the vantage of the descriptive sociologist, the outside observer – a non-citizen with no stake in what is being observed and described other than, perhaps, a desire for accuracy and clarity. This vantage rests as much as any on the plane of the copula 'is', of what happens to be the case or the fact of the matter.

Another is the vantage of the legislator or law maker. This person, as part of the group of all other legislators of some assembly, can turn policy options into law. To the extent that law involves force and duty-imposing rules carrying sanctions for non-compliance, the legislator (with enough of his or her colleagues) can bring these into being. Of course the legislator might look to morality, to wealth creation, to likely future consequences and much more in seeking to create a law. But at least as far as the 'general rules known in advance and applying to all' variety of law is concerned, it is the preserve of the legislator.

There are even more peripheral or ancillary vantages that will, on occasion, be of interest. Let me mention four such vantages now. They can be loosely denominated as the Omniscient Being's Vantage, the Moral Philosopher's Vantage, the Sanctimonious Man's Vantage, and the Law Professor's Vantage. Let us briefly take each in turn.

It will be helpful at times to be able to imagine being in possession of, say, all future consequences of some action or statute or decision, or of what is the morally right thing to do (assuming, for the moment, that moral rightness is a human-independent or mind-independent quality), or even of what some legislator intended when voting to enact the statutory words she did. We can, of course, sometimes only imagine a being in possession of such knowledge, given that we are limited biological creatures. From the Omniscient Being's or God's-Eye Vantage, though, we can at least put ourselves in the position of imagining a being (or Being) with access to all such knowledge. That might prove useful.

As the question of the relation between law and morality will come up – in fact we will start the first chapter on this topic – it might also be helpful at times to look at things through the eyes of a moral philosopher. Setting up this Moral Philosopher's Vantage will be helpful not least as an explicit counterbalance to the Judge's Vantage. Some judges (and some of their more enthusiastic proponents and followers) may think that they are experts in moral philosophy, or alternatively that they have superior moral perspicacity or more finely tuned moral sentiments, than their fellow citizens. Yet the former claim is a claim to professional expertise in moral philosophy – and one that very, very few actual judges (no real-life ones of whom I am aware) could meet by producing their doctorates or published books in some area related to moral philosophy. Meanwhile the latter claims, to judges' superior moral insight or perspicacity (as opposed to more pedestrian-type arguments for letting judges decide certain things on balance of power or institutional superiority grounds) are downright implausible. Spending three years at law school and then a dozen or more usually practising law in a big law firm or as a top courtroom lawyer is not obviously linked to engendering finer moral qualities in oneself than in those who follow different career paths – just about any alternate career path at all!

Accordingly, and Ronald Dworkin's interpretive theories notwithstanding, we will want to be able to distinguish the Judge's Vantage from the Moral Philosopher's Vantage. And we will want to be able to do this even though we are well aware that moral philosophers – top moral philosophers too – disagree amongst themselves on virtually every important issue, including over the relative merits of moral realism (or moral objectivism) versus moral scepticism (or non-cognitivism) and over the competing attractions of a Humean or Kantian theory of reason. This Moral Philosopher's Vantage is *not* the vantage of someone who has science-like right answers to moral disputes, nor even a science-like method for attempting to resolve such disputes. Its usefulness will lie in showing us what judges lack rather than in providing some technique or method for resolving moral debates by appealing to expertise.

What I have dubbed the Sanctimonious Man's Vantage is the vantage of the man or woman who is wholly self-assured in his or her moral judgments or evaluations. This person is convinced that he or she has a pipeline to God on all important moral issues; this person's evaluation or judgment on any contentious moral issue – same-sex marriage, headscarves in schools, euthanasia, affirmative action, capital punishment, anything at all – is always the right one. Or rather, *mirabile dictu*, this person is always wholly convinced that it is. So when his or her view fails to prevail in the legislature, or in the courts, our Sanctimonious Man tends to attribute the outcome to the moral blindness or stupidity or wickedness of some, or all, of those who disagreed.

The last peripheral or ancillary vantage I mention here is the Law Professor's Vantage. I include this perspective not because I am one, or because many readers of this book are likely to be one, or even because it is wise to flatter those whom you are trying to win over. (Well, these are not the only reasons for including this vantage.) To the extent that law professors indirectly sway the odd judge who happens to read one of their articles or books, or manages to shape future lawyers when educating them, or even contrives to influence a few citizens at large in, say, a newspaper column, this vantage is worth marking out.

So that makes three main vantages and some ancillary and even more ancillary ones that I have tentatively, and in a preliminary way, set out – those of the Concerned Citizen, the Judge, the Bad Man, the Visiting Martian, the Legislator, the Omniscient Being, the Moral Philosopher, the Sanctimonious Man and (perhaps leastly) the Law Professor. Yet a book concerned with the importance of vantage or perspective or standpoint in understanding legal debates, in giving grounds for preferring some interpretive theory or judicial approach to another, in thinking about whether law and morality should largely be kept separate, in pondering how best to appoint judges, in detailing the pros and cons of a bill of rights, and more, needs also to place those vantages in context. Not everyone lives in a nice, benevolent, liberal democracy where the vast preponderance of citizens think their system's laws not only are overwhelmingly good ones but also that they have come into being through a process that is by and large a morally good one too. Theories of law or of adjudication that presuppose (explicitly or implicitly) a nice, benevolent, liberal democracy may not transfer well – or at all – to less salubrious surroundings. And let us recall that for most of mankind's life in society the governing legal and political regime, at least from our perspective here today, has been something less than benevolent (to put it as kindly as possible). In terms of that same time-frame, democracy is a newborn baby, with a version that enfranchised only a very few emerging in classical Greece, then disappearing for millennia until the more modern, more enfranchising version showed its head little more than two centuries ago. And, of course, billions of people today still do not live under legal systems that could remotely be described as democratic.

Likewise, slavery has been a common practice in human affairs until extremely recent times – condoned by the Catholic Church, practised widely, including in Islamic countries and in some of the newly independent American colonies, and still alive today (albeit kept out of sight as much as possible).

My point is that any theory of adjudication, say, or of how law and morality do, and should, interact that necessarily positions itself in a thinly disguised modern-day United States or United Kingdom or Canada or jurisdiction in western Europe will be a most provincial one, even as regards the way the world is at present. In historical terms it will be of fringe interest at most. To discount, or be able to discount, the role of fear and violence in the operation of a legal system indicates good fortune, no doubt, but also the limited applicability of what is propounded.

That means that in addition to vantage, the sort of legal system can matter too. A concerned citizen in a nice, benevolent, liberal democracy might well come to different conclusions about the interrelationship of law and morality, for instance, or the advantages of a bill of rights than would a concerned citizen in a brutal dictatorship or cleric-dominated one (where law is given, or said to have, divine warrant and antecedents) or even one under direct threat of invasion or wartime attack.

I want to leave myself room to consider not just how vantage matters, but how the sort of legal system in place might matter too. My default assumption or position will be that we are in fact discussing what I have loosely called a nice, benevolent, liberal democracy. Yet for the purposes of clarifying what is at stake, and even of making certain claims more widely applicable, I will moot three other sorts of legal system. One is the Wicked Legal System. At its worst this could be a Hitleresque or Stalinesque or Maoist dictatorship under which tens of millions and more end up dead and violence and fear is pervasive. Less brutally and lethally (far less so in fact), it might be an apartheid South Africa-type regime or something along the lines of Mugabe's Zimbabwe or Milosevic's Serbia.

Another is the theocracy or caliphate-type regime, what I will call the Theocratic Legal System. Here, law is asserted to have an explicitly divine origin, and hence for all who accept such assertions is by definition wholly moral. If God is the ultimate author of this jurisdiction's laws, then those laws (ignoring interpretive disputes for the moment) cannot diverge from what is morally good and right nor command anything morally repugnant. 'Law as it is' correlates perfectly with 'law as it ought to be' because law, in this jurisdiction, has been laid down by God.

The benevolent, the wicked and the theocratic by no means exhaust the general sorts of legal systems on offer, or of those that have actually existed. One more will suffice for our purposes. Let us call this the So-So Legal System. In comparative historical and world terms things here are pretty good. But they are noticeably worse than in our nice, benevolent, liberal democracy. Perhaps we can think of Russia or Venezuela today or Britain in the eighteenth century as exemplars of a So-So Legal System (by our standards today, of course).

In addition to those vantages sketched above, then, I will also make use of these four sorts of legal system – the Benevolent Legal System, the Wicked Legal System, the Theocratic Legal System, and the So-So Legal System.

That leaves me only to introduce the topics I will discuss in this book. Broadly speaking, there are three. The first is a much-discussed one, which might be subsumed under this question: Is it good or desirable to keep separate law and morality, 'law as it happens to be' and 'law as it ought to be'? This is a 'should' question, not an 'is' question about the extent to which morality in fact is or is not interwoven into law. This claim or insistence, that what law is and what it ought to be should be kept separate, lies at the heart of the Benthamite project. You need to know what you have before you can improve it, reform it and make it better (and that holds true even if one is not inclined to measure 'betterness' in terms of increased utility or welfare or happiness).

Here's how Jeremy Bentham's disciple John Austin frames the issue:

> The existence of law is one thing: its merit or demerit is another. Whether it be or not be is one enquiry; whether it be or be not conformable to an assumed standard is another enquiry. A law, which actually exists, is a law, though we happen to dislike it, or though it vary from the text, by which we regulate approbation and disapprobation.[14]

Now that particular formulation, in severing so fully the 'is' question or questions ('Do people, as a matter of widespread fact, keep separate law and morality and in what ways do legal rules have moral components or involve moral evaluations at the point-of-application?') from the 'ought' question or questions ('Should people keep separate law and morality and should legal rules have moral components or involve moral evaluations at the point-of-application?') may oversimplify things.

---

14   John Austin, *The Province of Jurisprudence Determined* (Rumble, ed., Cambridge: Cambridge University Press, 1994 – first published 1832), p. 157.

For instance, as far as the amount of moral input or evaluating at the point-of-application is concerned, the 'should' question may be one of degree. Do we prefer our judges to have lots, some or as little as possible moral input, given that we live in a world where legislatures sometimes enact statutes that do little more than set out a moral test (e.g. 'best interests of the child' or 'good faith bargaining') and where many constitutions have bills of rights which, in effect, set out a series of vague, amorphous moral entitlements in the language of rights? Put differently, the live debate (as we know from an 'is' judgment) may not be whether we should eliminate *all* dependence by judges on moral evaluations but rather whether we should aim to *minimize* that dependence.

In any event, this book begins with issues related to that broad topic of the separation of law and morality. Perhaps approaching these issues from some of the different vantages sketched above will be of some interest.

The second broad topic I will tackle is judges and judging. Here we will need to consider the extent to which we can expect or rely on unelected judges to constrain themselves, the appointment of judges, the tensions between the demands of certainty and flexibility, the notion of the rule of law, the desirability of referring to (and deferring to) foreign law, democracy and more. Again, vantage will be stressed.

The third and final topic will be bills of rights. Connected or related subjects will include ways of understanding rights, their connection to paternalism, a brief mapping exercise, the issue of their interpretation, a digression on statutory bills of rights, and how these instruments appear from the various vantages.

Each of these three broad topics – the desirability of separating law and morality, judges and judging, and bills of rights – is clearly related to the others. The first two have been perennially important; for better or worse all three are in today's world.

Chapter 1

Separating Law and Morality – I

There are various ways to ask about the relationship between law and morality. The sort of question you ask might affect the answer you receive. Who asks the question might also affect what answer seems most plausible or appropriate.

The old-fashioned Benthamite question might be any of these: Is 'law as it is' distinct from or separate from 'law as it ought to be'? Is it good or desirable to keep separate law and morality, 'law as it happens to be' and 'law as it ought to be'? Should we insist that what law is be kept separate from what law ought to be?

Moving forward almost two centuries, Hart asked if there were any necessary connections between law and morality, though he argued and concluded that it is good to – hence that we should – keep separate law and morality (which is to answer one of the older Benthamite queries). Hart also asked the far simpler question of whether there were *any* connections between law and morality before answering that, contingently, there could be some. The legislators might draw on their moral convictions when deciding on the need for, and then wording and then enacting a statute. The point-of-application judges, when deciding how to interpret a statute where the application of that statute to the particular facts leaves the outcome uncertain and debatable – where it falls into the 'penumbra of doubt'[1] – might resolve the case and the uncertainty by appealing to their moral sentiments. Indeed Hart could have made the same point as regards the exercise of prosecutorial discretion, say, or the allocation of police resources.

And even in a Wicked Legal System, some few people, such as the top dictator and a few close allies, presumably think the bulk of the laws are good – that the ones facilitating this pogrom or that mass starvation will pave the way to some utopia or an improved racial strain or what have you. And this is true even if the preponderance of the officials in this same Wicked Legal System apply the legal rules solely out of fear or hope of advancement, all too aware that these legal rules they are applying are morally revolting or despicable.

That there can be *some* connections between law and morality for some few people even in a Wicked Legal System makes it extremely likely that there will be more such connections for more people in a So-So Legal System and a Theocratic Legal System, and more still in a Benevolent Legal System.

After Hart, the way to ask about the relationship between law and morality has become more and more conceptual. Rather than the Benthamite focus on separating law from morality for the eminently practical goal of reforming and

---

1   Hart, *Concept of Law* (Oxford: Oxford University Press, 1961), p. 119 *inter alia*.

improving the former, and so of increasing overall social utility and welfare, the questions asked today are more like these: Is there some possible legal system imaginable where the legality of a norm does not depend on any of its moral properties? Is it necessarily the case that there is no connection between law and morality? Can law be defined in a way that ensures no moral elements are included in it? Is there any conceptually necessary connection between what law commands and what justice demands? Or, back to Hart (who answered this in the negative), is it a necessary truth that laws reproduce or satisfy certain demands of morality?

In addition, especially when considering this issue from the Judge's Vantage, there is an element of intramural squabbling amongst those generally known as legal positivists. Does something, some moral principle say, count as law whenever the Judge appeals to it or relies on it to decide a case? Or is more than that needed? Must what is appealed to have a particular source-based warrant? Must what is observably – albeit, contingently – accepted by a jurisdiction's officials as a valid source of law have incorporated this moral principle into law for it to count (such as where a bill of rights might be said to incorporate certain vague, amorphous moral standards, enumerated in the language of rights, into law)? Or is even that not enough?

To varying degrees, the more conceptual formulations of questions related to the relationship between law and morality all divert attention away from the original Benthamite goal, namely that of reform and of making the law better. Most of today's legal positivists, in other words, are not much (if at all) concerned with whether it is desirable or good to keep separate law and morality, 'law as it happens to be' and 'law as it ought to be'. What is or is not necessary or imaginable or possible or definable can be speculated upon with little, if any, concern for what is desirable and good. On the Benthamite approach, it is the goal of good consequences that drives the analytical concepts and conceptualizing. It is not some stand-alone desire to construct the most philosophically sophisticated or satisfying theory of law that motivates the various concepts, conceptualizing, categorizing, and even intramural squabbling over what amounts to the meaning of the words 'law' and 'legal'. Rather, it is the recognition that law can be bad, and not just in the Wicked or Theocratic or So-So Legal Systems, but on occasion also in the Benevolent Legal System.

This illustrates one of the problems with framing this issue of the separation of law and morality in terms of labels such as 'legal positivism' and 'natural law'. As noted in the Introduction, such abstract, complex notions are both essentially contested concepts as well as ones that inevitably carry with them a penumbra of doubt or of uncertainty – meaning that there will be cases where there are good grounds for saying the label 'legal positivism' *does apply*, just as there are good grounds for saying it *does not apply*.

For instance, someone of the stature of Ronald Dworkin can discuss legal positivism with no mention of (or at the very least with no emphasis on) the old-fashioned Benthamite aspect of whether 'law as it happens to be' should be kept separate from 'law as it ought to be'. For Dworkin, legal positivism is about seeing law as a function of certain rules, rules that have the status of legal rules *not* because of their content but because of their source or pedigree. For him, legal positivism is about this rule-based conceptual notion, together with its concomitant, ancillary claim that these pedigree rules determine legal outcomes in the vast preponderance of cases, and where they unusually happen not to do so the point-of-application judges simply have discretion to decide on non-legal bases such as their policy preferences or moral druthers.

The label 'legal positivism' connotes for Dworkin this idea of law as a 'model of rules'. And in responding to and criticizing that idea – in arguing that some source-based test of legal validity, some rule of recognition, is *not* the ultimate and only arbiter or determiner of what counts as law because some moral principles can attain that status too, due to their content and goodness – Dworkin builds a theory of law out of a theory of adjudication. Or rather, Dworkin builds a theory of law out of a theory of how judges should (and, perhaps less plausibly, how judges in fact do) decide hard cases in Benevolent Legal Systems, or maybe only in some or one such Benevolent Legal System. His adjudication-propelled theory of law has next to nothing to say about our Theocratic or So-So Legal Systems, and nothing at all to say about our Wicked Legal System (other than baldly suggesting that judges here may have to lie). Moreover, even within the confines of a Benevolent Legal System it may be that the attractiveness and plausibility of Dworkin's theories vary with the vantage adopted, that they seem considerably more persuasive from, say, the Judge's and Law Professor's and even Sanctimonious Man's vantages than from those of the Concerned Citizen or Visiting Martian or Legislator or even Bad Man.

But that is to pre-empt myself. My immediate concern relates to the indeterminacy and contestability of the label 'legal positivism'. Hart seems to take the label to encompass the position that combines: *i)* a Benthamite insistence on separating law and morality; and *ii)* an equally Benthamite propounding of the gunman or 'orders backed-by-threats' or command theory of law; with *iii)* some concern for the analytical and conceptual study of law's language and sources and effects on human beings. Yet Hart himself does much to show the weaknesses of leg *ii)*, offering the alternative that, at core, law is best seen as a system of rules.

This new leg *ii)*, as I have suggested, is the one on which Dworkin concentrates. Other post-Hart thinkers, not least those more sympathetic than Dworkin to this particular task, make leg *iii)* pre-eminent. From them comes the emphasis on conceptual analysis (grounded to some degree or other in description), and the occasional bout of intramural squabbling.

Yet nothing in the label itself, or in the task of defending or attacking 'legal positivism', requires or mandates that any one of these legs be singled out. Henceforth, therefore, I put away almost all mention of legal positivism. What interests me is leg *i)*, the old-fashioned Benthamite set of questions linked to the separating of law and morality and asked in such a way so as *not* to obscure the fact that law can be bad and can be in need of reform and can require actions at odds with what the moral sentiments of most citizens deem right and proper.

Let us start with one particular formulation of the Benthamite desire to separate law and morality, namely: Should 'law as it is' be kept separate from 'law as it ought to be'? Anyone attempting to answer that prescriptive question must first make clear what criteria he or she considers relevant or appropriate in resolving issues lying on the plane of the copula 'ought'. Are we to measure and weigh up what people *should do* (either in general or in this specific instance) on the basis of likely future good consequences, or on some deontological or rights-based alternative?

Whatever the strengths of non-consequentialist moral theories in general terms, and I am one who admittedly inclines towards thinking that in any context they are few and far between, on this particular question of whether we should keep separate law and morality it is hard to see many bases on which non-consequentialism could come into play. Unless one thinks there is some duty or right (one *not* sounding in instrumental effects) that demands or entitles us to keep law and morality separate (or, obversely, to elide them together) – and even imagining that is difficult – then this is a question that will be answered in terms of good consequences. Certainly that is the battleground on which Hart and Fuller debated this issue.

So let us rephrase the question to make plain the criteria we intend to be dispositive, namely good consequences. Translated to make that explicit, our question becomes: Will there be good consequences or bad if we keep separate 'law as it is' and 'law as it ought to be'? And in attempting to answer that question, will it matter whose vantage we have adopted?

Recall that in chapter nine of *The Concept of Law* Hart set out the good consequences he thought would flow from keeping law and morality separate, from having a separate moral platform available on which one could stand to criticize, and with luck reform, the law. The main consequences focused on by Hart were related to the likelihood of disobeying wicked or evil or perhaps only egregiously wicked laws. Hart's claim was that we will be more likely to disobey such laws when we realize that legal rules are not – or need not be – a subset of morality and that in some circumstances moral rules may have a greater claim on our allegiance. Related to that main claim, Hart also put forward the ancillary assertion that keeping the two separate is more likely to enable us to see the variety of issues at stake in deciding whether or not to obey, and then how to disobey, a valid legal rule we judge to be a bad or wicked one. We will be better placed to decide whether to flee or to engage in civil disobedience or to take up arms and fight than we would be if we blended together the two evaluations; that is Hart's ancillary consequentialist claim.

Of course the range of consequences Hart considers may well be too narrow. In fact I think it is. In Chapter 2 I will suggest there are consequences that matter a good deal more than the ones that Hart raises and on which he focuses.

That said, we can for this chapter limit ourselves to these consequences bearing on encouraging disobedience to wicked laws and all related issues. And here a notable response to Hart can be made, one that is also in terms of likely good consequences, and one that again focuses on increasing the likelihood of disobeying wicked laws. It amounts to this: Most of us simply will not see this distinction between law and morality. Once a directive gets the label 'law' appended to it, most of us will obey it. On this view, an obligation to obey whatever is called 'law' is taken almost as a given, though it will not be totally clear whether the purported 'obligation to obey' is put forward as an empirical claim (i.e., this is the way most people happen to be) or as some sort of conceptual one (i.e., the very concept of law, and hence the label, carries with it an element of obligation or obligatoriness).

Hart's consequentialist claims could be wrong in a different (though arguably related) way. It is possible that people who think that a law only counts as a law if it satisfies some sort of moral test will, *pace* Hart, be more willing to disobey egregious statutes. It is possible that a natural law mindset, or a belief that nothing egregiously infringing human rights norms gets to count as law, will make one more likely – not less likely – to stand up to *in extremis* dictators and brutal regimes.

One need not even believe this himself. It is enough to think that most others believe it. Having in place an edifice in which the posited, laid-down rules emanating from a recognized valid source are regularly infused with references to vague, amorphous, indeterminate moral guarantees or entitlements (such as those expressed in, say, the language of rights) might deliver good consequences after all. If so, the Benthamite would opt for this path that achieves good consequences over the one that gives conceptual clarity or that prevents or significantly lessens the intermingling.

So how does one go about deciding whether separating, or not separating, law and morality is likely to lead more people to disobey wicked laws? Certainly Hart offers no empirical data to back up his consequential claim. But then neither do other eminent legal philosophers such as Fuller or Dworkin. At this point I think vantage matters, and it even matters were one simply trying to design empirical tests to throw light on the question.

The Concerned Citizen

Let us start with the Concerned Citizen. From his or her point of view, the question is what will be most likely to engender an outlook that at least considers the possibility of not obeying evil government directives (not to beg the question by calling such directives 'law' just yet). Will it be to insist on having a separate moral platform or grounding on which to assess the demands of these directives or laws? Or will it be to deny these directives the designation 'law'?

Down at the vantage of the Concerned Citizen what is most obviously relevant to answering these questions is that this citizen will not be in a position to do any of the designating. This is most clear in a Wicked Legal System. Here, the Benthamite and Hartian insistence on keeping separate law and morality provides a tool for the citizen to rebel against the diktats of the occupying Nazis, or the Soviets in Poland, or the Sudanese in Darfur. The fact that the authorities designated something as law did not prevent the building up of a resistance throughout Europe during World War II or the forming of Solidarity unions in Gdansk or the creation of rebel armies in parts of Sudan.

The Benthamite claim is that these egregious directives can be called law, for that is precisely how they will be designated by the government and officials, but they can all the same be rejected or rebelled against or escaped from by citizens on moral grounds. Indeed it is the citizen's ability to make this distinction that is crucial.

Those who wish to elide together law and morality are in a difficult spot when it comes to Wicked Legal Systems. They too think societies are better off when as many citizens as possible refuse to obey egregiously wicked official directives – directives designated as 'law' by the Nazi and Soviet and Sudanese authorities. All they can offer is that the official designation of 'law' is not determinative; that citizens need not obey because these wicked directives do not count as law, or are not wholly law or fully law or law in anything other than a half-dead sense. Put more prosaically, the only advice the anti-Benthamites can offer our Concerned Citizen in a Wicked Legal System is not to take the official or government designation seriously, to decide for him or herself what counts as law and on that basis choose whether to obey or not. In other words, all the difficult and tricky moral calculations and consequentialist weightings, including when and how to disobey, get collapsed into the one single issue of whether what the regime calls and labels a law is sufficiently moral to retain that label.

There is a seeming irony here. In a Benevolent Legal System the eliders or anti-Benthamites tell us we need to avoid separating 'law as it is' and 'law as it ought to be' – we need the label 'law' only to apply to what is not unduly bad on moral grounds – because once something is designated as 'law', then citizens will obey it. Yet that is flat-out something they cannot assert in a Wicked Legal System.

From the Concerned Citizen's Vantage it seems rather obvious to me that in a Wicked Legal System there will be more likelihood of disobedience to evil laws if we keep separate law and morality. In terms of that particular sort of good consequence at least, and as regards those sorts of legal systems, Hart was right. The Concerned Citizen will be better placed to decide whether to flee or to engage in civil disobedience or to take up arms and fight by keeping the two separate rather than by blending them together.

The same appears true of So-So Legal Systems. Concerned Citizens there will also be more likely to stand up to evil laws if they are able to understand that law and morality are distinct, with distinct claims on them, with the former not automatically trumping the latter.

The Theocratic Legal System raises different issues. Here, by supposition, many citizens believe that some or many of the laws have a divine origin or warrant or sanction. For those who believe this, such laws will not be seen as evil or wicked, almost regardless of their content. Indeed the Theocratic Legal System represents a version of natural law writ large, where law is a subset of morality.

Nevertheless, there is still room even here for the Concerned Citizen (one, let us assume, who accepts that God is the ultimate author of some portion of this jurisdiction's laws) to dispute what the officials or clerics propound as the specific content or articulation of divine law. From this vantage it does not follow that 'what God laid down' (and hence, we will assume, what must be morally right) aligns in some 1:1 way with what 'this clerical regime enacted in the name of God'. Separating morality and law, from the Concerned Citizen's Vantage, can be useful in disobeying odious directives here too, at least if one suspects with me that it is easier in such a society to claim 'this officially laid-down law is not in accord with God's prescriptions' than it is to assert 'God's prescriptions tell us this in fact is not really a law (or fully a law, or more than a half-dead law, or whatever one's preferred formulation)'. And, of course, not all citizens even here will accept the claimed genealogy of the laws. Surrounded by a majority of those who do, the ability to separate law and morality would appear to be particularly useful to them.

A more negative way to make this same point is to ask how eliding 'law as it is' and 'law as it ought to be' could ever help the Concerned Citizen to withstand evil laws in a Theocratic Legal System. A Benthamite separation of the two might prove insufficient, might pale against the fact that the vast preponderance of citizens accepts the divine origin of these officially laid-down laws to stone adulterers, say, or to chop off the hands of thieves. Yet it is only this Benthamite separation that offers any prospect of reform or amelioration.

That brings us to the Benevolent Legal System, the one most readers will think of as their own and the sort that is implicitly or explicitly under consideration in all (or virtually all) the modern rule-of-law talk, for example. From the Concerned Citizen's Vantage, and limiting our consideration of good consequences still to just the Hartian ones tied to making disobedience of wicked government directives more likely, is this the case if we keep separate 'law as it happens to be' and 'law as it ought to be', or if we elide them together?

The anti-separation argument is more plausible here than in any other sort of legal system, because there is more scope here to ensure that what gets officially designated as 'law' will be morally good, or at least will not be egregiously immoral. After all, our Benevolent Legal System will be a democracy and one with all sorts of institutional and legislative checks and balances and avenues for grievances. So, one way to approach the specific issue of wicked laws is to try to prevent them from being enacted or handed down in the first place. This is especially so if citizens do treat, or tend to treat, official directives with the label 'law' appended as carrying with them a requirement or an obligation to obey such 'law'-labelled directives. To put it differently, if citizens (as a matter of widespread fact) are going to obey anything that is officially designated as 'law', then we need to stop such designations. That is the best way to deal with wicked, evil, egregious, odious laws. Or rather, that is the gist of the anti-separation case in a Benevolent Legal System.

Notice immediately that from the Concerned Citizen's Vantage this anti-separation case is worthless. It leaves him or her wholly out of consideration. Remember, just as in a Wicked Legal System, the Concerned Citizen will not be in a position to do any of the designating of what will and will not receive the label 'law'. The Legislator will. And in various ways (*viz.*, through interpretation powers or via a striking down power) the Judge will. But *not* the Concerned Citizen.

True, the Concerned Citizen will have a vote along with everyone else in choosing who become legislators. He or she may even have the resources to challenge the validity of laws in the courts (though this does not equate to a power in the hands of the Concerned Citizen herself to invalidate them). And yes, nothing similar obtains in the Wicked Legal System; indeed our other mooted legal systems are in all likelihood deficient on this front too. Moreover, if we were looking for a causal explanation for why, in a Benevolent Legal System, most citizens tended to obey directives labelled 'law', we would start here. When citizens have real input into who makes legislation we would expect those majoritarian law-making institutions to pass laws that the majority thought were good laws, at least most of the time. And that fact may in large part causally explain why in such legal systems citizens tend to obey whatever gets designated as 'law', even when it is seen as bad or immoral.

Whether that be the case or not, it still begs the issue of whether a Concerned Citizen – as opposed to state officials – is more likely (in a Benevolent Legal System as much as any other) to disobey wicked directives if he or she understands that law and morality are distinct. And relevant to that enquiry is the fact that from his or her vantage the label 'law' has already been appended by the time the question of obedience or disobedience is before this Concerned Citizen.

The anti-separation position, from the Concerned Citizen's Vantage, seems to concede that the directive's having received the label 'law', people just are going to obey it. Or if that is too pessimistic, it certainly leaves the Concerned Citizen with nothing much more than being able to say 'that's not really law, though I recognize it has followed all the proper procedural steps, is officially valid and validated, differs in its pedigree not a whit from directives I do consider to be laws, will be treated as legally valid by officials, and will be considered as law by most of my fellow citizens'.

In trying to stand up to egregious, wicked laws (or directives labelled 'law'), the Benthamite separation of law and morality (with the realization that the latter's claims can on occasion outweigh the former's) seems to me to be far more helpful to the Concerned Citizen, even in a Benevolent Legal System. And we can see this in part because it is transparently untrue that what is designated 'law' is never disobeyed in a Benevolent Legal System. Nor do I mean disobedience of the sort shown by the common criminal, or the grossly immoral person, or even the amoral Bad Man. I mean disobedience motivated by the out-and-out belief or sentiment in the Concerned Citizen that some law or other is wrong. In the American context alone, we could point to Martin Luther King and much of the civil rights movement or to Vietnam War objectors or opposers such as Cassius Clay, or to those who recognize that the validly brought-into-being law allows abortion but who think the practice no different from murder and so picket clinics, harass doctors, seek to reshape the judiciary, and more. And in the United Kingdom we could recall those who refused to pay the poll tax. In all these instances people appear to have understood that what they object to counts as law, but that (in their view) it is bad law. To put it differently, the label 'law' does not in fact somehow guarantee obedience 100 per cent of the time.

From the vantage of the Concerned Citizen then, someone seeking to oppose or reform or disobey bad law, the Benthamite separation of 'law as it is' and 'law as it ought to be' appears to be a crucial, important tool, even in a Benevolent Legal System. Accordingly, when we consider the issue of increasing the likelihood of disobeying bad laws *from the Concerned Citizen's Vantage*, Hart's view is preferable to that of the anti-separation proponents, and is preferable in *all* legal systems.

And this is true even if it be correct, from the Visiting Martian's vantage, that most citizens, most of the time, are going to obey whatever has been designated as 'law' (especially in a Benevolent Legal System). For the Concerned Citizen, the consequentialist benefits of having a separate moral platform or grounding on which to assess the demands of these laws can potentially be immense. In particular, the ability of citizens to realize that some action X is what the officially validated law demands or forecloses, and yet that it is only a legal obligation and that one's moral views demand not-X, seems to me much more likely to engender good long-term consequences in the specific terms now under consideration, namely of likely resistance to egregious enactments, than will any natural law blending together of the two evaluations. Or rather, this seems much more likely from the vantage of the Concerned Citizen.

When the vantage shifts to that of the Judge, however, it is no longer obvious that this is the case.

The Judge

The anti-separation case or position seems strongest when the focus is taken away from the individual Concerned Citizen and placed firmly onto the Judge. From the judicial vantage, it is harder to separate law and morality – or rather, it is easier to blend together the two assessments, the legal and the moral.

Take the Hartian notion (a notion, by the way, that was put forward while at the same time explicitly recognizing that it was not all-embracing and that there will be gaps, lacunae and shortcomings) that law is best understood as a system of rules – the very notion attacked by Dworkin. If we sketch out this notion it becomes immediately plain how easy it is in some circumstances for the Judge to blend together and to elide the legal and the moral. On this Hartian notion laws will count as laws when they have the correct pedigree, when they come from a recognized source. These validating sources that amount to an ultimate test of legal validity, these Rules of Recognition, will vary from jurisdiction to jurisdiction. They have to be discovered by observation, by looking to see what the officials happen to treat as a law-creating source. And that may turn out to be the procedurally proper enactments of an elected legislature, or the decisions of a highest court, or the rulings of a body of top clerics, or the pronouncements of an absolute monarch, or the diktats of a Stalin, or something else.

On any such rule-anchored understanding of law there will be occasional instances where the application of the rule to the facts of the case provides no answer. Or rather, well-informed, reasonable people will once in a while differ on what the answer is or should be. This may be because of the open texture of language itself, as Hart suggested, or it may be because the point-of-application interpreters bring different moral (or more broadly, different normative) frameworks to bear on the task.

Whatever the cause of this indeterminacy, the judge will be left with discretion. She will be able to decide the issue one way or the other (assuming there are just two options falling within the penumbra of uncertainty). And, given that scope for judicial discretion, we might all expect this and similarly situated judges at least sometimes to turn to morality in order to decide the issue or case at hand in accord with what the judge thinks is just or fair or morally right.

On this rule-anchored understanding of law, then, the Judge is uniquely situated. Her view of what is moral, because of her position as authoritative resolver of disputes, can become law. In this situation of adjudicating a penumbral case, and from this Judge's Vantage, it really is difficult to separate law and morality.

Of course in saying that we can also all recognize with Hart that such penumbral cases, cases where the judge has discretion, are failures in the system (however unavoidable the existence of some failures will be). We can concede that the vast preponderance of disputes in our well-run Benevolent Legal System never get to a higher court or any court – the rules are sufficiently settled and clear to ensure most people never contact a lawyer, and most of those few who do never end up having the lawyer issue proceedings or commence a lawsuit, and most of those fewer still who push on end up settling before trial, and most of those fewer, fewer still who advance through to trial do not appeal. In other words, we can admit that the sorts of cases that reach a jurisdiction's highest court are very, very unrepresentative of how the legal rules affect and resolve most disputes in our Benevolent Legal System. To put it differently, the exceedingly few disputes that get this far are all, or almost all, what Dworkin would call Hard Cases. Or framed from the Judge's Vantage, it is not surprising that the legal world appears full of uncertainty and indeterminacy – from that perspective, that is the way things are!

The fact remains, however, that from this Judge's Vantage, when deciding one of these exceptional cases that has wound its way up to the jurisdiction's highest court, law and morality seem closely intertwined. They are difficult to separate. What the outcome should be, according to the Judge's own moral sense, can become or translate into what the law is. Hence, the more inclined we are to adopt the Judge's Vantage – and let me say straight out that this is by far the preferred perspective of the Law Professor – the more difficult it is to keep separate 'law as it is' and 'law as it ought to be'.

None of this is meant to deny that it is nevertheless possible for the Judge to separate law and morality. She can. For a start, there is *stare decisis*. Judges lower down the judicial hierarchy are required to follow the ratio of decisions from higher courts. Yet sometimes a judge following a binding precedent will think it morally suspect, even wrong. That judge will be able to keep separate what the law does require (in the shape of the rule laid down in some binding precedent from a higher court) and what she thinks the law should require.

Now it is assuredly true that when rules have to be inferred from the ratio of past decisions, it will generally (though not always) be the case that such rules have less specificity, less of a core of settled meaning, and less constraining effect over future circumstances than do rules laid down in statute form by a legislature. There will be more wiggle room, in other words, for the judge anxious or even determined to avoid the strictures of the precedent-generated rule. Yet that is certainly not to say that the honest judge will never be constrained by case law. There is no doubt that for the honest or non-prevaricating judge the common law can sometimes produce a body of rules as determinate as any statutory rule, as Hart himself reminds us. And those rules need not in every case align with what some particular person thinks is morally good or morally tolerable, even if that person be a judge.

Of course our mooted Judge is an appeal court judge at, or near, the top of the judicial hierarchy. Let's assume for the moment that she sits on the jurisdiction's highest court, where precedents are merely persuasive, not binding. Perhaps in that situation, as one of nine members of the US Supreme Court, say, or one of ten judicial members of the former House of Lords, it will not really be possible to separate law and morality – at least on the Hartian notion of law as a system of rules where the overwhelming majority of cases that reach that far up the court pyramid are those which fall into the penumbra of uncertainty and of judicial discretion?

In fact, not so. Even in the extremely rarefied world of a US Supreme Court Justice or House of Lords judge – where virtually all the cases reaching that far are uncertain and debatable ones as regards their outcomes, where no further appeals are possible and where strict *stare decisis* does not apply – even here the Judge is able to separate 'law as it is' and 'law as it ought to be'. For a start, such a Judge may not be in the majority in a particular case. As a member of the dissenting minority, she can quite easily distinguish between what the majority just said the law is, and what she said it should be. That is clear cut and obvious.

Less clear cut are those instances in which such a Judge feels compelled to follow a precedent even though she does not have to. Take an example from Australia. An issue arose over the meaning of the Australian Constitution. The High Court (Australia's highest) split 4–3. Shortly thereafter one of the judges who had been in the majority in that case retired and was replaced by someone expected to side with the minority. Another case was quickly brought on the same issue. As expected, the newly appointed judge sided with the earlier dissenters. And yet one of those dissenters changed his vote. He still thought the law *should be* what he had earlier ruled. But he placed greater weight now on certainty and on respect for precedent.[2]

One way to understand what that judge was thinking is in terms of distinguishing between 'what the law is' and 'what the law should be' (together with crediting him with a near superhuman level of self-restraint and respect for non-binding precedent, an approach we know, from experience, many other judges would not mimic).

My claim thus far is that vantage matters in so far as keeping separate 'law as it is' and 'law as it ought to be'. For the Judge, the anti-separation case is much stronger than it is for the Concerned Citizen. The Judge, but never the Concerned Citizen, is at times in the authoritative position to be able to elide her 'oughts' and the legal system's 'ises'. At any rate, that is so if one adopts the Hartian notion of law as a system of rules, a notion that carries with it inevitable judicial discretion when a few rare cases fall outside the core of settled meaning or expectations.

That notion or understanding of law does not imply or suggest that judicial discretion is pervasive, or even common. But the fact that it can and does on occasion arise opens the door to the Judge – and to no one but the Judge – to blend together the legal and what she sees as the moral. And that in turn buttresses the claim that the anti-Benthamite, anti-separation position is strongest from our Appeal Court Judge's Vantage. True, there is still scope for even the highest of judges to separate 'law as it is' and 'law as it ought to be'. But actually doing so, or thinking she should do so, is much harder for her (on both fronts) than for the Concerned Citizen.

Still, that is on the Hartian, system-of-rules understanding of law. Would the same be true if one were to adopt a more Dworkinian understanding? Would it still be easier for the Judge to elide law and morality than for the Concerned Citizen? The simple answer is an emphatic 'yes'. In fact, on any sort of Dworkinian understanding of law the Judge finds herself obliged regularly and routinely to blend together law and morality, 'law as it is' and 'law as it ought to be'. That in turn means that it is even harder for the Dworkinian Judge to separate law and morality than it was for the Hartian Judge. Hence the gap between the Judge's ability to separate the two, and the Concerned Citizen's, only widens under any sort of Dworkinian notion of law. It certainly does not narrow.

Recall the basic outline of a Dworkinian notion of law. As Jeremy Waldron puts it, 'Ronald Dworkin has made *Riggs [v. Palmer]* the leitmotif of an entire jurisprudence, arguing that law comprises deep legal principles as well as rules embodied in texts and precedents'.[3] So, in what he terms Hard Cases, when the

---

2   See *Western Australia* v. *The Commonwealth* (1975) 134 CLR 201 and *Queensland* v. *The Commonwealth* (1977) 139 CLR 201.

3   Jeremy Waldron, 'Foreign Law and the Modern *Ius Gentium*' (2005) 119 *Harvard Law Review* 129, at p. 136 (internal footnote omitted).

rules do not clearly apply, Dworkin suggests that judges do and should construct what amounts to the best background fit theory that explains and justifies those rules, something that best explains and justifies that jurisdiction's constitutional provisions and statutes and precedents and conventions.

In doing this our Judge will *not* be free to impose directly her own first-order moral values or judgments or preferences to decide these cases. Instead she will be constrained by these existing materials, not unlike the way a chain novelist asked to write the tenth chapter of a book is constrained by the preceding nine chapters written by others. So in that direct or first-order sense, when adopting a Dworkinian understanding, the Judge's moral views of what 'the law ought to be' do not become what 'the law is'. The first nine chapters, the deep legal principles infusing all the settled legal materials, constrain the Judge.

Of course, at the second-order or meta level of constructing such an all-explaining and all-justifying best background fit or understanding of those materials that puts them in their best light, the Judge's moral (or more broadly, normative) views do matter. Her view of what this should be, for the purposes of deciding the case at hand (and so, perhaps, even of announcing what the Constitution means as regards abortion or what some key statute is to be taken as saying or of how far a series of precedents extends) turns into what it is. The Judge's moral view of what the best background fit should be, because of her unique authoritative position, becomes or turns into what it is in fact (assuming, for the moment, that our Judge is in the majority and not dissenting).

In stark terms, the Dworkinian judge is regularly and routinely blending together her 'oughts' and 'ises', or transmogrifying the former into the latter. True, she is not simply substituting her own first-order moral preferences or judgments for the laid-down legal rules. But in a Benevolent Legal System there is certainly scope, because of the general benevolence of the materials with which the Judge is working, to shape her all-encompassing best justifying theory, to achieve much of what she might like, had she been free simply to substitute her 'ought' for the imposed 'is'. At least a good many commentators on the effects of a Dworkinian understanding of law, including me, think this is the case.

In more prosaic terms, when a point-of-application interpreter understands her job to be to make the best she can of the materials before her – to write the very best chapter ten she can – it is open to question just how constrained she really is in a Benevolent Legal System. My view is that she is much less constrained than on the Hartian understanding, under which the point-of-application interpreter once in a while has out-and-out discretion but in the preponderance of cases (at least for the honest interpreter) is wholly constrained.

On a Dworkinian understanding of law, in the search for those deep legal principles that are nowhere laid down in a recognized, source-based rule, it would appear to be even easier for the Judge to elide law and morality than on a Hartian understanding of law. And this claim is further buttressed to the extent one suspects, with me, that for Dworkinians *all cases* that reach a judge are in fact potential Hard Cases – that the only way to decide if the clear rules apply (or should apply) or not is to first build this best background fit that infuses 'how things should be' into 'how they are'. Even rules that at first sight appear clearly and unambiguously to apply to the case at hand – as in the *Riggs* case itself of the murderer claiming under inheritance rules that seem on their face to apply to him and say he inherits – might be held not to apply on a Dworkinian understanding. Every case, in other words, is potentially a Hard Case. And the Dworkinian judge can only know for sure by first constructing her all-encompassing best background fit that elides the 'ought' and the 'is'. In the right circumstances, what she constructs can override even the clearest of laid-down rules. And this prompts one to wonder what the difference is – from the Concerned Citizen's Vantage – between deciding a case retrospectively and deciding it based on rights that the parties were unaware existed. From the Concerned Citizen's Vantage, the Rule of Law problems tied to after-the-fact rule or decision making apply to both.

Having sketched out both the extremely judge-centred Dworkinian notion of law, and the much, much less judge-centred Hartian notion, we can turn back to the question we earlier considered from the Concerned Citizen's Vantage, namely: Does eliding law and morality together or keeping them separate do more in terms of engendering disobedience to wicked or evil, or perhaps only egregiously wicked, laws?

Adopt the Judge's Vantage, and immediately one sees how matters differ from when the vantage was that of the Concerned Citizen, and how the anti-Benthamite or anti-separation position has become so much more attractive. First off, in this Benevolent Legal System in which we are assuming our judge is operating, there is a sense in which what counts as law has not yet been determined – at least from the Judge's Vantage. In other words, she (unlike the Concerned Citizen) will get to designate what gets the label 'law'.

For instance, it may be that there is a US-style constitutionalized bill of rights that allows our Judge to invalidate or strike down what otherwise would have been valid legal laws. Or there may be a UK-style statutory bill of rights, with a potent reading down provision, that has been interpreted in such a way[4] as to allow judges significant scope to rewrite or redraft statutes, however clear and unambiguous they might be and however much the rewritten end product is in opposition to what is conceded to be the intentions of the legislature. Or it may simply be that the unelected judges have carved out for themselves, under the guise of 'common law constitutionalism' say, a role that amounts to one giving them the power to ignore or invalidate or interpret away provisions in statutes they (the judges) happen to find morally offensive.

The point in any of these scenarios is that what a law means, or whether it gets the label 'law', will be determined wholly by the judges. Not surprisingly, therefore, from the Judge's Vantage better consequences may well flow from eliding together law and morality. When the Judge, in effect, can say to herself something close to 'this directive labelled as "law" by the legislature will not

---

4   See *Ghaidan* v. *Mendoza* [2004] 3 All ER 411 discussed in Chapter 5 below.

continue with that label – or, alternatively, will continue with the label but will be given a fundamentally different, even opposite, meaning – whenever I think such a course is morally required', then it becomes plain and obvious that the anti-separation position *can* prevent wicked laws. It *can* foster disobedience (of an elitist rather than ground-level sort) either by preventing what is perceived to be wicked or evil from gaining the designation 'law' in the first place, or by gutting the offensive parts in the course of interpreting it and giving it meaning.

Either way, the anti-separation position is much more plausible from the Judge's Vantage. *If* most regular citizens are likely to obey anything officially designated as 'law', then stopping such designations or rewriting the content of the laws themselves seems a good way to deal with wicked, evil, egregious, odious directives or 'pre-judicial vetting' laws. It is a way that is only open to the Judge, of course. For her alone is this sort of disobedience an available option.

Moreover, the more that one is inclined to understand law in Dworkinian terms, the less this even counts as a form of judicial disobedience. Why? Because, on the Dworkinian understanding, what would otherwise be a form or theory of judicial disobedience (and when it is justified) translates into a theory of interpretation, albeit of a souped-up variety. More brusquely put, when interpretation stops being a search for intended meaning, and becomes a sort of moral-best-case-scenario-imagining, the line between a theory of interpretation and a theory of justified disobedience to law all but disappears. In fact, it probably does disappear.

Still, the fact is that from the Judge's Vantage the anti-separation position offers more scope to prevent and to disobey wicked laws. As it happens, it also offers the Judge more scope to prevent or rewrite laws that are *not* wicked. The same tools that allow the Judge, and only the Judge, to do what the Visiting Martian would characterize as rewriting or nullifying certain laws, laws seen to be particularly odious, are available to the Judge at other times too.

This shows that when calculating the likely future good consequences of opting for Benthamite separation or anti-separation elision, Hart's focus on disobedience to wicked laws was too circumscribed. Other consequences matter as well. For instance, who ends up deciding contentious moral and political issues, the elected legislature or the unelected judiciary, matters too. Good and bad consequences flow from that as well. Indeed, consideration of this important issue – I would call it the central and most important issue – I leave to Chapter 2. Here, I notice simply that the more one is inclined (with the Visiting Martian?) to see the world in Waldronian terms, where reasonable, smart, well-informed, even nice people simply disagree on all sorts of (if not all) moral issues, including what is the rights-respecting answer issues – where dissensus and disagreement over where to draw the whole array of lines that need drawing in society when it comes to abortion, immigration, how to balance criminal procedural entitlements against the need to lessen drunk driving, euthanasia, what limits to put on speech and religious practices and so much more is simply to be expected and is not a sign of pathology – the more one will worry about handing too much power to unelected judges.

At least that will be so for those whose starting point in resolving such inevitable disagreements is to count everyone equally and let the numbers count.

Putting that aside until Chapter 2, though, we can simply note that there will always be some sort of trade-off. The more scope judges, and only judges, have to instil or infuse their own moral views into law when the latter is egregiously bad (at least according to them), the more scope they are likely to have to do so as well when the latter is good or okay or not too bad (at least according to plenty of non-judges). Different people will opt for different sides, or positions along the continuum, of this trade-off; some will be more inclined to trust or to rely on judges than others. What is difficult to deny is simply that some sort of trade-off has to be made (at least in so far as we are considering a Benevolent Legal System).

My strong opinion is that any counter-balancing worry about over-powerful unelected judges in what is a more or less well-functioning democracy will not be nearly as evident from the Judge's Vantage as it would be from the Concerned Citizen's or the Legislator's, or arguably even the Bad Man's perspective. So the more one tends (explicitly or implicitly) to adopt the Judge's Vantage, the more it is true not simply that the anti-separation position is more attractive and persuasive but also the more it is that worries about over-powerful judges tend to stay out of sight and out of mind.

To recap this section, then, the claimed good consequences tied to disobeying wicked laws, should one elide 'law as it is' and 'law as it ought to be' are far more evident from the Judge's Vantage than from the Concerned Citizen's Vantage, where they appear virtually non-existent. Moreover, on a Dworkinian understanding of law, that gap widens even further. Indeed on that understanding it may often prove almost impossible for the Judge to separate the two; certainly it will be harder for her than it would be under a Hartian rule-anchored understanding of law.

That leaves us briefly to consider the merits of the separation and anti-separation positions from the Judge's Vantage when we leave the Benevolent Legal System for some other. Move first to the Wicked Legal System. The Judge's Vantage here comes close to collapsing into that of the Concerned Citizen's Vantage. In the most wicked of these jurisdictions the Judge will simply not be the authoritative interpreter of directives, ordinances or enactments promulgated by the dictator or ruling clique. She will do as she is told or she will lose her job, full stop. And attempts by her, alone, to subvert this wicked system will be futile. Benthamite separation is for her, as with the Concerned Citizen, the only option.

In less extreme cases, apartheid South Africa for example, there evidently will be room, at the margins, for the Judge to ameliorate the harshest aspects of the regime simply because that regime is not as ruthlessly brutal as it could be. There are limits to what it will do. So by blending morality and law the Judge can give interpretations that have comparatively better consequences – for those involved in the case at hand, that is – than had she not done so. Her position has not wholly collapsed into that of the Concerned Citizen.

Still, any ameliorations the Judge can effect at the margins come at a cost, namely the giving of a veneer of respectability or at least 'within-the-Paleness' to the regime. That is why the issue of whether an apartheid South African judge should have, or should not have, resigned is so difficult and debatable. Both courses of action are likely to provoke good and bad consequences; these consequences will vary in unknown ways depending upon what the other judges decide to do, on how the regime responds, on what citizens do, on how far this judge can go before being slapped down, and more – none of which can be known by the Judge with any certainty at all when making her decision either to stay (and do what she can to lessen some of the odious outcomes) or to resign.

What we can say for sure is that even from the Judge's Vantage, the anti-separation position is less persuasive and in some senses less attractive when we move from the Benevolent Legal System to malign varieties. In some cases the Judge's Vantage will, in practice, amount to nothing more than the Concerned Citizen's. Hence all of the arguments favouring the keeping separate of 'law as it is' and 'law as it ought to be' for the Concerned Citizen will here apply to the Judge too.

And as a slight digression, though one not unrelated to this issue, notice that the Dworkinian understanding of law simply does not work outside the context of a Benevolent Legal System; it has nothing to say as regards the vast preponderance of societies that have existed and as regards many that still exist. Where the settled law with which the Judge has to work in formulating her best background fit is on the whole not benevolent (from our point of view or even from the Judge's herself) – the statutes oppress women, freedom of speech and of religion are virtually non-existent, majoritarian democracy is unheard of, and worse – then the outcome she can reach by blending in her moral views at the second-order, create-a-justifying-theory-for-those-materials stage will not be a good one either. This is true no matter what she does in honestly performing her second-order task. Dworkin comes close to conceding the inapplicability of his notion of law outside the context of Benevolent Legal Systems, though with something of an equivocation and hedging of bets, when he says:

> If the judge decides that the reasons supplied by background moral rights are so strong that he has a moral duty to do what he can to support these rights, then it may be that *he must lie*, because he cannot be of any help unless he is understood as saying, in his official role, that the legal rights are different from what he believes they are.[5]

The basic point is that in Wicked Legal Systems there is little, if any, scope for the Judge to infuse her moral views into what the law is held to be. In that sense she is in the same position as the Concerned Citizen. She cannot stop odious directives from being designated as 'law', or gut them of their intended meaning. Reform and

---

5 Ronald Dworkin, *Taking Rights Seriously* (London: Duckworth, 2nd impression, 1978), pp. 326–7, italics mine.

improvement require the separate Benthamite moral platform, the one facilitating the distinguishing between 'law as it is' and 'law as it ought to be'.

Much the same seems to be true of So-So Legal Systems, the uniqueness of the Judge's Vantage there varying inversely to the extent the negatives (i.e. the morally objectionable aspects) of such a system happen to outweigh the positives.

As for Theocratic Legal Systems, and as noted when considering them from the Citizen's Vantage, many judges too in such jurisdictions will believe that some or many laws have a divine origin or warrant or sanction. Indeed we would be surprised if all judges in such a jurisdiction did not at least pretend to accept the claimed genealogy of the laws. We might even expect a good many judges in such a legal system to be clerics, but whether that be the case or not the Judge here will certainly find it hard to separate law and morality. Both will be seen as functions of 'what God laid down', though there will be some room to distinguish the interpretations and rulings of other judges and officials as immoral ones or ones against God's meaning or not in keeping with the divine law.

As with the Concerned Citizen, though, it is difficult to see how reform and betterment and amelioration of the law in a Theocratic Legal System, even from the Judge's Vantage, is impeded by adopting a Benthamite outlook that refuses to elide 'law as it is' and 'law as it ought to be'.

The Bad Man

Oliver Wendell Holmes' Bad Man is the amoral actor unaffected by morality. As I noted in the Introduction, he is a thinly veiled stand-in for the office lawyer, though the correlation is by no means 1:1. Such a Bad Man's Vantage is unhelpful in thinking about disobeying evil, odious, wicked laws. Our Bad Man just does not care about their immorality. He is indifferent to the fact that his jurisdiction's laws keep some races at the back of the bus, say, or deliberately imprison political dissidents or worse. By definition, this is the vantage that simply *does* – as a matter of fact – separate law and morality.

Having mooted such a vantage, anti-separation proponents have an obvious reply. They can say that such a vantage is purely illusory. Such amoral people, careful to stay within the law's ambit but completely unmoved by moral considerations, do not exist. That would be a straightforward anti-separation response to the mooting of the Bad Man's Vantage. The trouble is that any response along those lines just seems so implausible. One hundred per cent Bad Men, those with no moral feelings at all, may, thankfully, be rare. But as an empirical matter, plenty of people surely exist who come close. And the less we ask for complete amorality and the total absence of even a scintilla or two of moral feeling, the more people we include under this general rubric. One does not have to be a dyed-in-the-wool Hobbesian to see that altruism is not just limited, but in some (though not most) of our fellow men far too limited.

More interesting, however, is to use the Bad Man's Vantage as a proxy for the Client-Advising Lawyer's Vantage. Yes, as I conceded in the Introduction, lawyers have constraints imposed on them other than straightforwardly legal ones. There are constraints imposed by professional ethics, by obligations to the court and by their own consciences (most lawyers, like most people in society, not being themselves Bad Men). Yet, save at the margins, the advice a lawyer gives to a client will look very much like what a Bad Man would advise. It will be indifferent to morality but punctiliously concerned about law.

I think that is what Holmes was getting at. That the many graduating law students sitting before him when he first gave 'The Path of the Law' as a graduation address at Boston University were going out to be lawyers, not judges. Law school spends far too much time educating students from the implicit vantage of the judge. Having now been graduated, they would largely have to adopt the Bad Man's Vantage (at least until such time as they became judges themselves, or moved over to become Law Professors, who not infrequently see themselves as ersatz judges).

Still, if Holmes' Bad Man's Vantage shows that some people just will separate law and morality, that this vantage is one that can be and is adopted without any of the attendant Benthamite and Hartian concerns for the reform and amelioration of the law, and that lawyers are some of the first to do this, that nevertheless leaves the issue of disobeying wicked laws. How does that issue look from the Lawyer's Vantage? Well, unless the Lawyer is himself an amoral actor, this will be another of the relatively few instances in which the Lawyer's Vantage differs from the Bad Man's.

In most respects it appears to me that when it comes to deciding on whether to disobey odious laws, and if so how best to do so, the Lawyer's Vantage collapses into that of the Concerned Citizen. True, it will be that of a remarkably well-informed citizen, but the lawyer has none of the authoritative point-of-application interpretive powers of the judge. Better connections than most other citizens? Yes. Uniquely situated as far as bringing cases before those judges who do have such authoritative powers? Undoubtedly. When it comes to disobeying evil laws (or anything else, for that matter) does this somehow transform lawyers into subordinate or acolyte or even pretend judges? No.

As with the Concerned Citizen, keeping separate 'law as it is' and 'law as it ought to be' is important for lawyers. It is important in the Benevolent Legal System and absolutely crucial in the Wicked and other Legal Systems.

Back to the Concerned Citizen and Other Vantages on Other Matters

When assessing the good or bad consequences attaching either to the separation of law and morality or to their concatenation, the focus solely on how each option might further the disobedience of wicked laws is clearly too narrow. Other consequences matter as well. Who ends up deciding contentious moral and political issues, the elected legislature or the unelected judiciary, is one such consequence related to the blending together (or not) of morality with law. It is perhaps the most fundamental consequence we need to consider and so is a topic I postpone for now. It will be the subject of Chapter 2.

Of course, in choosing between separation or elision, the weighing of likely future good consequences tied to disobeying wicked laws and to who ends up deciding contentious social issues does not exhaust the range of relevant consequentialist concerns. We will look at two more, one raised by Hart and one not.

The first of these can be thought of as the War Crimes dilemma. It is an offshoot of the disobedience issue already discussed. What is the best way to proceed when someone who was living and operating under one legal regime finds that there has been a coup or a military defeat or a revolution or for some other reason the old Rule of Recognition has been discarded and a new one put it in place? And this someone is now – under the new Rule of Recognition or new legal system – considered to have done something morally wicked back under the old regime and old Rule of Recognition. And this someone's defence is that everything he did back then was wholly and completely legal at the time and under the existing laws. Indeed he may even assert that the then-existing laws compelled him to do what he did.

Which outlook delivers better consequences here, the one that seeks to keep separate law and morality or the one that blends the two together? And does it matter whether the someone so indicted was a top official in the former regime, or just a border guard or collaborating informant?

The outlines of the two opposing positions here are well known. The core of the anti-separation view generally involves both *a)* some sort of belief in the existence of mind-independent moral values together with *b)* a preparedness to allude to those same values when making an appraisal of legal validity. Holders of this view need not (and few today do) take the hard-core Augustinian line and make legal validity depend upon some sort of 1:1 mirroring with the mind-independently morally right (be it divine law or a secular alternative). More would travel down the Thomasonian path of recognizing that some bad laws should nevertheless be obeyed. Legal validity *can* attach to the morally bad (say, to a law that is against what will further human goods), though a point will be reached at which it is so iniquitous that legal validity stops attaching, or at least attaches only in the most tenuous sense. Perhaps there is a focal sense of law and a peripheral sense. It is not so much, then, that an odious law does not count as a legally valid law at all; rather, the idea is more that there are a range of senses to 'legal validity' and morally wicked enactments only count as such in a peripheral or half-dead sense – certainly not in the fullest sense.

The point is that, for the anti-separation subscribers, a point will be reached where the former regime's laws cannot be called in aid. They were too egregiously evil to count as law for the purpose of our indicted someone's legal defence now. We may be talking about the East German border guard who shot a fleeing teenager and is on trial in the newly united Germany. Or it may be some top-ranking Nazi, a Goering or a Hess, on trial after World War II. Or it may be one of the tens or hundreds of thousands who were paid informants on their fellow citizens in the formerly Soviet-controlled Poland or Hungary or Baltic States who, with the collapse of the Berlin Wall, now face legal sanctions of some sort.

The anti-separation response to the dilemma is to say that at some point – and views will differ as to where that is – what was done back then, and done legally back then and even was legally obligatory back then, was just too immoral for the then-existing law to count as law today (for the purposes of providing a legal defence to today's charges, at any rate). The old law was not fully law, due to its wickedness.

The Hartian, separation response to the War Crimes dilemma is quite different. If it is a good thing to keep separate law and morality, to see that law is one thing and morality another and that the demands of the latter can sometimes outweigh or trump those of the former, then there is no room to claim that some previous regime's laws are somehow not fully laws because of their moral content. What needs to be done, if we wish to prosecute someone today, is to pass new laws that retrospectively make what was done back then a crime (even though it was not one at the time, under the then-existing laws).

In other words, Hart's position is that you must weigh the evils of passing such retrospective laws (for it is overwhelmingly, though not always, the case that passing retrospective laws is a bad thing) against the evils of what our someone did and the concomitant need to punish him for it. Neither course of action, prosecuting or not prosecuting, is free from a moral downside. But at some point – and again views will differ as to where that is – the evils of enacting retrospective laws will be outweighed by the wickedness of what this someone did (and not punishing him for it today). Once that point is passed, or clearly passed perhaps, you opt to enact the retrospective legislation.

So is it the anti-separation view or the separation view that delivers better consequences when it comes to this sort of War Crimes scenario or dilemma? Let us assume for the moment that there is no international convention in place or applicable to our someone that gives a non-retrospective, positive law basis for prosecution. (And clearly the benefits of such a treaty or convention are precisely that it *does* provide such a basis – any arguments against such a convention would presumably rest on the claimed failings of international prosecutions, perhaps on the claimed failings of the international order itself, and on the difficulties such conventions put in the way of striking a deal to rid countries of evil leaders who might otherwise be persuaded to leave for sanctuary, Idi Amin-style, in some third country.)

One answer is that in this context there is less difference between these two outlooks than one might suppose. On the anti-separation footing one has to decide when a former regime's laws (or law) are wicked enough – and what they condoned wicked enough – to become peripheral or half-dead and so to provide no protection to anyone who acted in accord with them. On the separation footing one has to decide when a former regime's laws (or law) are wicked enough – and what they condoned wicked enough – that the protection they provide to someone should be overridden by retrospective legislation today. Either way, on either footing, the same line might be drawn as regards when our someone should be prosecuted without the protection of those then-existing laws.

However, the separationists will argue that their outlook makes clearer what is at stake; that to prosecute your collaborating informant or 18-year-old border guard or even some ex-dictator or one of his henchmen comes at a cost, and whether it is worth paying that cost might vary depending upon whom it is that is being suggested for prosecution. The costs might be worth paying to prosecute a top Nazi, but not worth paying when it comes to young border guards or informants. And this is obscured, they will claim, when one adopts the anti-separation outlook. In fact, it goes further than that. The anti-separation outlook, for all its grand appeals to morality and its tendency to see law through moralized lenses, ironically ends up being harsher and less merciful than the separation outlook. Or so proponents of the latter, echoing Bentham, will assert. They will be less likely to prosecute than their anti-separation cousins.

Consider this debate from some of our vantages. For the Concerned Citizen, the keeping separate of law and morality will accentuate and make more transparent the costs involved in prosecuting someone today. And that in turn will make it easier to distinguish the case of calls to prosecute former border guards, say, and calls to prosecute former high-ranking Nazis or top Serb militia leaders. It may also make clear the Rule of Law difficulties inherent in this War Crimes scenario, which for the separationists are ones tied to retrospective law making (while for anti-separationists the less immediately obvious Rule of Law difficulties relate to the uncertainty of the law and the problem of citizens not knowing what they can and cannot legally do). For citizens living through the death throes of a brutal regime, the separationist outlook may arguably even make it easier to bring an end to some tyrant's regime by lessening the prospects that he will face prosecution rather than an Idi Amin-style exile or some truth-and-reconciliation type exercise.

That said, many Concerned Citizens (who suffered under the former regime) may favour prosecution and for that reason (rather than causation flowing the other way round) prefer the anti-separation outlook.

Things look quite different from the Legislator's Vantage. From that perspective the attractions of the anti-separation position when it comes to this War Crimes dilemma are perfectly clear – and note that they are perfectly clear whether or not the Legislator himself happens to believe in the existence of mind-independent moral values against which the former regime's laws can be appraised. The simple fact is that on the anti-separationist outlook our Legislator is not required (today, in the present) to pass a law that retrospectively makes what was done back then a crime. The prosecution of the border guard or the collaborating informant or the top Serb militia leader can proceed without having to enact any retrospectively applicable provision. And from our Legislator's Vantage that is a significant, in all likelihood a decisive, advantage.

Even were the Visiting Martian to say that the same basic line-drawing exercise was required (of whom to prosecute of the former regime and whom not to prosecute), whichever outlook be adopted, the practicalities involved in drawing these lines are different for the separationist and anti-separationist legislator. The latter is not required to do anything explicitly to legitimate any prosecutions undertaken and the potential conflicts with Rule of Law concerns are less apparent. A newly enacted retrospective law will be more discernibly a concern on these grounds than will the plight of citizens in the former regime unable to tell (at least from our vantage today) what is and is not valid law for the purposes of later reliance on it.

So we know which position or outlook will be most attractive or alluring to the vast preponderance of legislators; it will be the anti-separation elision one.

Oddly enough, this War Crimes dilemma scenario may be one of the few situations where the Judge has as much, if not more, reason than the citizen to prefer the separation position or outlook. The Judge presiding over the prosecution of the teenage East German border guard or of the Polish collaborating informant may see herself as part of a 'victor's justice' trial. From her perspective, from this Judge's Vantage, having in place some piece of Hartian retrospective legislation that has been publicly debated and its costs and benefits widely surmised and aired, may at least counter-balance (if not remove) the 'victor's justice' taint or stigma – always assuming the particular judge is modest enough to desire a modicum of legitimacy-enhancing trappings, that she is not herself inclined to adopt the Sanctimonious Man's Vantage.

I said above that the range of relevant consequentialist concerns in play when choosing between the separation or elision positions encompassed more than which one better engenders disobedience of wicked laws and which has preferable outcomes as regards who will end up deciding contentious moral issues. We have just looked at the War Crimes dilemma scenario. The last one we will consider is perhaps the most straightforward, if only because it is one in which the anti-separation outlook or thesis is a non-starter from any of our mooted vantages.

I am talking about deliberate, planned law reform, be it through the agency of some Law Reform Commission or via public input into some mooted legislative reform or part of an overseas trip by legislators to study how, say, the legal provisions surrounding workers' compensation work elsewhere and so can be improved or even by means of top judges setting out to alter the laws of marriage or to fill in the interstitial gaps related to some aspect of negligence law. When the specific goal is law reform and the improving of 'law as it is', then the blending together of law and morality can never be more than half hearted. This is true from the Concerned Citizen's Vantage, and the Legislator's Vantage, and yes even the Judge's Vantage (as the many judges who regularly head Law Reform Commissions serve to illustrate). This is clear even from the Visiting Martian's Vantage or the Bad Man's Vantage (neither of whom cares about or needs to endorse the desire for reform). And it is true in any of our four mooted types of legal system.

Benthamite separation of 'what law is' and 'what law ought to be', and the erecting of a separate evaluative platform from which to pass judgment on what happens to be the existing state of affairs, is a pre-requisite to any deliberate changes to the law, changes the initiators hope will be improvements.

When law reform is the aim, the separating of law and morality will always be an explicit or implicit fact of life. This is not surprising. It was just such reform and amelioration of the law that motivated Bentham after all, and led him to insist on the good consequences that flowed from keeping separate law and morality.

'Is' or 'Ought' or Both?

I conclude this first chapter with a section on how the 'is'/'ought' distinction affects the issue of separating law and morality. We have seen that from the premise 'judges often resort to moral principles and make moral judgments in the course of rendering legal decisions' it does not in any way follow that the Concerned Citizen or the Bad Man or the Visiting Martian or the Legislator cannot keep law and morality separate. From these other vantages, the fact that the Judge is sometimes in a position to blend her view of what is moral and best into the determination of what is law in no way forecloses separating the two for those others. The Judge's view of what is best and most moral is not self-certifyingly correct; no one really thinks any particular judge has a pipeline to God on issues of morality; when it comes to morality, disagreement and dissensus are a fact of social life and simply to be expected. There is no science-like method or set of widely endorsed procedures for convincing those who disagree with you about the rightness or wrongness of abortion or same-sex marriage or capital punishment or where to draw the line in limiting free speech or certain religious practices (whether you believe there are mind-independently right answers to these issues, or not). In fact, as we have seen, even the Judge, who has this unique authoritative power to blend morality and law, even she can keep the two separate – when she is in dissent, when she feels compelled to follow precedent she thinks morally bad, when she is honestly interpreting some statutes, and more.

The fact that at any given time five of nine US Supreme Court justices might be able to decide what law *is* by appealing to what it *ought to be* does not make impossible (or even very difficult) the keeping separate of what it is and what it ought to be for all non-judges (not to mention for the four dissenters and all the lower court judges who disagree with this majority). For all of them, the existence of law is one thing,[6] its merit or demerit another thing entirely. Keeping in mind the various vantages in play in a legal system has made this indisputably clear. There are more vantages from which to think about law, Horatio, than are dreamt of in Dworkin's judge-centred philosophy!

---

6   And yes, for some of them its existence may be determined by the rule 'the law is what the judges say it is'.

And should a society choose to incorporate a moral test into its test for legality, one that experience of today's world tells us would be a test operated by the judges and *not* by citizens or legislators, that would in no way prevent the Visiting Martian from describing this society's legal system as one in which 'law as it is' remained distinct from 'law as it ought to be' (for some or many citizens, for some or many legislators, for the Bad Man, for a modicum of law professors, and even for a few judges). What is seen to be good by the preponderance of a select few judges can nevertheless be seen to be bad by a minority or even by a majority of others in society. 'Law as it happens to be' simply is not 'what it ought to be' for any of them, at least not in any complete and thoroughgoing sense.

My point is that the so-called separation thesis – that what law *is* and what law *ought to be* are separate matters – is descriptively true unless you insist on adopting the Judge's Vantage. Even law filtered by judges (or rather by a majority of judges) through a moral test or lens can be bad law from some, many, most or all other vantages. That is a straightforward empirical fact. It is a descriptive claim that is true. That a select few judges may resort occasionally or even all the time to moral principles in deciding cases and settling what the law is does not settle the moral rights and wrongs of that decision for everyone else. It simply settles what the law is. That judges *claim* their settlement of what the law is to be a good and moral one (assuming they do) does not, *mirabile dictu*, somehow make it so.

A good many law professors, keen to adopt the Judge's Vantage, seem to think or assume or write as though no other vantage in fact exists. Yet any understanding of law from the Concerned Citizen's Vantage will always distinguish between 'law as it is' and 'law as it ought to be'. As noted above, the Concerned Citizen, beyond exercising his vote, is never given a role in designating or determining or deciding what the law is. From this Citizen's Vantage, the separation thesis is a descriptive fact, not some imagined or conceptual possibility.

There are a few other things to note as regards the 'is'/'ought' distinction. Take these two questions. 'Do people separate law and morality?' 'Should people separate law and morality?' The first query asks an 'is' question about the extent to which morality, in fact, is or is not interwoven into matters or determinations that are legal in nature. As we have seen, different vantages and different sorts of legal systems will give rise to different answers. The sorts of 'is' determinations that are legal in nature might include: How do judges decide hard cases or penumbra of doubt cases? Do people always, almost always, or at least the vast preponderance of the time obey whatever is labelled 'law'? What sort of people, and in what sort of circumstances do they, disobey wicked laws? What happens when one group of officials gets to give more specific content to vague, amorphous, indeterminate moral guarantees articulated in the language of rights? Do leaders of disintegrating legal regimes stop fighting and step down more quickly in circumstances where they have plausible grounds for thinking they will not be prosecuted?

Whatever the answers to these and other questions on the plane of the copula 'is' – of what happens contingently to be the case as a matter of observable fact – the copula 'ought' rests on a different plane. How judges do decide cases, for instance, is logically distinct from how someone thinks they should decide cases. This much is clear at least since David Hume, and his insights that today are often referred to as 'Hume's Law' or as 'the naturalistic fallacy' or as 'you can't derive an "ought" from an "is"'.[7]

That said, nothing in Hume's Law demands some rigid dichotomy between description, on the one hand, and prescription, on the other. For instance, one might *describe* how the *ought* operates in law or a legal system. Hart does this. Recall that he tells the reader that people (or rather some people) in a functioning legal system have an internal point of view, a critical reflective attitude, about the law and its rules; they feel obliged to carry out its prescriptions; there is, to put it differently, an internal aspect to legal (and indeed other social) rules that operates in the minds of (most, or at any rate some, of) the individuals in the particular legal system.

These claims by Hart are descriptive claims about how the prescriptive 'ought' operates, about how legal 'oughts' involve feelings of obligation at the level of the individual actor; in essence, they are descriptive claims about the role of moral beliefs or moral feelings in a legal system. It is a description from the Visiting Martian's Vantage of the role of prescription in the participant's decision making. But '[d]escription may still be description, even when what is described is an evaluation'.[8]

In addition to describing the 'ought', one might also move back and forth between the 'is' and the 'ought', the explanatory and the evaluative, observing and recommending (without any attempt to go so far as to derive one from the other). Take Ronald Dworkin, a prescriptive legal theorist if ever there was one. Even Dworkin does some of both. Of course Dworkin is famous for his prescriptions. He tells us how judges *should* decide hard cases; that they *should* emulate a fictional

---

7   In fact, Hume actually put the point in these terms in his *A Treatise of Human Nature*: 'I cannot forbear adding to these reasonings an observation, which may, perhaps, be found of some importance. In every system of morality, which I have hitherto met with, I have always remark'd, that the author proceeds for some time in the ordinary way of reasoning, and establishes the being of a God, or makes observations concerning human affairs; when of a sudden I am surpriz'd to find, that instead of the usual copulations of propositions, *is*, and *is not*, I meet with no proposition that is not connected with an *ought*, or an *ought not*. This change is imperceptible; but is, however, of the last consequence. For as this *ought*, or *ought not*, expresses some new relation or affirmation, 'tis necessary that it shou'd be observ'd and explain'd; and at the same time that a reason should be given, for what seems altogether inconceivable, how this new relation can be a deduction from others, which are entirely different from it. But as authors do not commonly use this precaution, I shall presume to recommend it to the readers; and am persuaded, that this small attention wou'd subvert all the vulgar systems of morality....' (David Hume, *A Treatise of Human Nature*, L.A. Selby-Bigge, ed., 2nd edn, rev. by P.H. Nidditch (Oxford: Oxford University Press, 1978), the last paragraph of Book III I 1, 469–70 (italics in the original)).

8   Hart, *Concept of Law* (2nd edn, Oxford: Oxford University Press, 1994), p. 244, 'Postscript'.

Hercules and construct the background political morality that best explains and justifies the jurisdiction's settled law and then decide the case at hand in the way that accords with that background fit better than any other. In other words, we *should* think of law as providing one right answer to disputes in any well-developed legal system. As well, Dworkin tells us why we *ought not* to worry about any purported threat from external scepticism – as external scepticism collapses into internal scepticism, according to him.[9] And he tells us how we *should* interpret the US Constitution and how we *should* understand the American abortion debate and even how northern ante-bellum judges *should* have decided fugitive slave cases.

Yet even Dworkin's theories are at times descriptive and adopt the observer's vantage. For one thing, Dworkin does not deny (at times he seems even positively to assert) that his theory also is meant to describe how judges *do* decide cases – that when hard cases arise some process resembling the one invoked by Hercules is *in fact* employed, an empirical claim that is most plausible, if at all, in the United States. Again, at least the early Dworkin's theory argued that there *are* right answers (a much more provocative, noteworthy and intriguing assertion than the fairly pedestrian one that there *should be* right answers). And even Dworkin's theory of how to interpret the US Constitution, a recurrent element in his writings and one of the pillars of his reputation, is not simply prescriptive. For one thing, his constitutional interpretation theory rests on the alleged fact that the constitution's framers intended parts of it to be interpreted in a broad, 'moral', visionary, abstract way (requiring re-interpretation as attitudes change), *not* in accord with their own particular understandings of what the outcome should be. Ironically, that is, Dworkin's theory of constitutional interpretation is itself a sort of originalist interpretive theory in so far as he believes some of the language used (e.g., 'due process', 'equal protection', 'freedom of speech') indicates an intent not to limit the application of the provision to the particular substantive intentions of the enactors.

And there are more ways in which one can combine 'ises' and 'oughts' without succumbing to Hume's Law and logical error. One can attempt to derive 'oughts' from 'oughts', as some modern versions of natural law theory purport to do. Whether one finds the end-product convincing or the premises self-evident, there is no invalidity in the steps. Or one might follow the moral sceptics and dissolve all 'oughts' into 'ises', asserting that moral evaluations are actually nothing more than a function or projection of people's feelings, sentiments and desires (albeit ones that are in part socially shaped and constructed). Where moral values – right and wrong, good and bad, moral truth and moral falsehood – are tied ultimately to nothing more than the contingent and observably varying responses of human beings, 'oughts' simply become a function of 'ises'; they become a function of the actually held sentiments and feelings of people, and *not* what is generally meant by an 'ought' or a 'should'.

---

9   I disagree. See my 'Truth's Empire: A Reply to Ronald Dworkin's "Objectivity and Truth: You'd Better Believe It"' (2001) 26 *Australian Journal of Legal Philosophy* 61.

Again, one might combine the 'is' and 'ought' in an allowable way by simply leaving the latter assertion understood. Such arguments, in syllogistic and highly simplified form, would look like this:

1. The world *is* X. (A description of observed fact.)
2. We all know or agree that X is bad. (An unstated normative premise.)
3. We *should* eliminate X.

This sort of argument occurs all the time. In no way does it infringe Hume's Law either, though its author may be criticized for smuggling in a hidden prescriptive claim (number 2) that would be better made explicitly and defended openly.

Let me finish with one last variant, the obverse of the first possibility I noted above, that a writer might *describe* how the *ought* operates in a legal system. The obverse of that is to rest one's normative claims, one's 'shoulds' and 'oughts', on the way things happen to be. So one might argue along these lines:

> Since at least the end of World War II, and in an ever increasing manner, judges in the western world do decide contentious moral and political issues in the course of giving their judgments. Today, it *is* simply a fact that unelected judges in the West are an aristocratic elite. This trend, this experience of most of the western world, is undeniable. Therefore we ought to accept that trend. Anyone who argues such a state of affairs should not exist, and should be opposed, has his or her head in the sand. He's a crank. Or she's stuck in a sterile research framework or programme. At the end of the day, all our 'oughts' must take account of the way things happen to be, of the existing 'ises'.

Of course any such argument along those lines, no doubt made in less clear-cut and facetious terms, in no way infringes Hume's Law. Moreover it is a logically valid argument, to be sure. Yet when it comes to 'ises' in the realm of politics and law, it is also a very odd sort of argument to make, one strangely combining an implicit Whiggish view of moral improvement with a sort of conservativism. Or rather, this sort of argument is only remotely attractive for those who happen to like the current trend, the existing state of affairs, or the fact that unelected judges have massively increased their political power in the last half century. Yes, this sort of argument has the enticing side-effect of allowing those opposed to these recent trends to be characterized as 'opponents of progress'. But ultimately it rests on an implicit defence of the status quo. The argument is not really of the form 'we ought to support or base our theories on what is'. No, the argument is really of the form 'we ought to support or base our theories on what is because what is – for us – happens to be good and desirable (at least for the moment)'.

No one who rejects that last subordinate clause, however disguised or implicit it may be, is foreclosed from attacking the way things are in politics, law or the role of the judiciary. Any sort of argument explicitly in those terms would be preposterous. Of course it is true that the way things happen to be can be hard to change. And, yes, 'what is the case' can last a long time. But no man-made state of affairs is immutable. And no argument can silence critics writing on the plane of the copula 'ought' by pointing to the existing contingencies on the plane of the copula 'is'.

And readers will have noticed that this sort of 'ought based on what is' argument is a mutant version of the anti-separation outlook or position generally. It is the inherently conservative side of blending together law and morality ('this is good because it is the law'), rather than the inherently radical or revolutionary side of the same outlook ('this is not law because it is bad'). It also leads us back to the question of who *should* end up deciding society's contentious moral and political issues, a question not answered by the prevailing facts or states of affairs, and one we turn to now.

Chapter 2

Separating Law and Morality – II

When calculating the likely good consequences of opting for a Benthamite separation of law and morality or a Fullerian elision, any focus restricted to which option makes disobedience of odious laws more likely is too restricted and circumscribed. Other consequences matter as well.

To the extent that moral determinations are contentious – to the extent, that is, that large groups of people in society differ and disagree over where to draw the whole array of lines that need drawing when it comes to such things as immigration, police powers, abortion, euthanasia, same-sex marriage, what limits to put on speech and religious practices, which punishments are acceptable and so much more – then it may be that the choice between separating or blending together law and morality will have effects on who gets to make these sort of line-drawing decisions. More specifically, it may be that the relative roles of the elected legislature and the unelected judiciary will differ depending upon the degree to which law and morality are kept separate.

In fact, this is almost certainly the case. Where judges have more scope to instil or infuse their own moral views into law, they also have more power to make the sort of aforementioned line-drawing decisions for society. The choice between Benthamite separation of law and morality and anti-separation elision, then, or something in between even, has ramifications in terms of judicial power. Good and bad consequences will flow from the choice that is made. And these sorts of consequences may prove more important in many ways than the sorts of consequences that were considered in Chapter 1. Indeed, in today's world this issue is almost certainly the most important one related to the question of separating law and morality. Or rather, in a Benevolent Legal System these seem by far the most relevant consequences worth considering.

The Benthamite's basic position is this: The fact that a select few unelected judges may be authorized to resort occasionally or frequently or even all the time to moral principles in deciding the cases before them and settling what the law is does *not* settle the moral rights and wrongs of that decision for everyone else. It simply settles what the law is. These judges' views of what is most moral are not self-certifyingly correct. The fact they *claim* their settlement of what the law is to be a good and moral and rights-respecting one does not somehow – simply by virtue of their having made the claim – make it so. In fact, giving unelected judges this power has bad consequences, at least in the long term. It lessens democratic input and decision making, which is likely to lead to more bad consequences than good ones over time. Another reason to keep law and morality separate, then, a very important reason, is to keep to a minimum the moral input of the point-of-application judges. Such input has bad long-term consequences.

It is that Benthamite position that I turn to examine now. It is that focus on the likely future consequences related to who ends up deciding contentious moral and political issues, and hence the tangential desirability (or not) of curbing the judges, that is the subject of this second chapter.

Of course where the legislature is not elected or the judiciary not independent it is most unlikely that there will be overmuch moral or political input at the point-of-application. That is just a raw empirical assertion, I recognize. But it seems clear enough to me as regards Wicked Legal Systems, and only marginally more open to question in So-So and Theocratic Legal Systems. If the grievance is that overall bad consequences flow when too much moral and political input is handed to (or indeed taken by) the point-of-application judges, then that grievance is most relevant in a Benevolent Legal System. At any rate, let us assume as much and situate this chapter's discussion in that context.

Moral Dissensus and Disagreement

The greater the degree of consensus across society on moral issues, the less the issue of the relationship between law and morality matters or is a live one. Put differently, if almost everyone agrees on the morally correct outcome as regards how to legislate or how to decide cases, then the debate on whether we *should* keep separate law and morality becomes a most strange, other-worldly one indeed. Or put differently still, the Benthams and Harts and Waldrons of the world want to keep the moral input of the point-of-application judges to a minimum because they see a world of moral disagreement and dissensus, not one of near-universal agreement.

Jeremy Waldron, perhaps more than anyone, has emphasized this lack of moral consensus. Indeed if Ronald Dworkin can be characterized as having 'made *Riggs [v. Palmer]* the leitmotif of an entire jurisprudence, arguing that law comprises deep legal principles as well as rules embodied in texts and precedents'[1] then, in a similar spirit, it would not be unfair to say that Jeremy Waldron has made this emphasis on dissensus and disagreement – reasonable disagreement amongst reasonable, smart, well-informed, even nice people where there are no agreed or uncontentious procedures or methods for resolving that disagreement – the leitmotif of his discussions of legal philosophy, rights and bills of rights. Indeed Waldron points to the sorts of issues that can come before the top courts in the United States and Canada (and ever increasingly in the United Kingdom). He points to disputes over abortion, immigration, euthanasia, racial and other group preferences, how to balance criminal procedural entitlements against the need to lessen drunk driving

---

1   Jeremy Waldron, 'Foreign Law and the Modern *Ius Gentium*' (2005) 119 *Harvard Law Review* 129, at p. 136.

or sexual assaults, what limits to put on speech and religious practices, what punishments are acceptable, and so much more and he says that disagreement on all these issues is simply to be expected. It is not a sign of pathology.

From the Visiting Martian's Vantage, Waldron is clearly correct (at least in so far as the existence of widespread disagreement is concerned). Pick any Benevolent Legal System and, viewed from the disinterested observer's perspective, there appear to be plenty of differences of opinion – differences that cannot be resolved by appealing to the substance of the dispute because each side believes (or feels) that substance favours its view. Any method of resolving such society-wide disputes must ultimately be procedural. One possible method would involve some variant of counting each citizen or resident equally and having him or her vote for elected representatives who in turn would vote to resolve these issues, the side with the most votes prevailing. The resolution here, at core, would turn not on which side was in fact morally correct but rather on which side had the greater strength of numbers thinking it was morally correct. It would ultimately be a procedural test, a letting-the-numbers-count test, though before any final vote both sides would have opportunities to persuade the other. And such attempted persuasion would no doubt rely heavily on appeals to the moral rightness of the position being defended or advocated.

Another possible method would involve handing such decisions to the unelected judges. As Waldron continually points out, though, any resolution they reached would also turn, ultimately, on which side had the greater strength of numbers. It, too, would be a procedural, letting-the-numbers-count decision making rule. It is just that the five-votes-beat-four size of the franchise would be somewhat more circumscribed under this method.

Of course here too those voting might attempt to persuade others by appealing, *inter alia*, to the moral rightness of their position. Yet the fact would remain that neither the quality of the moral argumentation nor the extent of references to J.S. Mill or Milton or the International Covenant on Civil and Political Rights would be determinative. Five morally bankrupt or morally bereft judgments beats four morally uplifting and highly quotable judgments remains the rule.

If that sort of Waldronian dissensus and disagreement is what the Visiting Martian would observe, how might things alter when we adopt the Concerned Citizen's Vantage? Not very much at all is the short answer. Our Concerned Citizen would observe the same disagreements and dissensus as the Visiting Martian. His moral views would not align perfectly, or in some instances all that regularly, with those of the majority of the justices on the highest court. The main difference would be this. On most of these issues the Concerned Citizen would himself have strong, heartfelt views. The temptation to see those who disagreed or took opposing positions as ill informed or morally blind or in need of re-education would be ever present. Or to make the same point in less kindly terms, there is always scope for the Concerned Citizen's Vantage to slip into that of the Sanctimonious Man. When it comes to contested moral issues, it is certainly not unheard of for people to betray an attitude that seems to rest on the implicit proposition that they, somehow, have a pipeline to God – one denied to those with opposing views.

What of the Judge's Vantage? From this vantage, is the extent of moral disagreement and dissensus in society less apparent? It can certainly seem that way at times. Take the manner in which moral values are articulated in various areas of administrative law or family law or contract law or criminal law or, more explicitly still, in bills of rights. Such values are often sold – or articulated – up in the Olympian heights of consensus-achieving moral abstractions. In other words, they are enunciated in vague, amorphous and indeterminate terms. They are framed in terms that finesse disagreement. Of course such values play out, and have real effect, down in the quagmire of detail, of drawing debatable and contested lines as regards acceptable hiring and firing procedures, say, or which actions, taken in reliance on pre-contractual assurances, to compensate, or campaign finance rules, or hate-speech provisions, or where precisely to balance access to a lawyer against lessening the occurrence of drunk driving, and so much more.

The more the Judge's Vantage deals in terms of the 'freedom of expression' side of the ledger, rather than the side having to answer where precisely to draw the line when it comes to acceptable campaign finance rules, the easier it will be to exaggerate the extent of moral consensus across society.

Such downplaying of moral dissensus by framing issues in consensus-achieving moral abstractions is not a fault (or practice) of the judges alone. Some citizens do it. Plenty of law professors do it. The Sanctimonious Man revels in it.

The issue for now is simply whether one is more prone to do it from the Judge's Vantage than from the Legislator's or Concerned Citizen's. And the answer to that may well be 'yes'. Certainly the judges talk in such terms frequently enough. Consider, for instance, claims made when interpreting constitutional or quasi-constitutional texts about the need to ensure that the legislature is held to a standard that is 'progressive', 'keeps pace with civilization', is 'constantly evolving', 'keeps abreast of changing social values' and so on and so on. All such judicially uttered metaphors implicitly downplay reasonable disagreement.

Other factors may also work to make the extent of moral disagreement less evident from the Judge's Vantage. There are the well-known claims about judges' relatively privileged backgrounds – the far-greater-than-in-society percentages who have attended private schools or Ivy League universities or Oxbridge. And there are the high numbers who worked in big law firms or had successful litigation careers. And of course some point to their far higher than average wealth. If these and other shared characteristics tend to narrow one's moral perspectives or to induce higher degrees of consensus than in society at large – and such claims may or may not be convincing – then the extent of expected dissensus and disagreement will be downplayed, if not ignored completely.

In addition, there is the possibility that judges are not as exposed to competing viewpoints as legislators or regular citizens. True, on a top appeals court or a supreme court one has to reckon with one's colleagues' views. A vigorous, even strident, Scalia or two can force one to think again. But such outliers are noticeably absent on Canada's top courts. And the United Kingdom's. And New Zealand's. (Australia's top court is an unusual one in that the outlier of recent years was the one who was *not* interpretively conservative, though that is changing.)

In places like Canada, there is the additional uniformity-of-outlook enhancing fact that all superior judges, federal and provincial, are chosen by the federal government (unlike in the US and Australia). And for over four-fifths of the last 45 years there, the centre-left Liberal Party has been in power in Ottawa. The illusion of apolitical judges and fair degrees of moral consensus might just be created, or nearly created, when the same political party chooses the preponderance of superior court judges over long periods of time.

This in turn raises issues about the appointment of judges. The American method for Federal and Supreme Court appointees is the most overtly political, and for that reason may give rise to the greatest breadth of outlook or of moral sensibilities. Jurisdictions with judicial appointments committees, on the other hand, and depending on the extent of residual political input, are most in danger of creating a self-selecting caste or body of judges with a narrower set of moral views than those in the wider society. Were that so, this would be another way in which the extent of moral disagreement and dissensus could be less apparent from the Judge's Vantage.

Let us turn to three other vantages before concluding this section. Start with the Bad Man. By definition this Holmesian literary device adopts a viewpoint that cares only for law. He is wholly amoral. At first glance, then, the extent of moral consensus or dissensus across society does not concern him, not in the least.

Yet that is not quite right. If we suppose, say, that the period since the end of World War II can be characterized as one in which American constitutional notions (broadly speaking as involving in part the articulation of amorphous moral standards in the language of rights in an instrument that has legal force and allows for some sort of judicial review on the basis of those standards) have gradually triumphed almost everywhere that can plausibly be said to have a Benevolent Legal System, then it is also the case – as a matter of fact – that judges in those jurisdictions have become comparatively more powerful. They have more scope than they did to resolve at least some contentious cases (call them 'penumbra of doubt' cases with Hart or 'Hard Cases' with Dworkin or something else again) on the basis of *their* moral views, be that directly or be that indirectly working through some sort of Dworkinian 'best fit' edifice. And in addition, because of these instruments, more cases in turn become penumbral or hard cases.

This means that for the Bad Man, one who cares solely what the law is and who is in need of predictions as to the *law's* scope and demands, it may at times be necessary to consider the judges' moral views – on abortion, affirmative action, hate speech, gun control, same-sex marriage, etcetera. Or more to the point of this section, it may be necessary for the Bad Man to consider the extent of moral dissensus *amongst the judges*.

In this context the Bad Man's Vantage is there to remind us that moral abstractions incorporated into law (or read in by the judges themselves) are *not* self-defining. One who cares not a whit for morality in general, nor about the extent to which there may be disagreements across society on morally laden issues, may well care about the extent of judicial disagreements on such issues. He will care about judicial disagreements on such issues precisely to the extent that judges' moral views will be determinative in deciding what the law is. No more, no less.

The Law Professor's Vantage is worth a brief consideration solely because it seems plausible to argue that the moral centre of gravity there is noticeably to the left of society's. Or more relevantly here, the range of acceptable moral opinions – at least in a bell-curve sort of sense – is narrower. Within the law schools, the extent of moral disagreement and dissensus may accordingly be less apparent. At any rate, it may be less acknowledged or less countenanced.

It may follow, if Waldronian moral dissensus is less acknowledged, that it is easier to call for greater judicial moral input at the point-of-application from this vantage. If so, it is easier still to do so to the extent one suspects the judges will deliver more of one's own first-order moral preferences than the voters and their elected representatives. (A corollary of that is that a perceived-to-be-right-wing top court should engender new-found scepticism as regards judicial review and judicial powers from legal academics.)

That leaves us to conclude this section on moral dissensus and disagreement by considering the Moral Philosopher's Vantage. One obvious question I have thus far side-stepped is whether mind-independent (or in some other sense transcendent or real or objective) answers actually exist when it comes to moral issues and dilemmas.

From the Moral Philosopher's Vantage we can see that this is a hotly contested second-order issue in its own right, namely, what is the status of moral evaluations. Broadly speaking there are two camps. On the one side are those who might on a theistic, or Kantian, or natural law, or of late Dworkinian, or any other deontological basis subscribe to what might be described as moral realism or moral objectivism. They argue that there is a mind-independent quality – a rightness or wrongness independent of the way some, most, or even all people happen to feel – to moral evaluations. On the other side are those who might for Humean, or utilitarian (because while utilitarians can in theory be moral realists, it is in practice difficult to think that the right thing to do is that which, looking forward, tends to increase overall human welfare and that that outcome is divorced from contingent human sentiments in some mind-independent way), or Mackiean error theory, or Blackburnian quasi-realist, or any other basis subscribe to what might be called moral scepticism or moral subjectivism or non-cognitivism. They argue that ultimately all moral evaluations are mind-dependent and linked to the feelings or sentiments people happen to have. On this side, then, there is a certain etherealness or insubstantialness or variability to moral evaluations, though the degree varies within this camp.

Our Moral Philosopher would tell us that this is a long-standing and still live debate in moral philosophy. No side or camp has clearly won the intellectual argument.

So why mention it at all? One such reason is to note the temptation that might exist for some of those more inclined towards the moral realist or moral objectivist camp to downplay observed moral disagreement and moral dissensus on the basis that the fact people disagree in no way disproves the existence of mind-independently right moral answers to all the issues that are provoking the observed disagreement.

This is Dworkin's line of argument. From the fact that three, four, twenty, thousands or even tens of millions of people might disagree, it does not follow that there is no right answer. And, clearly, Dworkin is correct as far as he goes. The existence of observed disagreement does not prove the moral sceptic's or non-cognitivist's case. John Mackie conceded as much in arguing for that sceptical case. Of course it is equally true – in a way Dworkin obscures or never makes explicit – that the existence of observed disagreement does not itself prove the moral realist's case either. From the that fact that people disagree about the rightness and wrongness of X, it in no way follows that there *is* a mind-independent right answer (any more than it follows that there is not one).

Jeremy Waldron insightfully shows how this live and interesting and unresolved debate in moral philosophy in no way undermines the relevance of observed and real moral dissensus and disagreement when it comes to the 'who should decide these issues' question. For as Waldron notes, even if *ex hypothesi* moral realism of some form be ultimately true and correct and so mind-independent answers to contested and disagreed upon moral issues and evaluations do exist (the metaphysical issue), it remains the case that we humans do not know what those answers are in any sense beyond our own individual beliefs (the epistemological issue). So when moral realist disagrees with moral realist on the issue of same-sex marriage, or euthanasia, or refugee policy, each can claim his or her view is more than just a moral sentiment – is in some sense mind-independently correct. But neither can appeal to any agreed procedure for convincing the other. (And the difference with empirical and scientific disputes is at this point abundantly clear. Anyone who rejects the mind-independent existence of gravity can be ushered up to an eighth-floor office and asked to jump. The issue will be settled independently of the contingent views either of us might hold.)

In more succinct terms, the fact of observed moral dissensus matters even for moral realists. The fact that someone claims a particular moral evaluation to be a mind-independently true one does not, in and of itself, make it so. Worse, people claiming the same second-order status (i.e., 'this is a mind-independently correct moral evaluation') will disagree as to the first-order substance of the claim. ('You said abortion was morally permissible. I say it is not.')

From the Moral Philosopher's Vantage we would see all that, and so would be able to withstand the temptation to say observed moral dissensus in society is irrelevant to (or, less strongly, weakens the importance of) the 'who should decide' question.

A second reason for adopting the Moral Philosopher's Vantage is more speculative. It is simply to raise the possibility mooted by Stephen Smith. This is the possibility that our Benevolent Legal Systems need the implicit support of some sort of moral realist or natural law scaffolding, even if many or most legal actors and commentators reject the plausibility of moral realism and natural law and even if that scaffolding and support is erected at such a high degree of moral abstraction that it finesses all or most of the actual moral dissensus and disagreement in society.

The claim is an intriguing one, and a plausible one, though I do no more than repeat it here. That said, it in no way answers the question of whether unelected judges' moral input at the point-of-application should be kept to a minimum. So we turn to that next.

The Consequences of Keeping to a Minimum the Moral Input of the Point-of-Application Judges

From the Judge's Vantage we have already seen that the extent of moral disagreement across society – and perhaps, too, the felt intensity of that disagreement – can appear to be less than from other vantages. It is not as obviously present. Not only that, the attractions from that same vantage of keeping to a minimum the moral input of the judiciary are likely also to be less apparent.

Of course any discussion of the most desirable level of moral input from the unelected judges in a Benevolent Legal System begins with the clear, observable fact that judges' moral input nowhere is zero. Common law legal systems, for example, refer to and force the point-of-application judges to consider all sorts of moral principles – the 'reasonable person' test in tort law, the 'best interests of the child' test in family law, 'duress and unconscionability' in contract law, 'undue influence' in the law of succession, the notion of 'novelty' in intellectual property law, plus such determinations as what amounts to 'confidential information' and 'restraint of trade'. And that is without even leaving what is broadly the private law side of the ledger. Administrative, constitutional and criminal law, the public law side of the ledger, make even greater use of moral and wider normative tests.

Our starting point, in other words, is not one in which the judge's moral judgment never enters into his or her decision-making in some puritanical, extremist sense. We all recognize that legislatures (however much we may or may not want to condemn them for it) will sometimes enact statutes that do little more than set out a moral test (e.g., 'good faith bargaining') and then hand the decision to the point-of-application judges. Whether the consequences of such statutes be good or bad, the blending of morality into law is not here initiated by the judges. The same goes for any justiciable bill of rights brought into being with a modicum of democratic credentials.

Similarly, judges deciding a case that falls into Hart's penumbra of doubt, where the valid rules provide no clear answer, need for practical reasons to decide the case one way or the other. As Hart himself recognized, it would be undesirable on efficiency grounds to send such cases back to the legislature. And when one of these penumbral cases does arise, we would expect it to be resolved often enough (at least in part) on the basis of morality. In fact, Hart probably undersells the frequency of such penumbra of doubt and uncertainty cases because he ties the uncertainty and doubt solely to the nature of language. Yet moral dissensus and disagreement of the sort discussed above can also give rise to penumbral cases, because of all the existing moral tests.

In this section, then, we are not considering why judges might have the levels of moral input they do in a Benevolent Legal System, or who is most to blame for that state of affairs. We are, instead, considering the consequences of minimizing it, or perhaps just of reducing it, or maybe even of preventing it from increasing any more than it already has in the last half century. We are looking at the consequences of curbing the judges' moral input. If for no other reasons than those Hart gives as regards the inefficiency of sending penumbral cases back to the legislature, eliminating completely judges' moral input may not be possible; nor is some puritanical excising of it palpably desirable or something likely to lead to good consequences.

That said, our focus in this second chapter is on the likely future consequences related to who ends up deciding contentious moral and political issues. In other words, the focus is on who has the last word. A system in which judges have scope, plenty of scope even, to bring their own moral sentiments and judgments to bear in deciding the cases before them is also wholly compatible with a system in which those very same judges never have the last word. So they might develop a very morally driven body of negligence law related to personal injuries, and yet the elected legislature overrules them with a statutory no-fault personal injury regime, as happened in New Zealand. Or the judges might stake out a strong entitlement to cross-examine one's accuser in criminal trials, but the legislature partially overrules them as regards complainants in rape cases.

Who ends up deciding? Who has the last word, not just in form but in substance? That is the live issue. Whatever one thinks about the extent of judges' moral input generally, whether it might be beneficially lessened in all sorts of ways or not, there is a major difference between the situation where that judicial moral input can be gainsaid by the elected legislature, and the situation where it cannot.

It is the 'last word' moral input of the judges, the latter of the two situations, that I will concentrate on in the rest of this section. What are the consequences of minimizing that? Admittedly, the distinction between 'the morality of the judges is the last word on some issue' and 'it is not the last word' is nowhere near as clear cut as I may have implied. There will be cases where the judges evidently do have the last word. (Think of any constitutionalized moral tests, most archetypically in the form of an entrenched, justiciable bill of rights.) Yet there will also be cases where it is debatable whether the judges have the last moral word, cases that fall into the penumbra of doubt or the open texture of the distinction. (Think, perhaps, of a statutory bill of rights that nominally retains the sovereignty of parliament, though as I will suggest in later chapters my opinion is that these statutory instruments in fact often work out in practice to be near on indistinguishable from their constitutionalized, entrenched cousins in terms of giving a moral last word to the unelected judges.)

For now, though, I merely flag the sometimes tenuous nature of any claimed distinction between instances where judges' moral input is determinative – where they have the last word – and those where it is not. As noted, I will return to the point below in Chapters 5 and 6 when considering bills of rights. Here, I simply gloss over the indeterminacies related to when the unelected judges do, and do not, have the last word and turn to the consequences of minimizing their moral input in all last-word situations.

The Judge

The more it is true that judges' moral judgments and sentiments can be overruled by the legislators' moral judgments and sentiments, the less room there will be for judges to ameliorate what they see as the harsh effects of legislatively laid-down rules. In a parliamentary sovereignty jurisdiction with an unwritten constitution – say, the United Kingdom before the introduced complications of its entry into Europe in 1972 and its recent statutory bill of rights or New Zealand before its 1990 statutory bill of rights – the scope for the legislature to have the last word and to overrule the judges even as regards Hart's penumbral cases will be very great indeed. Yet even in this situation the judges will have the last moral word sometimes, be it, say, on the status of enactments passed without the consent of the legislative House of Lords[2] or on the status of European laws.[3]

In Australia, a federal jurisdiction with a written constitution but no national bill of rights, the judges' moral views will prevail more often again, but still nowhere near as frequently as in all those other Benevolent Legal Systems with some sort – any sort – of bill of rights.

The point is that even limiting ourselves to the issue of the judges' moral input in a last-word, determinative, cannot-be-overruled sense, we are talking about minimizing or reducing it, not eliminating it completely. We are talking about real-life options ranging at one end from New Zealand and the United Kingdom (at least as they were 20 or 30 years ago), through Australia today, out to the United States and Canada at the far other end where judges have the most 'cannot be gainsaid' moral input. Other countries fall somewhere between these two poles.

It follows from what I argued in Chapter 1, and indeed is in keeping with most people's first instincts, that the consequences of minimizing this sort of moral input will generally look worst from the Judge's Vantage. Judges, more than any others, are likely to trust the beneficial consequences of the judges' own moral

---

2   See *Jackson* v. *Attorney-General* [2006] 1 AC 262 and my analysis of that case in 'The Paradox of Sovereignty: *Jackson* and the Hunt for a New Rule of Recognition?' (2007) 18 *King's Law Journal* 1.

3   See *R* v. *Secretary of State for Transport ex parte Factortame Ltd* [1990] 1 AC 85 (HL).

input and welcome any authorization to resort to moral principles in deciding the cases before them. This might be seen in terms of counteracting any tyranny-of-the-majority dangers or acting as a check and balance or providing a sober second thought or upholding rights-based principles against utilitarian-calculated policies. Whatever the metaphor, the core notion is related to the judiciary's being in a better position, or better able, to deliver moral judgments than are the elected branches.

In other words, if blending law and morality together has ramifications in terms of the greater scope judges will have to infuse their own moral views into law and so to decide morally contentious social issues – who gets the last word on where to draw the line when it comes to such things as campaign finance rules, same-sex marriage, immigration, abortion, which punishments are acceptable and much more – then that greater scope will be most attractive and easily defended from the Judge's Vantage. And attempts to minimize that scope for judicial input, obversely, will appear least beneficial and least justified from the Judge's Vantage.

As I have claimed in Chapter 1, for the Benthamite advocate of separating law and morality, this will be the set of consequences that matters most, and even more so in today's world. Limiting judicial power (in the sense of minimizing judges' last-word moral input) is far more of a live issue in Benevolent Legal Systems than is promoting a greater willingness to disobey odious laws or knowing how best to deal with possible War Crimes suspects. As for deliberate, planned law reform, important as it is, it simply does not engage the pro- and anti-separation debate in the way questions tied to the desirability of curbing judicial line-drawing powers do. Everyone is a Benthamite when it comes to deliberate law reform. Many judges, many law professors, a surprising number of citizens and even some legislators are not when it comes to minimizing judges' last-word moral input.

Accordingly, I would say that Hart uncharacteristically misfired when he argued why we *should* keep separate law and morality. He misfired by leaving out of his account the bad consequences that might flow from too much judicial moral input, though as he was writing in 1961 that may be unfair – at least unfair in relation to everywhere outside the US. Nearly half a century on, however, and with the triumph of American constitutionalism a plausible description of those intervening years as regards Benevolent Legal Systems, any answer to why law and morality should largely be kept separate must include John Gray's 'puncture of windbags'[4] type response. Hence, it may be good to keep separate law and morality because none of us, the judges included, has a pipeline to God on contentious moral issues, even where those issues are articulated in rights-based terms, decided by committees of ex-lawyers required to issue written reasons for their decisions and presented in terms that finesse and downplay actual disagreement – that prefer the Olympian heights of moral abstractions to the quagmire of specific line-drawing details.

---

4   See John Gray, 'Some Definitions and Questions in Jurisprudence' (1892) 6 *Harvard Law Review* 21, at p. 23.

Any elision and blending together of law and morality runs the risk of producing a legal system where too much moral say is handed over to the point-of-application unelected judges. Different people, not least because they come to the issue from different vantages, no doubt disagree about when that point has been reached and, relatedly, about the consequentialist benefits of keeping judges' last-word moral input to a minimum. I have said already that the Judge's Vantage is the one least likely to see the benefits of puncturing puffed-up moral windbags (or, more precisely, even to see the issue in those terms).

That said, adopt the Judge's Vantage and one might point in response to the under- or over-inclusive nature of all rules, and hence to the consequentialist benefits of flexibility at the point-of-application. As Hart and many others have noted, all legal systems must strike a balance between the two sometimes competing values of certainty in the operation of rules and flexibility as regards their application. We want certainty so people can know in advance what the rules demand, shape their conduct and actions accordingly and generally find their expectations satisfied. This sort of certainty is closely tied to the older, procedural incarnation of Rule of Law talk where one is said to value general rules whose application (or not) can be known in advance. But we also want flexibility at the point-of-application because we know that all rules, however fanatically detailed, will be under- and over-inclusive; a time will arise when the rule fails to cover instances intended to be covered and another when it covers instances not meant to be covered. There is absolutely nothing novel in that insight. It is just that from the Judge's Vantage the value and attractions of flexibility at the point-of-application tend to get emphasized, in part because the arguably under- and over-inclusive instances are the ones that motivate people to spend large amounts of money to litigate in court.

Having scope to instil morality (or more accurately put, to appeal to and place some reliance on the *judge's view* of what is morally appropriate) when deciding cases is no exception. Flexibility here too can have good consequences. Moreover, it is from the Judge's Vantage, perhaps more than from any other, that the advantages of flexibility are most obvious and those of certainty least evident.

A temptation that needs to be resisted at this point is to see the issue of judges' last-word moral input in terms of rule utilitarianism and act utilitarianism. Flexibility at the point-of-application, on this understanding, more or less equates to act utilitarianism, to deciding on a case-by-case-by-case basis. Rule utilitarianism, just applying the rule, then stands in for certainty. The reason for resisting the temptation to characterize the issue in these terms is not because rule utilitarianism might be inherently unstable, as some have suggested, and so be prone to collapsing into act utilitarianism in extreme cases. That may well be true (though it is more debatable when one body makes the rules and another applies and interprets them). Nor need anyone deny the truth that no rule – however fanatically detailed – will ever have a 100 per cent hit rate in terms of applying when it should and not applying when it should not. In any situation in which we have to decide between case-by-case decision making and application-of-a-rule decision making we know, going in, that both methods will deliver less than 100 per cent of the time. (And our Visiting Martian might be inclined on occasion to remind the odd real-life judge of this fact.)

Hence, we opt for a strict 'vote when you turn 18' rule in the full awareness that many 17-year-olds are more civically aware and politically involved than a host of 18-year-olds, or indeed of those of any older age. We opt for the rule because we think its hit rate of enfranchising those we want voting – be it a 92 per cent or 88 per cent or something else rate – will outscore any possible or practical case-by-case procedure. We suspect, in other words, that the costs and potentials for corruption and fraud of having panels of people decide who can vote will do worse than the rule. Neither the strict application of a rule nor the flexible case-by-case decision making by an individual or group will ever deliver 100 per cent results. In some situations, such as who can vote, we predict that the rule-based method is the way to go and in others, such as who can drive, we opt for individualized decision making, fully apprised of its extra costs and different potential frailties. But no one is foolish enough to expect either route, ever, to be perfect. Both routes will be under- and over-inclusive.

The temptation when it comes to looking at the consequences of judicial moral input from the Judge's Vantage is to think this is a scenario in which we are deciding between flexibility (and the relative hit rate of case-by-case decision making) and certainty (with the hit rate that would come from always applying a rule). But in fact it is not that sort of scenario at all. When the judges are to some extent authorized to resort to moral principles in deciding cases that come before them, let us suppose by means of a US-style or Canadian-style bill of rights, it is in the context of there being a hierarchy of courts, *stare decisis* and an observable infrequency in the top court over-ruling itself. All this gives you what amounts to recognizably rule-governed outcomes. *Roe* v. *Wade* decided that all women can have abortions, not merely that the particular woman before the US Supreme Court in her particular situation could have one. The same goes for decisions by top judges to allow or legalize same-sex marriage. In Massachusetts and Canada all homosexual couples can marry, not simply the ones who appeared before the judges. It is not like getting a driver's licence. Again, as far as those claiming refugee status in Canada goes, all are entitled to an oral hearing and government-provided lawyer, due to the moral input of the top judges, not simply the litigants who first raised the issue.

Where judges have that sort of scope to infuse their own moral views into law the result cannot be characterized as an act utilitarian one. It is similar, if not identical, to a rule-based outcome. It is just that the judges, or rather the top judges, or rather still a majority of the top judges, have made the rule – constrained, no doubt, to the extent one thinks the relevant entrenched bill of rights is constraining (or rather, constrained to the extent that the interpretive theory used, be that some version of originalism or pragmatism or best-fit Dworkinianism or 'living tree' progressivism or anything else, in fact constrains those judges).

That means that even from the Judge's Vantage the consequentialist benefits of withstanding attempts to minimize judges' last-word moral input do not really sound in terms of flexibility *per se*. Rather, they will have to sound in more accustomed terms: Of judges not being swayed by the next election; of having (at least some of) the affected parties there in front of them; of deciding based on principle and rights rather than policy and overall social welfare calculations; of all the variations on the Ulysses-tying-himself-to-the-mast Siren-song theme; of being a check and a balance on the legislature; and any I have inadvertently left out.

All of these accustomed and regularly heard grounds for *not* minimizing judges' last-word moral input are most persuasive and most plausible from the Judge's Vantage.

The Concerned Citizen

The consequences of *minimizing* judges' 'cannot be gainsaid' moral input are most obviously attractive from the Concerned Citizen's Vantage. Or at least that is what one might expect. One might expect the Concerned Citizen to think his moral sentiments every bit as finely attuned as any judge's, those of the top Supreme Court included. If judges are deciding based on morality, and moral sentiments and moral judgments, the Concerned Citizen might well think that *legally* trained judges have no more moral expertise than plumbers or secretaries or teachers or CEOs of large companies or even of bond traders.

And of course from the Concerned Citizen's Vantage, more than from the Judge's, the consequentialist benefits of democratic decision making are likely to be more apparent. Nor are there obvious grounds uniquely to exclude moral matters from being best resolved by 'letting the numbers count'. After all, the Concerned Citizen will know that letting the numbers count has delivered the modern welfare state; it has extended the vote to women and blacks and indigenous peoples; it has produced elected politicians who stood up to and defeated Hitler and fascism and later on a decrepit communism; it has in most places ended capital punishment; it has brought in compulsory schooling and vastly extended tertiary education opportunities; it has legislated into existence anti-discrimination commissions, and ombudsmen.

This is all pretty clear from the Concerned Citizen's Vantage. Just as clear from that vantage is that democratic decision making procedures and institutions have not glossed over and made disappear fundamental moral disagreements between people in society over matters such as abortion, euthanasia, same-sex marriage, economic refugees, the most desirable criminal procedures and countless other things. They may, perhaps, have made it somewhat harder to think the world divides easily into those on the side of the angels and those who are wicked, ignorant or just dumb. But if so, the Concerned Citizen might consider that a further good consequence.

What else might our Concerned Citizen list as a benefit flowing from minimizing moral input at the point-of-application? From that vantage what stands out is the process itself. The less last-word moral input the unelected judges have in this Benevolent Legal System, the more these contentious, social line-drawing issues will be decided on the basis of a process that looks something as follows: Count each adult citizen equally in terms of granting him or her a vote to elect representatives who will, on a majoritarian basis, decide all these contentious, debatable, morally laden, social line-drawing issues such as the rights and wrongs of capital punishment or how to organize society's immigration procedures and campaign finance rules or what limits to put on abortion and euthanasia. Leaving aside for a moment how well outcomes produced by this sort of letting-the-numbers-count procedure fare as against one with more moral input from the unelected judges – meaning which option's outcomes are seen to produce better consequences, to get it right more often – and focusing solely on 'who gets to make the decision' grounds, the Concerned Citizen might be expected to prefer this process over one that abdicates a few, some or plenty of moral calls to the judges. To put it more bluntly, if the outcomes produced look pretty similar, neither option being indisputably or self-evidently more productive of good outcomes, then the more democratic process with all its 'related good consequences' should carry the day. Or so we might anticipate the Concerned Citizen to say.

Those related good consequences are well known. They include all the virtues (or good consequences) normally emphasized in republican theories, benefits such as having an involved citizenry that is responsible for the decisions taken in its name – one where people are encouraged to participate in political life, to debate key issues, and to play an active role in the polis. Lon Fuller, despite holding views more sympathetic to systems where judges have a larger ambit for infusing their own moral views into law, nevertheless put this version of the republican case into the mouth of his hypothetical Justice Keen in his famous 'The Case of the Speluncean Explorers':

> Judges have been celebrated in literature for their sly prowess in devising some quibble by which a litigant could be deprived of his rights where the public thought it was wrong for him to assert those rights. But I believe that judicial dispensation does more harm in the long run than hard decisions. Hard cases may even have a certain moral value by bringing home to the people their own responsibilities toward the law that is ultimately their creation, and by reminding them that there is no principle of personal grace that can relieve the mistakes of their representatives.
>
> Indeed, I will go farther and say that not only are the principles I have been expounding those which are soundest for our present conditions, but that we would have inherited a better legal system from our forefathers if those principles had been observed from the beginning. For example, with respect to the excuse of self-defense, if our courts had stood steadfast on the language of the statute the result would undoubtedly have been a legislative revision of

it. Such a revision would have drawn on the assistance of natural philosophers and psychologists, and the resulting regulation of the matter would have had an understandable and rational basis, instead of the hodgepodge of verbalisms and metaphysical distinctions that have emerged from the judicial and professorial treatment.[5]

Those sorts of process values and claimed good consequences related to a fully involved and responsible citizenry are most visible from the Concerned Citizen's Vantage. And anyway, from that vantage the competing outcomes produced in no way look to favour processes where judges have comparatively greater moral input. Australia, without a national bill of rights, compares well in moral terms to the US, Canada and the UK. The outcomes – the moral outcomes in those three just-mentioned jurisdictions where judges' last-word moral input is considerably greater – do not appear noticeably better. In hosts of areas across the spectrum of contentious moral and political issues many would say Australia has done the better job. Nor do the outcomes in New Zealand before its 1990 statutory bill of rights or in Canada before its 1982 entrenched model or in the United Kingdom before its 1998 statutory version appear worse than the outcomes that came afterwards. (At any rate that appears plausible, provided one does not just assume that politics and democratic decision making somehow would have become frozen on those bill-of-rights-producing dates and that no elected legislature would ever have gone on to enact, say, abortion-liberalizing laws or same-sex marriage-type laws or anti-discrimination and affirmative action laws or whatever it is that you happen to like about what the judges have done since these moral-input-for-judges-enhancing instruments came into force. Somewhat bizarrely, however, some people do make this sort of unwarranted assumption!)

Next, we might expect our Concerned Citizen to point to Rule of Law advantages that flow from minimizing point-of-application, last-word moral input. Think back to Hart's penumbra of doubt or penumbra of uncertainty cases, those that fall into a rule's open texture. As I have suggested above, Hart attributed these cases to the nature of language alone, and that is implausibly too reductionist. Another cause of penumbral cases – cases where the rule itself does not dictate an answer or even suggest a most plausible one to the vast preponderance of interpreters – is moral dissensus in society (and amongst judges) where the law happens to build in a moral test at the point-of-application. A rule that awards custody based on the 'best interests of the child' or another that prohibits 'cruel and unusual punishment' will throw up penumbral cases just because there will arise certain factual situations where people split more or less evenly in their moral evaluations or judgments. Lots of people will think the moral test points one way. Lots of people will think it points the other way. The same divide might split the judiciary.

---

5   Lon Fuller, 'The Case of the Speluncean Explorers' (1949) 62 *Harvard Law Review* 616, at pp. 636–7.

In these situations, it is the built-in moral test itself that is giving rise to the rule's open texture. And that, at least from the Concerned Citizen's Vantage, raises Rule of Law issues. Or rather, it raises Rule of Law issues in the older, procedural understanding of 'the Rule of Law', where good consequences are thought usually to follow on from having a system in which people are regulated by general rules, known in advance, applying to all, by which they are capable of abiding and so can shape their expectations and conduct without waiting for some authoritative interpretation. Moreover, the good consequences here are independent of the substantive content of any of the particular rules.

Reducing judges' last-word moral input would shrink a rule's penumbra of doubt. It would further this procedural, non-substantive understanding of the Rule of Law. And that, in turn, would appear most attractive from the Concerned Citizen's Vantage. Or rather, we would expect this vantage, more than the judge's or any other's, to see this diminishing of the scope for last-word moral input at the point-of-application as a plus, as likely to generate good long-term consequences.

To recap, then, our Concerned Citizen might be expected to see good consequences flowing from minimizing the last-word moral input of unelected judges. These perceived benefits or good consequences might relate to the legitimacy of democratic decision making itself, and the republican values associated with that sort of process. They might relate to not obscuring the moral and political divides and dissensus in society. They might relate to the good things that having a procedural Rule of Law regime produces. Most basically, they might simply sound in better outcomes – that letting the numbers count when it comes to society's difficult, contentious, highly disputed moral line-drawing exercises achieves better outcomes than incorporating some sort of point-of-application moral test and so increasing judges' last-word moral input and hence decision making powers.

And, of course, many Concerned Citizens do think all that. But by no means all Concerned Citizens subscribe to those expectations. Many prefer *not* to minimize last-word moral input at the point-of-application. They prefer the unelected judges to the elected legislators. (One has only to observe the popularity of the *Canadian Charter of Rights and Freedoms* to see this as a possibility, the Canadian *Charter* being a much more popular instrument, it would seem, than the related instrument in the United Kingdom.)

Why might these other Concerned Citizens prefer not to limit judges' last-word moral input? Three possibilities spring to mind. The first is the most straightforward. Here we have the self-interested citizen who simply calculates that the judges are more likely to decide his way – to satisfy more of his first-order moral and political preferences – than the elected politicians (and, relatedly, his fellow voting citizens). So across the spectrum of contentious social issues ranging from same-sex marriage and capital punishment to affirmative action and acceptable criminal procedures (even as regards suspected terrorists) this citizen calculates that the judges' moral views are more closely aligned to his own than are the elected legislators'.

That is a wholly understandable point of view and reason for preferring higher levels of judicial moral input. It may, or may not, be short sighted in terms of its assumption that the judiciary's views will continue to more closely reflect one's own. Likewise, it may too easily forget that it is harder to replace the judiciary than the elected branches when their outcomes are repeatedly diverging from one's preferred outcomes. Likewise again, it may too readily discount the good long-term consequences of letting-the-numbers-count decision making procedures, though such a self-interested motivation might be combined with the virtue of being honest and open in conceding that its judge-focused preference is less democratic, perhaps not democratic at all in some senses or instances.

A second possibility is that our judge-preferring Concerned Citizen, by focusing upon the Olympian heights of moral abstractions, thinks there is a greater degree of consensus across society on moral issues than she might had she focused on more specific line-drawing moral and political disputes down in the quagmire of detail. As I suggested in the last section, the more moral consensus one perceives there to be in society, the easier it is to hand moral-input powers to unelected judges.

A third possibility is that our judge-preferring Concerned Citizen believes both *1)* that there are mind-independently right moral answers to contentious and disputed social line-drawing issues *and 2)* that the unelected judges are more likely to find or discover such answers than the legislators. Notice that *1)* alone is not enough. Notice, too, that this third possibility tends to ignore consequences related to *how* a decision was reached, concentrating largely or exclusively on whether the outcome reached is (or is likely to be) a good one. It implicitly assumes that there cannot be more value in using the right (or better) procedure to reach a wrong (or worse) outcome. Or, taking account of the fact that we are weighing dynamic, ongoing situations where decisions will need continually to be made over time, it seems to assume that a few more right (or better) outcomes here and there cannot be outweighed – in terms of long-term consequences, at any rate – by a more participatory, legitimate decision making process. Or, in more realistic terms still, it does this in a world in which there is no agreed method for showing or convincing others that one's own moral right answers – what I say are the answers that deserve the label 'upholding fundamental human rights' – are in fact correct and the equally sincerely held or felt or believed answers of others are not.

There, then, are three possible grounds for a Concerned Citizen to prefer greater, not lesser, moral input from the judges. No doubt there are others. Nevertheless, and in no way seeking to ignore or downplay the existence and extent of such judge-preferring Concerned Citizens, it remains the case that the good consequences and benefits of minimizing judges' 'cannot be gainsaid' moral input are most obviously apparent and attractive from the Concerned Citizen's Vantage.

The Law Professor and the Legislator

How does the issue of limiting or minimizing judicial power (in the sense of reducing or just constraining judges' last-word moral input) in Benevolent Legal Systems look from the Law Professor's Vantage? Certainly many, many, many law professors in the United States, in Canada, in the United Kingdom, in New

Zealand and in Australia are opposed to minimizing judges' last-word moral input. For example, given a choice between some version of parliamentary sovereignty (where the legislature is *legally* unlimited in what it can do but, of course, faces a host of political and moral constraints) and a system where the legislature is legally limited (which means that the judges will be in the position of authoritatively interpreting and applying those legal limits, and hence what constrains the judges are political considerations and morality), most law professors in the above countries prefer the latter. At least that is an empirical claim I am confident would stand up to any and all forms of testing, surveys and sampling.

The three possible grounds mooted above for why a Concerned Citizen might prefer *not* to limit judges' last-word moral input could apply here too, to the preponderance of law professors in the Anglo-American common law world who share that preference. As regards law professors, there is a further possible factor at work. It is the one raised by Oliver Wendell Holmes over a century ago in his famous 'The Path of the Law', namely that the dominant way of teaching law (in the common law world at any rate) is to have students put themselves in the shoes of the top judges. Law schools feed students a steady diet of cases from the top courts. They devote significantly less time to having students read statutes than to having them read cases. They rarely point out, with Hart, that legal rules often provide clear answers and hence that most disputes never lead to the hiring of lawyers, that those that do overwhelmingly settle, that few first-instance decisions are appealed and that cases reaching the level of appeal court studied by law students are grossly unrepresentative (not least in distortingly accentuating uncertainty of outcome). More often than not law schools implicitly ask law students to consider, ponder and learn the law from the Judge's Vantage, not the Lawyer's.

Complaining about this was one of the themes in Holmes' famous paper, written to be delivered in 1896 to the first-ever graduating class at the then brand-new Boston University Law School. Given that Holmes' complaints about the overwhelmingly judge-centric approach to legal education still today largely apply – the various legal aid and lawyers' skills programmes notwithstanding – and perhaps this sort of day-to-day emphasis on what judges do contributes to shaping the attitudes of some of our judge-preferring Law Professors (not to overlook the similarly inclined law students).

Meanwhile, if any vantage is going to see the attractions and consequential advantages of limiting the last-word moral input of the judges it will be the Legislator's Vantage. She will consider her *moral* perspicacity every bit as good as the legally trained judge's. And she knows that she is elected, and in that way accountable, unlike all judges in most of our jurisdictions and all top judges even in the United States.

Much of what I said above about why the Concerned Citizen could be expected to favour minimizing last-word moral input at the point-of-application applies also to our legislator. Yet there can exist the situation in which a fairly high degree of last-word moral input has, as a matter of fact, been given to or taken by the judges in some jurisdiction or other. Against that backdrop it will sometimes be very convenient for the legislator who happens to be in favour of some particular contentious decision made by the judges – say, to allow flag burning or to legalize same-sex marriage – to pretend that she is not. This legislator can blame the judge for what she thinks (*sotto voce*) is the morally good or right decision. She can vote to pass statutes banning flag burning, secure in the knowledge that they will be struck down by the United States Supreme Court. She can vote against same-sex marriage, knowing the Canadian courts cannot be gainsaid in any practical sense. In this sort of situation our legislator need not take responsibility for how she votes. She can grandstand. Indeed, the very fact that the unelected judges have the last word on these issues encourages the legislator to do so.

In at least one sense, then, having a fair degree of last-word moral input at the point-of-application might be seen as a good thing from the Legislator's Vantage. But it is in the cynical sense of leaving her relatively free to abdicate tough, contentious decisions to others, and then possibly to complain about them (sincerely or insincerely) later.

Now it may be that any time unelected judges have last-word moral input this is a possibility, even a likelihood. But from the Concerned Citizen's Vantage, its long-term bad consequences are yet another reason – one not mentioned above – for minimizing instances in which judges' moral judgments and sentiments are determinative. It is yet another reason for separating law and morality, for restricting the scope judges have to instil or infuse their own moral views into law.

Back to Bentham

This chapter has looked at the issue of separating law and morality *not* as it bears on how best to promote a greater willingness to disobey odious laws or any related variant of that long-standing debate. Rather, it has turned back to a more Benthamite concern, namely who gets to decide contentious social issues. In a Benevolent Legal System, at least, the blending together of law and morality in statutes, in constitutions, in bills of rights can affect who or which branch that will be, in the sense of shifting some of the decision-making power away from where it would lie in the absence of such a blending together. So the less the two are kept separate, the greater the scope the point-of-application judges will have to take enunciated moral abstractions, give them specific content in the cases that arise, and in that way be the ones who decide morally contentious – and yes, morally debatable – social issues.

Whether the consequences of authorising a select few unelected judges to resort occasionally or frequently to moral principles in deciding the cases before them and settling what the law is, whether that be seen as generally good or bad may be influenced by one's vantage. The Benthamite vantage that sees as bad such an authorization is clearly not that of a judge. Most plausibly it is that of the legislator, and perhaps implicitly too of the concerned citizen.

It is from that Concerned Citizen's Vantage (and the Legislator's Vantage) that this aspect of blending together or eliding law and morality appears least attractive and least beneficial, or so I have argued. From that standpoint it is most likely that good consequences will be seen to result from minimizing moral input at the point-of-application. Conversely, they will be least apparent from the Judge's Vantage, the vantage Bentham shuns and belittles.

As I have made explicit above, these 'who gets to decide' ramifications of separating or not separating law and morality are live ones in a Benevolent Legal System with an independent judiciary and an elected legislature. In a Wicked Legal System they are not, because there is little prospect there of moral (or political) input at the point-of-application – or indeed coming out of what passes for a legislature. The political and moral decision-making will take place elsewhere, a circumscribed elsewhere at that. In So-So and Theocratic Legal Systems the importance of the 'who gets to decide' issue, and hence the ramifications of minimizing point-of-application moral input, will fall somewhere between these other two poles. But the Benthamite grievance that overall bad consequences flow when the elision of law and morality leads to overmuch moral and political input being handed to – or taken by – the point-of-application judges is virtually always and everywhere one that is most relevant in a Benevolent Legal System.

That being the case, I finish this chapter by making explicit one of the trade-offs involved in varying the extent of last-word moral input at the point-of-application in a Benevolent Legal System. This trade-off is frequently obscured.

Take any two Benevolent Legal Systems. Call one country X and the other country Y. Let us assume that the former one, country X, has to a significant extent blended together law and morality – perhaps by entrenching a justiciable bill of rights or by repeated incorporations of broad moral tests into the statute book. Country Y, by contrast, has not done so. In comparative terms it has minimized the last-word moral input of its unelected judges.

Now assume some sort of extreme situation arises. The elected branches of government of these two jurisdictions proceed to act in a way that most people, in calmer times, would consider heavy handed, if not morally odious. Perhaps the legislature enacts certain anti-terrorism provisions that would result in suspects being detained without trial for unusually long periods. Or the executive branch keeps non-citizen suspects off-shore. Or members of an identifiable minority, one linked to the causing of the extreme situation, are rounded up and moved elsewhere.

In such extreme circumstances it is abundantly evident that the judges in country X – because there is less separation of law and morality there – have more legitimate scope to soften the harsh aspects of such laws and actions than do their judicial colleagues in country Y. The judges in country X may even be able to annul or strike down or re-interpret such enactments or declare unconstitutional such executive actions.

Accordingly, if we focus on such extreme situations, and especially if we judge the responses of the elected branches in hindsight and with the standards we use when times are generally good and calm and peaceful, then country X's arrangements will appear preferable to country Y's.

Put differently, the option *not* to minimize the judges' last-word moral input generates better consequences than doing so in these sorts of extreme situations. At least that appears *prima facie* likely.

However, in order to put the unelected judges in that position should such extreme situations arise, they must also be put in that position when times are not extreme. Where judges can legitimately infuse their particularized moral views into law on the basis of some set of moral abstractions' having been incorporated or blended into law, they can do so in bad times *and* good. Yes, they can do it in extreme situations. And if they actually do do so, that will be seen by many as beneficial. The price for enabling that judicial safety net, though, is a not insignificant one. To enable that, you must also enable the judges to decide various legalized moral issues where the elected branches are *not* acting in haste or without consideration of issues of rights, when times are good, calm and peaceful and there just happens to be fundamental disagreement across society. Smart, well-informed, reasonable, even nice people simply disagree about where to draw debatable, contentious lines when it comes to campaign finance rules, say, or hate-speech provisions, abortion, euthanasia, religious practices such as women wishing to cover their faces with veils when passing through airport security, how precisely to balance criminal suspects' entitlements against the safety of the general public (think about whether drunk drivers ought to be able to call a lawyer before blowing into the breathalyzer or whether the cross-examination of rape complainants can be circumscribed in non-standard ways) and so much more. In these standard, non-extreme situations country Y's minimal judicial moral input arrangements will appear preferable to many people.

By focusing on the extreme situation and attempting to justify last-word moral input at the point-of-application as a safeguard in those sort of instances, what that entails in terms of the non-extreme situation can be obscured. There is a trade-off involved in a Benevolent Legal System in choosing not to keep to a minimum the judges' legitimate last-word moral input.

The trade-off needs to be resolved by asking which of the following is the greater risk. Is it that an elected legislature and executive will do something everyone, or almost everyone, will at some future point concede is wicked? Or is it that in normal, non-extreme situations the unelected point-of-application judges will become overly powerful and unrestrained and that their moral-line drawing views will too frequently trump those of the majority of citizens in their country?

That is the trade-off issue in stark terms. Obviously there are a host of ancillary issues that might affect which of the two is seen as the greater risk. For instance, how likely is it that these extreme situations will arise where the elected branches grossly over-react? And when they do arise – when times really are grave and bleak because Pearl Harbor has been bombed or the Germans are sweeping across Europe or two skyscrapers have been demolished by suicidal fanatics – is it in fact true that the unelected judges will be able, or indeed inclined, to stand up to the elected politicians?

The less-frequent the likely instances of extreme-situation abuse, the more country X's and country Y's arrangements will be measured on the basis of the day-to-day scenario in which moral dissensus and disagreement in society between reasonable, well-meaning people is an observable fact and some procedure to resolve it needs to be adopted.

Similarly, the less likely it is that unelected judges in country X will be able to stand up to the elected branches when times are very bleak, the more the non-extreme situation (and which arrangement is preferable there) becomes the basis for choosing between country X's and country Y's arrangements.

And related to that, I suppose, is the further issue of whether the judges in country Y, judges who have little or no *legitimate* authority to instil their own moral views into law, might in extreme situations nevertheless feel compelled to lie. Will they cheat, in other words, and say the law they have sworn to uphold means something other than what they honestly take it to mean? Will they opt for morality over law *in extremis*? (And we saw in Chapter 1 that by no means must such a choice always be condemned from any or all vantages.) The point here is not so much the philosophical one, that a theory of when disobedience is warranted is distinct from a theory of how best to interpret, but rather that extreme situations may not be the best basis for choosing whether to incorporate morality into law. In extreme situations one might find either that the judges support (or are unwilling to gainsay) the elected branches, thereby nullifying the predicted advantages of incorporating morality into law. Alternatively, one might find that in extreme situations the judges in country Y sometimes disobey the law in favour of morality, thereby narrowing the differences between country X and country Y *in extremis* – though not in the non-extreme situations.

All these considerations and factors, and the weight to give them, are likely to be influenced at least somewhat by the vantage point from which they are assessed and felt. They affect differently the Judge, the Concerned Citizen, and the Legislator. That is what our Visiting Martian would observe.

I turn now to the general topic of judges and judging, where that same observation is likely also to apply. Few would deny that the role of judges in most Benevolent Legal Systems has increased in importance (if importance be measured in terms of their moral input at the point-of-application at any rate) since the time Hart was writing *The Concept of Law*. He paid comparatively scant attention to issues related to judges and judging. I will pay more, not least because these issues today are often more evidently connected to the original Benthamite goal of making the law better.

Chapter 3
Judges and Judging – I

Imagine for a moment that there exists a smart, well-read, articulate Law Professor, one who is well versed in constitutional law and more so in legal philosophy (indeed in moral and political philosophy as well). Somewhat exceptionally, this Law Professor (or if you prefer, Lawyer), or so we will imagine, favours minimizing judges' last-word moral input. He is no advocate of bills of rights, then, perhaps because he thinks these instruments fail to take seriously each citizen's right to participate in social decision making, including decisions about rights and how rights ought to play out and rank against each other. In terms of the preceding chapter's discussion, his views align with the Concerned Citizen's rather than the Judge's.

Now imagine further what would happen if this Law Professor, *mirabile dictu*, were called up by the President of the United States (or for that matter the Prime Minister of Canada, or even of the United Kingdom or New Zealand) and asked to serve on the Supreme Court. Could he accept? And if he were to accept, what would it be like for him as a judge? How would he decide the cases that came before him, including bill of rights cases?

Notice that in so far as minimizing judges' last-word moral input is concerned, this is probably more of a live issue than is whether or not to adopt (or jettison) a bill of rights or whether to repeal those statutes which have incorporated broad, indeterminate moral tests. For those who think the role given to unelected judges under these sort of instruments and statutes is a puffed-up, illegitimate one, then considering how a Judge – one with that same general view himself – might decide cases seems an instructive, and different, way to approach the issue of how to limit the judiciary. How can we keep to a minimum the moral input and rights-based social decision making of these committees of ex-lawyers and so maximize the role of Legislators and Concerned Citizens? Imagining the travails of our Law Professor newly appointed to a top judicial job is a vehicle to explore that very live and relevant question. It is how we will begin this chapter.

To start, let us name our new judge. Let us call him Judge Waldron. And let us assume that his jurisdiction is one where the electoral and legislative arrangements are in reasonably good shape. It is what I have been calling a Benevolent Legal System.

This matters. It matters not least because our Judge Waldron thinks bill of rights-style (and any functional equivalents) judicial review is illegitimate for such jurisdictions. So how he would decide these cases that came before him would presumably be affected (at times decisively affected) by whether his was a Benevolent Legal System jurisdiction or one of our other variants.

One's initial instinct would be to say that the United States and Canada, and for that matter the United Kingdom, Australia and New Zealand, are obviously Benevolent Legal Systems – countries with democratic institutions in reasonably good working order. If not these, then who?

This instinct is buttressed by a willingness not to demand perfection in the electoral and legislative arrangements. So the fact that all of us can point to what we see as imperfections in the electoral and legislative arrangements of Judge Waldron's jurisdiction is far from enough to disqualify it from Benevolent Legal System status. True, Canada has an unelected Upper House filled with appointed placemen and party hacks. And the United Kingdom, too, also lacks a genuine, elected House of Review, to say nothing of the democratic deficiencies that some would claim flow from membership in the European Union. And the United States has notorious problems with gerrymandering; with the effects of that gerrymandering, which include such vices as political party nominations or primaries counting for more than the actual elections and so driving candidates away from the political centre in their quest to appeal to less centrist party activists; and with campaign finance deficiencies that overplay the role of money in elections. Tiny New Zealand, meanwhile, has no Upper House, genuine or otherwise, and also lacks federalism. Only Australia (with federalism, a genuine elected House of Review Senate, no American-style gerrymandering, a preferential voting system, indeed compulsory voting and good campaign finance rules) appears immune from easy fault-finding.

Again, though, much more is needed to move a jurisdiction into the So-So category than an ability to spot imperfections. On any comparative basis none of the Anglo-US countries mentioned above looks anywhere near being classed as anything other than Benevolent. This is no surprise, of course. I make it explicit here solely to emphasize that there will be no easy way out for our Judge Waldron. He has accepted a job on the top court in a country where he believes 'decisions about rights made by legislatures [ought not] to be second-guessed by courts',[1] where society's 'disagreements about rights [ought to be settled] using its legislative institutions'.[2]

How then, given the political illegitimacy he thinks attaches to the task, might Judge Waldron decide those cases that come before him? Speculating on that, and on whether Professor Waldron could even accept the job on the top court, is the subject of the rest of this chapter.

What to Do?

So what ought he to do? Our Judge Waldron might surprise even himself. Once in the job he might find he adopts something like the Frankfurter or Posner or Holmes approaches – or stated approaches – to dealing with last-word moral input

---

1 Jeremy Waldron, 'The Core of the Case Against Judicial Review' (2006) 115 *Yale Law Journal* 1346, at p. 1360.

2 *Ibid.*

cases. Let's call this the 'can't help it' or 'puke test' approach. Judge Waldron's basic stance, on this approach, will be one of deference to the elected legislature. He will accept that disagreements about rights and morality ought to be settled by the legislature. Or rather, he will accept that that is the appropriate stance to take in the vast preponderance of cases.

Judge Waldron recognizes that authorizations of last-word judicial moral input – let us focus most obviously on the rights in a bill of rights – are expressed in indeterminate, amorphous terms; they are expressed as moral abstractions. When cases come before him he will be asked *not* to approve the fine sentiments that lie behind these abstractions (who wouldn't?) but rather to apply them to specific situations down in the quagmire of social-policy line drawing. He will be asked to rule on the desirable scope and ambit of these indeterminate rights, on how they might rank against one another, and on what limits on them are thought to be reasonable and justifiable. And on all these questions people just disagree. That disagreement is a fact of social life. More importantly, that disagreement takes place between reasonable, well-meaning, smart, even nice people and does so on questions over which the judiciary has no obviously greater moral perspicacity than anyone else. Or this is what our Law Professor *cum* Judge thinks. This is what makes him believe the elevated, puffed-up role and powers of unelected judges operating a last-word moral test are so illegitimate. That is why Judge Waldron will think his task at core illegitimate.

And yet the odd case, more likely only the exceptionally odd, rare and unusual case, may come before him where deference to the elected legislature would make Judge Waldron want to puke (metaphorically, at any rate). How optimistic can we be – how optimistic can our Judge Waldron himself be – that in such situations he will swallow hard or hold his nose and defer? Do not forget, he has accepted a job in which *his view* (assuming he happens to vote with the majority of others on the top court) *is determinative*. He can strike down legislation he wants struck down (under the constitutionalized bills of rights of the US and Canada). He can use the reading-down provision (section 3 in the UK and section 6 in NZ) to rewrite any legislation[3] he wants to rewrite (under statutory bills of rights).

A clear and present danger, or at least likelihood, is that Judge Waldron may not be able to help himself in such situations. He has been given the power to second-guess. He believes the contested statute to be morally deficient, and considerably so. Most human beings, rather than resign (an option I will consider below), would at some point exercise those powers. Odds are, I think, that Judge Waldron would too.

Of course few judges who, like our Judge Waldron, accept the basic illegitimacy of committees of ex-lawyers and of ex-law professors having this last moral-word second-guessing power will also follow Posner and Holmes in so explicitly setting out or articulating a 'can't help it' or 'puke' test. Some may even come to rationalize what they are doing in other, less troubling terms.

---

3   See Chapter 5 below.

Notice, too, that I am *not* mooting some moralizing judge who is wholly convinced of his or her own ability to achieve justice, to be on the side of the angels, to do the right thing, to keep pace with civilization, to know what highly indeterminate rights (and other moral) guarantees require down in the quagmire of social policy-making detail, to keep flowing the pipeline to God – though, of course, we could all quite easily begin to compile a list of this sort of judge from all of the jurisdictions under consideration. That is partly the problem. I am mooting just the opposite of that sort of judge. Yet under the dynamics of last-word moral input at the point-of-application adjudication, even our Waldron-type judge will find himself, I suspect, second-guessing the elected legislature, though of course much, much less frequently than those who have no doubts or qualms about the legitimacy of what they are doing.

Still, if our promoted Law Professor's goal is to limit and keep to a minimum the moral input (largely exercised via rights-based decision making) of unelected judges, this sort of Holmesian or Posnerite or Frankfurterite approach will likely appear attractive – not perfect, but possibly as good as it gets in practice. It may even lessen the tendency of judges to fall victim to moral self-righteousness or sanctimoniousness. Of course there will still be the 'thin skin' problem. The threshold of what makes some judges want to puke will be markedly lower than for others. And this is true even if all judges were open and honest about what they were doing when applying this puke test (which seems to me to be a highly implausible assumption).

Nevertheless, our Judge Waldron might himself come to see the attractions of the relative moral minimalism (as regards judges) of this 'can't help it' or 'puke' test. As I said, he might surprise himself. Whether he did or not would depend on how constraining other interpretive approaches proved to be when it came to bill of rights-type adjudication.

The various forms of textualism or literalism or plain-meaning interpretation would not appear to be overly constraining in the context of instances in which law and morality have been blended together by incorporating amorphous, indeterminate moral tests or standards (such as the rights in a bill of rights) into law.

Does the text of a bill of rights secure predictability? Or is it 'general, ... ambiguous, ... vague, and ... [full] of terms that would leave the citizen at the mercy of the interpreter's judgment or discretion'?[4]

Let us consider the case law for a moment. The texts of all our Anglo-US bills of rights make mention of a right to 'freedom of speech' or to 'freedom of expression'. Canada's and New Zealand's also make explicit that bill of rights rights can be limited by laws where the limit is deemed (by the judges) to be reasonable and justifiable.[5] In the United States this is implicit.

---

4 Jeremy Waldron, *Law and Disagreement* (Oxford: Clarendon Press, 1999), pp. 83–4.

5 See section 1 of Canada's *Charter of Rights* and section 5 of New Zealand's Bill of Rights Act.

So how constraining on the point-of-application interpreters is this injunction to guarantee freedom of speech and expression, where reasonable? How does it affect, say, campaign finance rules, hate-speech provisions or defamation regimes? To my mind, it seems abundantly clear that the citizen is largely at the mercy of the interpreter's judgment or discretion. Just compare *RAV* v. *City of St Paul*[6] with *R* v. *Keegstra*[7] (re criminalizing hate speech in the US and Canada) or *New York Times* v. *Sullivan*[8] with *Hill* v. *Church of Scientology*[9] and with *Lange* v. *Atkinson*[10] and with *Reynolds* v. *Times Newspapers*[11] (re defamation laws in the US, Canada, New Zealand and the UK). Or look at how the right is interpreted to affect campaign spending,[12] or the openness of trials.[13]

Or take just about any of the other rights enumerated in a bill of rights. Does a textualist interpretive approach tell us where to draw the line when it comes to voting,[14] or who can marry,[15] or limits on advertising?[16] Does it help us decide what does or does not constitute 'cruel and unusual punishments', 'due process of law', 'unreasonable search and seizure', 'reasonable and demonstrably justified limits' or any of the other openly moral mandates? Does it foreclose finding or discovering some further broad right, say one to privacy, in the 'penumbras, formed by emanations' of existing rights to due process, freedom from unreasonable searches and against self-incrimination (then finding a more specific further unwritten right in the penumbra of this discovered privacy right's emanation)?[17] Are any of the rights in a bill of rights, say, 'specific rather than general, univocal rather than ambiguous'?[18] Is a bill of rights like a tax statute or campaign finance statute or criminal statute (or code) or corporations statute in terms of its determinacy, specificity and core of settled meaning?

---

6   505 U.S. 377 (1992).

7   [1990] 3. SCR 697.

8   376 U.S. 254 (1964).

9   [1995] 2 SCR 1130.

10   [2000] 3 NZLR 385 (C.A.).

11   [2001] 2 A.C. 1217 (H.L.).

12   Compare *Buckley* v. *Valeo* 424 U.S. 1 (1976) and *Harper* v. *Canada (Attorney General)* [2004] 1 SCR 827.

13   Compare *Nebraska Press Association* v. *Stuart* 427 U.S. 539 (1976) with *Gisborne Herald Co. Ltd.* v. *Solicitor General* [1995] 3 NZLR 563 (C.A.).

14   See *Sauve* v. *Canada (Chief Electoral Officer)* [2002] 3 SCR 519.

15   See *Halpern* v. *Canada (Attorney General)* (2003) 65 O.R. (3D) 161 (Ont. C.A.) and *Quilter* v. *Attorney-General* [1998] 1 NZLR 523 (C.A.) and *Joslin et al* v. *New Zealand*, Communication No. 902/1999, UN Doc. A/57/40 at 214 (2002) and *Goodridge* v. *Department of Public Health* 440 Mass 309, 798 N.E. 2d 941.

16   Consider *RJR – MacDonald* v. *Canada* [1995] 3 SCR (1995).

17   See *Griswold* v. *Connecticut* 381 US 479 (1965) and *Roe* v. *Wade* 410 U.S. 113 (1973).

18   Jeremy Waldron, *Law and Disagreement*, pp. 83–4.

I do not think anyone can answer 'yes' to these questions honestly or while keeping a straight face. Our Judge Waldron may believe that in normal circumstances democratic considerations dictate that 'legislators are entitled to insist on the authoritativeness of the text and nothing but the text',[19] supplemented only by 'the meanings embodied conventionally in the text'.[20] This may even be a powerful position to take as regards interpreting the vast preponderance of statutes. As regards bills of rights and other instances of last-word moral input at the point-of-application, however, it is akin to handing the judiciary (and himself) a blank cheque. Textualism or a plain meaning approach constrains the bill of rights-interpreting judge hardly at all.

Hence, our Judge Waldron, a judge convinced of the political illegitimacy that attaches to second-guessing the elected legislature and one intent on minimizing the judiciary's moral input, would have to shun plain meaning textualism as regards this sort of adjudication. Even more obviously, he would have to eschew progressivist or 'living tree' or 'living constitutionalism' type modes of interpretation – approaches grounded on the notion that the meaning of moral incorporations into law evolves and changes in accordance with the needs of contemporary society (or more honestly put, in accord with the judges' views of those needs).

That is why I began by mooting that our Judge Waldron might surprise even himself and come to see the attractions of a Holmesian or Posnerite or Frankfurterite approach.

Another possibility is this. Perhaps our Judge Waldron, a student of Ronald Dworkin's (literally), might decide that broadly speaking he likes the Herculean best fit approach to interpretation, but that in his jurisdiction the best understanding of the first nine chapters – of all the settled law, cases, constitutional provisions, and conventions – is an overarching commitment by society to a right to participate in social decision making, even about rights. In other words, all the provisions in a bill of rights would need to be interpreted against this synthesizing, all-embracing, fundamental, best fit commitment to letting the numbers count when it comes to resolving where to draw the myriad lines rights-based adjudication gives birth to. Judge Waldron would direct himself, in other words, to interpret bill of rights (and other last-word moral input) disputes in the light of society's strong *prima facie* commitment to majority rules.

On this sort of approach, our Judge Waldron might end up with a very strong presumption in favour of the challenged piece of legislation that was the product of the democratically elected legislature. Having regard to bills of rights, then, only where some enumerated right appeared to give him abundantly clear warrant to strike down (under a constitutionalized model) or to re-write under the guise of interpreting (under a statutory model) some statute would our Judge Waldron use the bill of rights to do so.

---

19   *Ibid.*, p. 145.
20   *Ibid.*, p. 142.

In a sense, this would be a sort of redirected Dworkinianism, one in which the mythical Hercules is taken to pay a good deal more attention to his homeland being a birthplace of democracy.

More to the point, this redirected Dworkinianism appears likely to produce just about the same outcomes as the more spartan, less varnished (and possibly more plain dealing) Holmesian or Posnerite or Frankfurterite approaches. There would be an awful lot of deference coupled with a scintilla or dash of juristocracy or kritarchy. The architectural designs and justifications would be much more elaborate; the finished product pretty much the same.

Here is yet another alternative. This one involves a John Ely-type distinction between those rights and incorporated moral tests that further or make possible voting and canvassing and campaigning and participating in social decision making and so majority rules and letting the numbers count, on the one hand, and all other rights and moral tests on the other. As Amartya Sen notes, '[e]ven elections can be deeply defective if they occur without the different sides getting an adequate opportunity to present their cases, or without the electorate enjoying the freedom to obtain news and to consider the views of the competing protagonists'.[21]

In other words, 'majority rules' or 'letting the numbers count' is a deceptively simple seeming notion, one that in fact requires some sort of moral overlay to give life to the notion of having a right to participate. Value judgments and choices need to be made about voting systems, campaign finance rules, access to media, district or boundary-drawing mechanisms, defamation regimes and more. At some point a jurisdiction's choices may mean that the numbers do not really count. People having to vote by raising their hands in the presence of men with machine guns is a blatant example. More debatable examples might include countries with only government-controlled broadcasting and newspapers or those with swingeing defamation laws or those with locked-in gerrymandering. At some point – and no doubt our Visiting Martian would observe that different people would draw the line at different places – the numbers stop really counting and who govern and become legislators is not really determined by the preferences and choices of the majority.

So maybe our Judge Waldron might consider adopting two different approaches as regards, most obviously, the rights in his jurisdiction's bill of rights. Those rights, those moral abstractions, raising issues related to how governments are chosen (so as to ensure the numbers really do count) might be treated one way. All other rights and value judgments – those linked to the scope of and reasonable limits on freedom of religion, say, or of privacy, or of search and seizure, or of immigration policy, or of how to spend society's limited resources on health or education, and so much more – might be treated in another.

---

21 Amartya Sen, 'Democracy as a Universal Value' (1999) 10 *Journal of Democracy* 9, at p. 9. For my response to Sen's advocacy of a fat conception of democracy, see 'Thin Beats Fat Yet Again – Conceptions of Democracy' (2006) 25 *Law & Philosophy* 533.

In instances of the latter our Judge Waldron would be almost wholly deferential; in instances of the former, however, perhaps he would be much less so. To ensure the numbers really do count, our Judge Waldron might be more prepared to second-guess, to inject his own moral input, to draw some of the social policy lines that rights-based instruments allow him (if he so desires) to draw.

And yet not so. Some may find attractive this Ely-type distinction with its two-speed approach to the level of judges' moral input and intrusiveness. As it happens, our Judge Waldron does not.[22] Even here, he thinks, it is not for the judges to intervene. Even here there are highly debatable and contentious decisions to be made, ones over which smart, reasonable, well-informed people will inevitably disagree.

Is there anything more, then, on which we can speculate as regards how our Judge Waldron might decide the last-word moral input cases that come before him? Recall that thus far we have speculated that our Judge Waldron will not be able to resort to plain-meaning textualism when interpreting the rights in a bill of rights; such an interpretive approach will hardly constrain the point-of-application interpreter at all; it will not minimize, or much reduce, the judge's moral input. Nor would any version of progressivist or living-tree interpretation. Instead, I have conjectured that our Judge Waldron might surprise even himself by coming to see the attractions of a Holmesian or Posnerite or Frankfurterite approach to interpreting in these sorts of instances. He might do this directly, or perhaps he might reach much the same end-point by means of some sort of more souped-up Dworkinian vehicle. I have also suggested that our Judge Waldron might also reject the Ely-type approach.

As we are imagining the situation in which our Judge Waldron himself – at least in his pre-judicial incarnation – thinks it a good idea to minimize judges' last-word moral input, their scope to infuse their own values into law, then another possibility is for him to decide these cases on the basis of some version of originalism. In other words, he might be inclined to adopt some version of originalism (be it a version of original intentions or of original understanding) because it will act as an internally imposed external constraint on him and on other judges who adopt it.

If a plain, ordinary meaning approach to interpreting the words in the constitution or the bill of rights – words like 'due process', 'equal protection', 'freedom of speech' and 'unreasonable search' – often fails to dictate an outcome or an answer to a dispute and so leaves our Judge Waldron more or less free to decide on other grounds; and if interpreting these words in a way that evolves and changes according to contemporary values, concepts, and contexts – or more accurately put, according to Judge Waldron's sense of changing contemporary values *et al.* – imposes even fewer constraints on him; and if interpreting these words in an openly moral way imposes even fewer constraints on him still; then

---

22   See Jeremy Waldron, *Law and Disagreement*, pp. 295–6 *inter alia* and 'A Right-Based Critique of Constitutional Rights' (1993) 13 *Oxford Journal of Legal Studies* 18, at p. 39.

what about some version of originalism as a means of limiting or minimizing the point-of-application judge's scope to instil his own values?

Recall that we are largely talking about interpreting constitutions and bills of rights. The former (and indeed the latter) cannot function well if they are too specific, detailed and determinate. A certain level of generality is needed. In comparison with a tax code or planning law regime or almost any decent-sized statute, a written constitution will be short, general rather than specific, and relatively indeterminate. A bill of rights is likely to be even more vague and amorphous, often setting out a catalogue of individual rights in near-absolutist language that is emotively charged. These sorts of instruments, when Judge Waldron is called upon to interpret them, will have a greater penumbra of uncertainty than most statutes. So the hope in adopting some version of originalism is to turn the interpretive exercise, at least in part, into a search for 'what the fact of the matter was' rather than for 'how things should be or ought to be today'.

For the judge who himself thinks minimizing point-of-application last-word moral input a good thing, originalist forms of interpretation might offer, as I just suggested, a sort of internally imposed external constraint. Our Visiting Martian might say that turning to originalism here is not unlike the person who believes there are no mind-independent, transcendent moral values but who nevertheless seeks to avoid raw subjectivism, 'sympathy and antipathy',[23] by opting for the external, inter-subjective standards generated by utilitarianism. Similarly here, the judge adopts originalism, thinking it requires him to give the particular provision or right the meaning intended by those who enshrined it or as it would have been understood at the time of adoption or enactment. So, for instance, capital punishment is left for the elected legislature to consider and possibly eliminate because one takes the late eighteenth-century external evidence to be clear that virtually no one considered it to be a cruel and unusual punishment. A particular judge today may herself think capital punishment wrong, even gravely immoral, but the protection against unusual and cruel punishments – she thinks – is not to be extended by her and her judicial colleagues. She constrains herself, but she does so on the basis of external evidence of what the set of rights were taken (or intended) to mean at the time of adoption.

Of course the perceived benefits of substituting 'what the fact of the matter was' questions for 'how things should be today' questions would disappear under an approach to interpretation that looked for what the enactors' intentions *would be today*. This might at first appear to be a version of originalism. But, on reflection, this variant seems as unlikely to constrain the judiciary as the 'keeping pace with contemporary values' approach or the plain meaning approach. Determining the enactors of the constitution's intentions *when the constitution was being drafted and enacted* is one thing. Saying what those intentions *would be today* is another.

---

23   The phrase was originally Jeremy Bentham's in his *The Principles of Morals and Legislation*, chapter 2, paragraph XI.

The former seeks to establish a matter of the historical record,[24] a matter of fact, though admittedly many facts cannot be known or determined to a sufficient degree of trustworthiness by limited biological creatures like humans. Still, to the extent that we can establish and determine a sufficiently trustworthy answer on the evidence available, that answer is independent[25] of today's deciding judge and his or her present-day beliefs, preferences, sentiments, biases and political desires.

The latter, by marked contrast, is much less a matter of 'what the case was'. It asks the judge to make a 'conditional dispositional' evaluation – 'dispositional' because it is an assertion of how a particular person or group is disposed to react and 'conditional' because that disposition is of how a historically real person or group of people would react (*not* did react, because this is *not* an attempt to determine an event that actually happened in the real world) were he, she or they able[26] or alive to do so today. Clearly this conditional dispositional evaluation does not seek, as well as is possible, simply to establish a historical fact. Rather, it asks the judge, like our Judge Waldron, to make an evaluation of what *he thinks* that real person would think today. It is beyond argument that this evaluation is more speculative, and certainly less tied to actually occurring, real events in the external world, than is the historical quest to establish actual intentions or actual understandings back at the time of enactment or adoption. Bluntly, such conditional dispositional evaluations give a fair degree of scope to the interpreting judge to decide as he or she thinks right. It imposes fewer constraints and external limits on Judge Waldron – it enhances his judicial power and discretion to make policy at the point of application – than would adhering to original intentions or understandings.

Meanwhile, if called upon to do so, our Judge Waldron might well be able to give a pretty powerful argument on behalf of adhering to those original intentions or original understandings (in the context of constitutional and bill of rights interpretation, that is, as opposed to statutory interpretation more generally). He could start by saying that constitutions, and bills of rights too for that matter, are about locking things in. They set out rules and standards that impose second-order constraints on the preferred legislative choices of the elected legislators. They lock in a particular set of protections that the people – at some point in the past – have decided to make unusually hard to remove or alter or change (either formally or

---

24   And some countries, like Australia, have quite full records of the statements and views of the participants who framed, drafted and have enacted their constitutions.

25   This is not to deny that history is in part a matter of interpretation. Rather, it is a claim that there are mind-independent occurrences in the real, external world which limit the plausible interpretations that humans can give those occurrences (e.g., that Hitler and Stalin were kind, tolerant, forgiving leaders).

26   In jurisdictions in which framers of the constitution or enactors of a bill of rights remain alive, judges, as far as I am aware, never seek to determine what these framers and enactors now think (or what they say they then thought) and then base their decisions accordingly. This, besides being somewhat suggestive of how little judges like being constrained, allows us to focus on the more typical case where framers and enactors are dead at the time the judge comes to interpret the text.

in practice). They give us a new floor level of locked-in protections above which matters are to be decided in the same way as in a pure parliamentary sovereignty – by voting and by majority rule.

Judge Waldron could go on. He could note that according to this view, the job of unelected judges is *not* to update the scope, ambit and application of rights, from time to time, in order to keep pace with civilization and abreast of changing social values. Nor, he might argue, is this an obviously unattractive stance, since it is clear that the locked-in rights are overwhelmingly a floor, not a ceiling. If some one-century-old or two-century-old locked-in bill of rights does not protect same-sex marriage or access to abortion or prisoner voting entitlements, nothing, anywhere, prevents the elected legislature from doing so by means of an ordinary statute. There is no need to amend the constitution or alter the statutory bill of rights to give extra protections. The locked-in rights very rarely constitute a ceiling or restriction on further liberalizations. So if access to abortion is not extended or same-sex marriage not enacted, one's gravamen is with the elected legislature and one's effort for change is focused on the political process – a state of affairs otherwise known as 'democracy'. That is what we might hear our Judge Waldron say in defence of originalism.

My suspicion, however, is that although our imagined Judge Waldron could say all that in defence of originalism, he will nevertheless find the Posnerite or Holmesian or Frankfurterite 'can't help it' or 'puke test' approach more attractive. Originalism can offer the desirable prospect (to Judge Waldron at any rate) of preserving a great deal of democratic decision making. Yet that is wholly contingent on what the original intentions and understandings happen to have been. In undertaking our historical 'what the fact of the matter was' research we might end up concluding, with Ronald Dworkin, that in using abstract moral terms the founders intended judges to apply their own moral beliefs and so to have the restrictions such rights impose on the elected branches be fluid and evolving ones. That, we may find, was their intention or that was the understanding at the time. A commitment to originalism, in other words, may end up being a commitment to Dworkinian interpretive methods rather than locking-in a set of floor-level protections.

What the actual intentions of the founders were, of course, is a question of empirical fact. Historical evidence may, or may not, be sparse. (If it is, that is a further problem.) In one jurisdiction the evidence, such as it is, might point in the Dworkinian direction; in another it might not – as I think is true of the United States and Australia.

For our imagined Judge Waldron who seeks to minimize last-word moral input at the point-of-application, that is one potential ground for thinking, with me, that he might surprise even himself and opt instead for the 'puke test' approach. The gaps he is likely to find in the historical record are another.

Yet, however our Judge Waldron might ultimately decide those bill of rights and last-word moral input cases, there is an earlier issue we have put to one side to which we must now return.

Can He Accept the Job?

We have thus far begged the most interesting question. Could Professor Waldron accept the job on a top court? I want to be deliberately provocative and suggest that the situation Professor Waldron faces is the obverse of that faced by some of the apartheid South African judges. They could either stay, and make a bad system more palatable and less harsh than any likely replacement, or resign. Professor Waldron can either take the job, and lessen what he sees as the illegitimacy of the system more than any likely alternative appointee (by keeping to a bare minimum any second-guessing of the elected legislature), or decline the job offer.

Yes, the degree or amount of political illegitimacy between the two systems differs substantially. An apartheid regime is far worse, far more politically illegitimate, than is a system in which society's rights-based decision making and line drawing is handed over to committees of unelected ex-lawyers.

Nevertheless, for a person like Judge Waldron, someone fundamentally committed to letting the numbers count and giving real effect to the right to participate as the right of rights, the difference is one of degree or amount (of illegitimacy) only. He faces the same calculation as the apartheid South African judge – either take part, because the likely replacement or alternative will be worse, or have nothing to do with the illegitimate system.

Observe that the choice to follow the first fork, to undertake politically illegitimate judging, appears defensible only on a utilitarian (or other consequentialist) basis. The thinking would be that I can do more to diminish second-guessing and the inputting of judges' moral views and sentiments[27] than the sort of person who is otherwise likely to be offered (and take) the job. The likely good consequences of my being in this position, in other words, outweigh the likely bad ones – including the perceived legitimacy the system garners by virtue of having someone like me in the job.

By contrast, the second fork, not to take the judging job or to resign from it, can be justified either on a consequentialist/utilitarian basis or on a deontological/non-utilitarian basis. It is the former when one decides that the bad consequences of being a part of the system – say, in terms of perpetuating it by reducing its rigours – are likely to outweigh any good one can do as a judge in the system. It is the latter when one forswears or disavows all appeal to consequences and just says 'this is wrong' or 'I will not be tainted'.

Here, I do no more than suggest that people of a non-utilitarian or deontological inclination are likely to lean towards not taking (or not keeping) the judgeship. Consequentialists have the harder task. Some will weigh up things and think it right to accept; others will reach the opposite conclusion. And the degree of perceived illegitimacy of the system will affect their calculations. The worse the system, the more offsetting good one needs to think he or she can do by being a judge. Thus, it is a possibility – because one scenario is more illegitimate than the other – that

---

27   Or in the apartheid context, I can do more to ameliorate the harshness of a wicked system.

the same person might calculate that he should resign from his job in the apartheid scenario but that he should take the judging job in the scenario we are considering in this chapter.

I suspect, as well, that any consequentialist or utilitarian weighing up of likely consequences – or at any rate any honest weighing up – needs to factor in the probability that, once in the job, anyone, even our Judge Waldron, will to some extent succumb to the temptations of moral second-guessing, of having a largely unchecked power to impose his own moral sentiments on the rest of us. Differently phrased, there is the possibility that what Professor Waldron would advocate be done in his role *as a professor* might not align perfectly with what he, as Judge Waldron, would in fact do *once a judge*. The job, as it were, might go to his head; he might start putting more stock than before on his own moral antennae; he might fail to spot all the sycophancy and flattery that goes with the job; the ability to achieve justice, do the right thing and know what is needed to keep pace with civilization might appear to be more judge-like attributes once he was in the job. In short, our Visiting Martian would remind us that there is no necessary 1:1 correlation between the opinions of Waldron *qua* professor and Waldron *qua* judge.

A thorough, consequentialist weighing-up of whether to take the job would need to factor in that possibility as well.

I say no more than that. Certainly I do not presume to say whether our mooted Law Professor should, or should not, take up the offer to become a top judge, or even whether there is a right answer (or indeed a right approach to finding an answer) to such a question.

Actually, I will say just a bit more than that because I have thus far overlooked the relevance of the judicial oath, 'to do justice according to law'. Were our Law Professor to take the top judging job, the very fact that he swore or affirmed the judicial oath might give rise to an interesting complication. Would our newly appointed Judge Waldron (because of the judicial oath) now have a legal obligation to enforce the bill of rights and other last-word incorporated moral tests and standards regardless of his political and moral objections to it and to them? More to the point, would he have a moral obligation to comply with his legal obligation?

Obviously that would depend, in part, on how constraining the enumerated legal rights and incorporated moral tests were taken to be, given that they are not self-defining. The more amorphous, vague and indeterminate these bill-of-rights' enumerated rights and other moral standards, the more this becomes a non-question. And that aside, it will remain the case that the decision of whether other considerations constitute a reasonable limit on the reach and scope to be accorded to a right will remain with Judge Waldron.

That in turn, though, raises issues about *stare decisis*. The rights themselves, for instance, may be phrased in woolly, ambiguous, vague terms, leaving much to the interpreting judge's discretion. But maybe the case law generated by the hyper-constitutionalized legal environment has significantly expanded the core of settled meaning pertaining to some of these rights? (If so, the puke test then becomes ambiguous. A legislative enactment could induce the puking reaction, but then so could some past precedent of the court. If it be the latter, can Judge Waldron circumvent that? Or does that constrain him, meaning his legal obligations are less than vague sometimes?)

Or perhaps not. Ironically, it is just those judges who are most attracted to progressivist 'living tree' modes of interpretation who are least likely to be bothered by the 'according to law' suffix of the judicial oath, at least if we take this as a contingent claim about the way the world tends to operate at present. There is a divergence, as regards the extent to which precedent is considered to be binding, between those who take progressivist, 'living tree' type interpretive approaches and those who do not. The former, keen to keep pace with what they see as the demands of civilization and the needs of contemporary society, are likely to be less constrained by past precedents. Our Judge Waldron, I suspect, will be far more concerned about pre-existing constraints.

Once we head down this road other issues spring up too. We would need to distinguish between a theory of interpretation and a theory of judicial disobedience – of when it is justifiable and defensible to disobey the law or to lie about what it requires. (And here one might want to claim that the degree of illegitimacy of the system *does* matter vis-à-vis a theory of judicial disobedience more tellingly than it does vis-à-vis a theory of interpretation.) We might also want to allow for the Waldronian judge who reckons it best (in a long-term sense) to overturn legislation as liberally as possible, to give the community just the juristocracy they seem to crave (in the hope that such activism might awaken them from their foolishness).

No doubt when it comes to these ancillary issues, there is much that is uncertain. All we can be sure of is that there exists an asymmetry here. The Waldrons of the world will hesitate and ponder and be unsure of whether to take the job as a top judge. They will see political illegitimacy in the task of last-word moral input adjudication such as with bills of rights and this will have a bearing on their decision. Meanwhile bill of rights proponents – at least those who see nothing illegitimate in unelected judges settling disagreements about rights and morality for the rest of us – will have no concerns about the propriety of their required task, no qualms about accepting the job.

Over time, and were all other things equal, our Visiting Martian would not expect to find many judges who favoured minimizing last-word moral input at the point-of-application on a Benevolent Legal System's highest court. And, of course, our Visiting Martian would go on to note that all other things are unlikely to be equal over time. For instance, we should expect law schools to produce a preponderance of bill of rights proponents, lawyers' groups to be strong supporters (for self-interested and non-self-interested reasons) and any bill of rights sceptic nominated for judicial appointment to be characterized or vilified (by bill of rights proponents) as beyond the Pale.

Reflections on the 'What to Do?' and 'Can He Accept the Job?' Queries

Let us turn now to consider some of the implications of this Judge Waldron hypothetical. We have been imagining a scenario in which the top judges of a Benevolent Legal System themselves wish to minimize point-of-application last-word moral second-guessing powers. In such a situation, an admittedly rare situation, it may be that the most minimizing approach such judges could, and perhaps would, take is some version or other of the 'can't help it' or 'puke test' approach. Yet even that is fairly uncertain. This hypothetical has shown that once in his new job as a top judge, even the Law Professor or Lawyer who earlier had been a strong critic of constitutionally (or pseudo-constitutionally) incorporating vague moral tests into law – and so of handing significant last-word moral and political line-drawing powers to the unelected judiciary – might find that things look different from the Judge's Vantage. There is a difference between considering this issue from the outside as an observer, be that as a Visiting Martian, a Concerned Citizen or even as a well-informed Law Professor with atypically sceptical-of-the-judiciary views, and considering it from the inside as a top judge oneself. Already there are grounds for thinking top judges will find it difficult to limit or minimize the extent of their own moral input under a bill of rights (or otherwise where broad moral tests and standards have been incorporated into law in a way that makes the specific content given to those broad standards by the judges formally or practically next to impossible to override).

In addition, there are good grounds for doubting that the sort of atypical Law Professor (or Lawyer) who favours minimizing judges' last-word moral input would very often end up in the top judge's job. If asked, he is more likely than most others to say 'no'. Moreover, and by virtue simply of those atypical views, he is less likely to be asked, or, where applicable, confirmed.

Accordingly, those who in good faith counsel reliance on the judges themselves (in Canada, the United States, New Zealand, the UK *inter alia*) to be generally cautious and minimalist offer us a counsel of hope over experience.

This hypothetical has also shown that the appointments process for judges matters. The chances of our imagined Law Professor being appointed a top judge will vary with the particular Benevolent Legal System's method of choosing people to serve on its highest courts.

Outside of the United States, most commentators in common law Benevolent Legal Systems dislike the American process for appointing top federal (including Supreme Court) judges. They think it too overtly political. They think the raw, probing and sometimes personal questions deter some – perhaps many – talented and eminently qualified candidates. This is the widespread view – outside the United States – not just from the Judge's Vantage and the Law Professor's Vantage, but also the Legislator's Vantage. It is not necessarily the view from the Concerned Citizen's Vantage, though. He or she may come to think that once top judges are given the sort of input that comes with bills of rights-type blending of law and morality, would-be appointees should first be subject to an openly (or less-than-openly) political vetting process.

The traditional alternative to a US-style Senate hearing process has been the absence of any formal constraints on the elected government in power. It appoints whomever it wishes, subject to very minimal thresholds being surmounted, such as the person having been a qualified lawyer for ten years or so. Generally the choice is made by the Prime Minister or Attorney-General, though no doubt Cabinet is consulted (at least in the case of the most senior vacancies) and informal soundings are taken of the existing judges and the various lawyers' bodies, perhaps of others too. In Canada, the United Kingdom, Australia, New Zealand and more widely still, this was the traditional judicial appointments process. It was itself a political process, though not an open and publicized one.

In the absence of a constitutionalized bill of rights (Canada before 1982) or a statutory version (New Zealand before 1990 and England before 2000) or some other innovation that noticeably increased judges' last-word moral and political input, this sort of process generally worked fine. The unelected judges knew that the elected legislature would have the last word, even on issues characterized in terms of rights. The legislature knew it was free to enact statutes overturning or reversing judicial decisions with which it disagreed. In such circumstances there is an incentive to appoint based on merit. That is not to deny that an incentive also exists to reward party stalwarts. It is simply to say, and especially as regards more senior judicial vacancies, that talented people with different party-political allegiances can and will be appointed. The Visiting Martian would observe that this happens noticeably more often than it does after bill of rights-type moral and political powers are given to the judges.

Once such powers are entrusted to the judiciary, however, our Concerned Citizen might prefer a more openly political appointments process. The greater the point-of-application last-word input, the greater the attractions of an overtly political appointments process that involves subjecting would-be appointees to aggressive, probing and even personal questions in public. At any rate, that is more true from the Concerned Citizen's Vantage than from the Judge's or Law Professor's or Lawyer's.

As it happens, however, the American-style judicial appointments process for top judges cannot easily be mimicked or copied. It requires, to start, real bicameralism with a genuine House of Review or elected Upper House. It works only because this Senate or elected Upper House will not always be in the control of the governing (or President's) party. Perhaps not always, but sometimes at least, there needs to be the prospect of nominees' receiving more than just a perfunctory questioning, and on occasion of being rejected. Of the common law countries I have mentioned above, only Australia would be in a position to emulate the US-style Senate hearing judicial vetting process. (For what it is worth, and mostly due to the voting system used there to elect Upper House members in Australia, combined with the fact an even number of Senators per State get elected each election, it is considerably less likely that the Australian Prime Minister's party will control their Upper House than it is that the US President's party will control theirs.) Meanwhile, Canada's Upper House has no democratic legitimacy whatsoever, being a body composed solely of appointees, many of whom would be seen as party hacks and placemen. The United Kingdom's Upper House, the House of Lords, not so long ago was a mostly hereditary body with some appointees for life. That mix has now been reversed, but it too has no democratic legitimacy – and whatever non-democratic legitimacy it might have would not be sufficient, one suspects, to leave it in a position to reject (even occasionally) judicial nominees. New Zealand, meanwhile, has no Upper House at all.

Where a US-style appointments process either cannot be copied or there is little desire to do so, there is still the fact that since the end of World War II there has been what our Visiting Martian would describe as a marked increase in the power of the judiciary vis-à-vis the legislature and executive throughout the Benevolent Legal Systems' common law world. And for some observers this ever-greater judicial prominence in social policy making, perhaps most notably in the area of contested rights claims, not only bears on the issue of how best to appoint judges, it tells against the traditional (or status quo) non-American appointments process. For them, the traditional process may have been fine where judges deferred to the elected Parliament and so governments had little incentive to appoint on the basis of the candidate's social, political and moral views. But with the observable decline in such deference, it is fine no longer. These sorts of people want now to take the appointments of top judges out of the hands of politicians and give them to some sort of non-party-political Judicial Appointments Board – this being a catch-all name for various indirect methods of appointing judges where politicians either choose from a short list drawn up by such a Board, or the Board approves or disapproves of submitted names, or recourse is had to any other such indirect nominating or screening process that gives real, significant say to a committee of experts or insiders. Advocates often argue for such a change on grounds more or less analogous to those used to justify taking the power to draw electoral boundaries away from politicians to prevent gerrymandering.

What is the strength or persuasiveness of that analogy and from which vantages will it seem most attractive?

Both the Concerned Citizen and the Judge, as well as the Legislator, Law Professor and Visiting Martian, would tend to agree that where judges are much less likely to defer to the elected politicians on major social-policy line-drawing issues, politicians in turn are more inclined to consider a candidate's views on these issues and to opt for seemingly like-minded judges, at least to some extent. It follows that the danger of the traditional or status quo judicial appointments process (as sketched above) is the over-politicization of the process. Too much weight gets put on vetting candidates behind closed doors to try to discover their political views on controversial issues.

This is more of a threat or a concern from the Judge's Vantage (and the Lawyer's and Law Professor's) than it is from the Legislator's. For the latter, the risk that such a screening process might plausibly lower the calibre of those prepared to consider judicial appointment is one well worth running. Those already on the bench, or in the ranks of potential nominees, are likely to see things differently.

Our Concerned Citizen might concede that the traditional, status quo appointment process in New Zealand, the UK, Canada, Australia and perhaps elsewhere may turn more political as the power of judges markedly increases. Yet she might also note the dangers of the more indirect, 'body of experts' appointments process. And this is more than simply the threat of the potential mediocrity of indirectly appointed judges. Our Concerned Citizen might think that a far greater danger than that flowing from these Judicial Appointments Boards is the danger of a lack of heterogeneity among those ultimately chosen as judges; she might fear that such indirect appointments processes produce an insulated, self-selecting lawyerly caste – mediocre or otherwise – whose views on euthanasia, capital punishment, abortion, same-sex marriage, immigration and other contentious issues are noticeably at odds with the general voting public's (her own included, though this need not be the case).

This is not obviously a worry from the Judge's Vantage or the Lawyer's Vantage or the Law Professor's Vantage. Or if it is, it is a much less widely felt one.

Nor, from our Concerned Citizen's Vantage, is this a far-fetched worry. She is able to compare the general views of most – not all, but most – lawyers, law professors and judges in Canada, Australia, the UK and New Zealand and surmise that the majority position within these groups differs from the majority of the public's views in various areas of social policy.

Our Concerned Citizen may also notice that an indirect, 'body of experts' appointments process can make it difficult for a political party that has been out of power for some time, but has now won an election, to appoint a judge from among those lawyers who hold minority views (for lawyers, that is; they may quite possibly be majority views among the public at large). Those on any Appointments Board may fall victim to the temptation to feel most comfortable with lawyers and law professors who share broadly similar world-views. Indeed the notion of merit itself may come to be viewed through this prism of a candidate's general, small 'p' political views – on the proper role and influence of the jurisdiction's bill of rights, for example.

For instance, what is the likelihood of any indirect, Judicial Appointments Board process ever nominating or approving the sort of law professor we imagined at the start of this chapter? If the chances of appointing a Judge Waldron are slight in a US-style process or in a traditional, status quo Westminster process, they would be next to non-existent in any indirect process. Once such a process were in place our Visiting Martian would predict that Law Professor Waldron could never make it onto any top court (in one of today's common law Benevolent Legal Systems) with his views about bills of rights and about minimizing judges' last-word moral input. Our Concerned Citizen may well consider that, in itself, as a reason to avoid such Judicial Appointments Boards. Or rather, it is far more probable and believable that a Concerned Citizen would think this, than that a Judge or Lawyer or Law Professor would.

Our Concerned Citizen might also point to yet another hazard or peril in opting for some sort of Judicial Appointments Board. There is the possibility that a political party that has been in power for some time, and that has already made a large number of judicial appointments, may come to see the advantages of moving to an indirect, Judicial Appointments Board-type process before losing power. The party having already chosen so many judges, the goalposts constituting what is and is not beyond the Pale will have shifted. One more judge in the same mould will appear to many – and most obviously to the judges, ex-judges, lawyers' trade group representatives, law professors, heads of non-governmental organizations and rights-related litigation advocacy groups who will staff such Appointments Boards – to be the apolitical choice.

If we were to put this 'bring in a new system after moving the goalposts' concern on one side of the scales, together with the dangers of creating an insulated, self-selecting lawyerly caste and of making virtually unappointable those with non-conforming views, such as our Law Professor Waldron; and if on the other side of the scales we were to put the danger that the traditional, status quo appointments process may turn too political in a world where judges have ever-increasing input at the point-of-application; then one question (for those outside the United States) is which is the lesser danger.

From the Concerned Citizen's Vantage, and from the Legislator's Vantage, over-politicization will probably be seen as the lesser danger. Certainly for those who favour as vigorous a democracy as possible in these days of powerful judges there will be strong grounds for preferring a highest court where homogeneity of background moral sentiments and outlooks does *not* prevail. Or if that is thought to over-reach likelihoods, then in more modest terms we might say – with the Visiting Martian – that such a preference will be held by the Concerned Citizen more often than it will be by the Judge.

In other words, Judicial Appointments Boards appear least attractive from the Concerned Citizen's Vantage.

Notice, too, that our Visiting Martian is now in a position to indicate why the analogy of Judicial Appointments Boards to non-party-political constituency or district boundary-drawing commissions breaks down. Our Martian, that is, can tell us why gerrymandering – politicians pick the boundaries – is unlike politicians picking the judges directly (whether there be a further, public, US-style, political vetting step for those judges or not). The analogy breaks down because, although in both cases (politicians pick boundaries and politicians pick judges) the danger of over-politicization is a real one, there is no obvious obverse and corresponding danger to put on the other side of the scales when it comes to district or constituency boundary-drawing commissions. In other words, taking party politics out of appointing top judges by handing such decisions to Appointments Boards comes at a cost (in terms of heterogeneity, self-selection, conformity and the rest). But taking party politics out of the drawing of electoral boundaries carries no such identifiable competing dangers. Set out in statute that boundaries are to be regularly shaped, to enclose roughly the same number of voters, to pay heed to topography and communities of interest, and what sort of danger is there in handing the final say over to a committee of 'the great and the good' that rivals the threat of gerrymandering?

This chapter, with its imagined hypothetical, has raised doubts about the extent to which a Concerned Citizen, or Legislator, can expect or rely on unelected judges to constrain themselves and be cautious and minimalist once broad moral standards have been incorporated into law in a way that makes gainsaying the judges' resulting social-policy decisions extremely unlikely (in practice, if not formally). Concomitantly, from those same vantages, it has questioned the desirability of any indirect Judicial Appointments Board-type process for appointing top judges. And as between a US appointments system and the traditional Westminster system, the attractiveness of the former varies directly with the extent of the last-word moral and political input of the judges. Or so more Concerned Citizens than Judges would see it.

Admittedly, this chapter has been almost exclusively occupied with Benevolent Legal Systems. Not least, and as I argued in an earlier chapter, that is because focus on what judges do is of far less importance in Wicked and Theocratic and even So-So Legal Systems. (This can be seen as a corollary of one of the now standard criticisms of legal positivism – or one strand of legal positivism at any rate – that it is largely irrelevant to theories of adjudication.) Nevertheless, we will remain focused on the judges for one more chapter.

Chapter 4
Judges and Judging – II

How does the notion or concept of the Rule of Law differ from, and how is it related to, Rule by Judges? That question, phrased in Hartian terms, is the starting point of this chapter. Again, we are most likely to be asking it in a Benevolent Legal System, though the query is a live one in a Theocratic Legal System as long as the point-of-application interpreters of the supposedly divine commands or revealed natural laws are taken to be fallible.

On one side of my proposed comparison is an ideal encapsulated by the phrase 'the Rule of Law'. That ideal is fuzzy and amorphous. And when any attempt is made to be more specific in terms of what this ideal means – about the contents of the ideal, about why it is thought to be desirable, about the practicality of achieving this more specific state of affairs – there is widespread disagreement. Smart, reasonable, well-informed and nice people line up on differing sides of any version of the Rule of Law that has managed to descend from the disagreement-disguising heights of abstractions down into an account that lays out specific precepts or recommendations. As a catch-cry warning against the evils of arbitrary power or the dangers of some sort of unchecked-in-any-way method of determining social policy, this phrase will command extremely widespread support (though a few do see it as an empty slogan). But ask if the Rule of Law concept is to be purely a procedural one or whether it is to have a substantive element, and answers diverge. Or ask those in the former camp if they accept Lon Fuller's set of procedural criteria – namely, that laws ought to be general, publicly promulgated, prospective, intelligible, consistent, practicable, not too frequently changeable and in line with the actions of real-life officials – or if they prefer some shorter, longer, modified or different set, and there will be dissensus. Likewise, ask those who want the Rule of Law to be understood as a substantively laden concept, as more than just a requirement that power be exercised via general rules, known in advance (plus or minus according to taste), and consensus is just as hard to find. Talk of law having to be in accord with reason may mask some of that disagreement in this camp, but not for long. It simply shifts it to the issue of what is, and is not, in accord with reason. And just how substantively laden one wants the concept to be – from the fairly minimal position of asserting that the Fullerian-type procedural requirements make it substantively harder to enact and apply wicked, egregious laws to the maximal one of thinking that any law that is in any way unpleasant or not nice or unfair in its effects on some person or group breaches the Rule of Law – is no less disputed and open to debate.

Let us for the moment concede all that, either in fact or provisionally. Instead of aiming for a specified delineation of this ideal, let us just pick out a few notions that most people who use the phrase would accept fall under its aegis. Of course some would want any fleshed-out version of the concept to be much more encompassing than these few notions, others only a bit more so, others again not at all so. But as we are not aiming for anything like a fully worked-out account, we can simply acknowledge yet another aspect of disagreement as regards the Rule of Law concept or ideal and move on to trying to pick out a few of these core notions.

One is the desirability, in some circumstances though not all, of constraining decisions by means of rules. Lots and lots of matters relating to the social interactions of thousands or millions can and will be left to be decided without any rule in place to constrain the decision maker's choices. The realm of relevant considerations here will not be narrowed by a pre-existing rule. This is case-by-case-by-case decision making. But a core notion (for most people who talk) of the Rule of Law is that decisions made under its aegis are different, more circumscribed, than they would be under a wide-open case-by-case-by-case set up; such decisions are constrained by general, known rules that apply to all. The relevant factors that are to determine the decision maker's judgment have been embodied in just these abstract rules, rules that are intended to be binding.

That is one core notion of the Rule of Law, that it is a system of decision making under which such decisions are constrained by rules.

A second core notion relates to why such a more constrained system might be desirable. And here a generally acknowledged corollary of the Rule of Law notion or ideal is that it promotes or furthers predictability, certainty and stability. People no doubt differ on how much we ought to value certainty and predictability of outcome in its own right; but very, very few people think it an insignificant or trifling consideration.

So talk of the Rule of Law or of a Rule of Law system of governance is also associated (to some extent) with this value of being able to promote certainty when it comes to predicting outcomes. It is thought to further people's ability to shape their expectations and plan their lives accordingly. A system of law in which some policy is embodied in a rule – a general, binding-on-all rule – and then that rule is left to be interpreted, implemented and executed by others is part of this notion of the Rule of Law.

Perhaps, or perhaps not, the post-dash part of that last sentence should be seen as constituting a wholly distinct notion that most people would see as falling under the rubric of the Rule of Law ideal. Or perhaps, or perhaps not, it ought to be seen more narrowly as an offshoot or codicil to what is needed to achieve stability, predictability and certainty, namely separating the two tasks of *a)* laying down (or otherwise formulating) the abstract, binding rule and *b)* interpreting and applying it.

Either way, there is this connection between the contested, debatable and elusive Rule of Law ideal and the equally contested, debatable and elusive Separation of Powers ideal. At its most basic the claim amounts to this: To have a modicum of confidence that the announced rules are in fact constraining and impinging on the decision maker's range of options and discretion, there needs to be some sort of separation of function. The rule maker cannot also be the rule interpreter or applier.

And the reason why not is solely empirical. Experience gives us grounds to doubt the constraints will be as strongly felt when the tasks are combined (though if this is the case it is a contingent, not a necessary, truth tied to human nature and the way most humans, most of the time, happen to be).

Whatever the links between the Rule of Law concept or ideal and the Separation of Powers one – and as with the two concepts themselves their inter-relationship or the extent of their connectedness will be disputed and disputable – we need say no more here. Instead let us point out a third core notion that most people who use the phrase 'the Rule of Law' would accept falls under its aegis. This third one, together with the other two of decision making constrained by rules and done so with the aim of fostering greater certainty and predictability of outcome, should suffice for the discussion in the rest of this chapter. And that third notion at the core of Rule of Law talk is the idea that the more a jurisdiction's citizens are ruled by rules rather than by men, the more closely it approaches the ideal of a Rule of Law regime.

I do not put forward this third notion as something that can ever be fully attained. Indeed many would point out – me included – that rule by men is inevitable in so far as men and women will be the ones making the legal rules, and interpreting them, and applying them, and enforcing them. Rules, legal rules included, are *not* self-enforcing nor self-interpreting nor self-executing. They never can be. There is no entity out and about in the world known as 'Law' that can independently and without human help rule any group of people, however small or big. Rather, we are talking about the degree to which human rulers operate through laws (i.e., legal rules). The more they do so in any particular jurisdiction, the more it can be described as a Rule of Law one. That, not some naive belief that governance by rules can somehow ever reach the point where humans are taken wholly out of the picture as regards the making of, giving concrete meaning to, and dealing with those who infringe such rules is the third core notion I attribute to the Rule of Law ideal.

Now admittedly there is overlap between these three notions. To some extent decision making constrained by rules and the goal of forcing human rulers to operate more frequently through rules are opposite sides of the same coin. And the extent of any certainty likely to be engendered by them may depend on the sort of rules that have in fact been created. In addition, we must reiterate yet again that these are nothing more than a few notions that I think most people – not everyone, but most people – would agree lie at the core of the Rule of Law ideal. Of those that do so agree there would nevertheless be much disagreement were any more fully worked-out account of the ideal requested. The proceduralists would differ with the substantivists, and each of those two groups would itself splinter.

Luckily for us, however, we will not require any more consensus over the meaning to attribute to the Rule of Law ideal than what has just been sketched out.

The remainder of this chapter will be divided into three sections. The first will ask how the Rule of Law concept differs from Rule by Judges. The second section will move on from there to consider how common law decision making, in the context of interpreting a constitution or a quasi-constitutional instrument such as a statutory bill of rights, differs from Rule by Judges. And the third and final section of this chapter turns to the question of the legitimacy or desirability of referring to, and indeed on occasion deferring to, foreign law. It will become plain to the reader how this third section relates to the foregoing two.

In each of these sections the vantage adopted matters. It will influence the perceived desirability of referring or deferring to foreign law; it will affect how one reacts to common law constitutionalism; and it will bear on one's assessment of the extent to which the Rule of Law differs from, and is related to, Rule by Judges.

Rule of Law v. Rule by Judges

The Judge

From the Judge's Vantage it is clear that the Rule of Law ideal – whatever added extras be welded on to our core notions and whether it be understood in procedural or substantive terms – is something different from Rule by Judges. Just as claims that 'law is whatever the judges say it is' do not resonate with judges, equating the ideal of the Rule of Law solely to judicial power that is legally (though not morally or politically) unconstrained does not mesh with how the judge sees things. Judges do not see themselves, always and everywhere, as free to decide on the basis of their own political and moral beliefs or preferences or opinions.

This is more obviously so the lower down the judicial hierarchy our mooted judge resides. But even as a member of the jurisdiction's highest and final court, there is scope to separate law and morality (and so policy in the wider-than-morality sense) from the Judge's Vantage – as I argued in Chapter 1. If we pick our example carefully enough, this is especially evident. Imagine a tax case or a company law case on appeal to the highest court and the pre-existing rules in place will often be felt, by the judge, to govern the dispute. Those rules, both the ones laid down in statute and the others that have grown up as past judges have ruled upon related and analogous disputes, will narrow the realm of relevant considerations open to our judge. Even outside the core of settled meaning of the particular set of tax laws or company laws this will be the case. From the Judge's Vantage it is the laws that here are dictating the outcome, at least in the sense of taking some options – not necessarily all, but some – off the table.

And remember, this is at the highest judicial level, where cases falling outside the core of settled meaning of the applicable legal rules are by far the most numerous. Even up here, if we focus on a tax appeal say, the Rule of Law is distinct from Rule by Judges, from our Judge's Vantage. It becomes ever more obviously distinct as we look at such a dispute in cases of first instance, then in the hands of lawyers before trial, then at the stage where parties are considering whether to sue, and then way back at the start when the would-be plaintiff is considering whether to hire a lawyer.

However, what if we picked a different sort of dispute or case as our model? What if we were to focus, instead, on cases having to do with those amorphously phrased and morally laden rights in a constitutionalized or statutory bill of rights (or, relatedly, with cases the top judges themselves characterized in human rights terms, whether one of these provisions was explicitly applicable or not)? Let us call these 'noble dream' disputes or cases, the allusion being to Hart. What do things look like from our Judge's Vantage when we ask, for these noble dream cases, whether the Rule of Law differs from Rule by Judges?

Certainly, in the last decade or so top judges in the United Kingdom, for example, have taken to appealing to the 'rule of law' ideal in a not insignificant number of such noble dreams decisions. Here is a small sampling. 'Unless there is the clearest provision to the contrary, Parliament must be presumed not to legislate contrary to the *rule of law*.'[1] 'What matters is whether the effect is to give the executive a power to make decisions about people's rights which under the *rule of law* should be made by the judicial branch of government.'[2] 'The *rule of law* enforced by the courts is the ultimate controlling factor on which our constitution is based.'[3] 'I myself would consider there were advantages in making it clear that ultimately there are even limits on the supremacy of Parliament which it is the courts' inalienable responsibility to identify and uphold. They are limits of the most modest dimensions which I believe any democrat would accept. They are no more than are necessary to enable the *rule of law* to be preserved.'[4]

Assume for the moment that there are judicially enforceable limits flowing from the Rule of Law, or from the need to preserve the Rule of Law, in these noble dream cases. The question then becomes, for our top judge who is appealing to this ideal, where does he look to find the constraining content of this ideal. From the Judge's Vantage, in other words, is appeal to the Rule of Law just a sufficiently indeterminate – and so convenient – abstraction, one that can serve as a proxy for 'outcomes that I think are more morally and politically acceptable'? To put it differently, what does our judge think is constraining him in these noble dream cases when he appeals to the Rule of Law as some over-riding precept?

I suspect few judges see themselves as free agents, unconstrained by anything outside their own moral and political values, beliefs and sentiments. More to the point, I suspect that is the case even in these (admittedly rare) noble dream cases. From the Judge's Vantage, appeal to the Rule of Law to resolve these noble dream

---

1   *R* v. *Secretary of State for the Home Department, ex parte Pierson* [1998] AC 539, at p. 591 per Lord Steyn (emphasis mine).

2   *Matthews* v. *Ministry of Defence* [2003] 1 AC 1163 at para. [29] *per* Lord Hoffmann (emphasis mine).

3   *Jackson* v. *Attorney General* [2006] 1 AC 262 at para. [107] *per* Lord Hope (emphasis mine).

4   Lord Woolf, extra-judicially, in '*Droit public* – English style' [1995] *Public Law* 57, at p. 68 (emphasis mine). This is just one of various examples of top UK judges arguing that in appropriate circumstances the judiciary has (or possibly should have, the claim is kept somewhat ambiguous) much greater constitutional power than orthodoxy allows. See, as well, J. Laws, 'The Constitution: Morals and Rights' (1996) *Public Law* 622 and S. Sedley, 'Human Rights – A Twenty-First Century Agenda' (1995) *Public Law* 386.

cases, on occasion to be the decisive factor in resolving them, is *not* a proxy for 'this is my personal view of what is the morally and politically best, or least bad, outcome'. (That said, to move beyond mere suspicions of judicial good faith would require an extensive empirical study, one so far not in existence and one able to overcome all the obvious difficulties, such as how to determine that 'what judges say they are doing' turns out to be consistently at odds with 'what judges think they are doing'.)

So where is the constraint on the judge coming from when reliance is placed on the Rule of Law ideal in these noble dream cases? Think back to the three core notions I suggested most people would say fall under the aegis of the Rule of Law ideal or concept. Decision making constrained by rules that narrow the realm of allowable considerations was the first core notion. Yet when judges in the House of Lords appeal to the Rule of Law to justify limiting what Parliament can do – perhaps, say, limiting its ability to remove judicial review of executive action – it is not obvious where the rule comes from that provides this constraint. Is it anywhere laid down by a representative body? Is it identifiable in the official decisions of past judges? If it be the latter, then what was its source when it was first cited in an official decision? Was it simply the stated opinions of other top judges, and maybe of law professors, including in other jurisdictions?

And if this first core notion of decision making being constrained by rules seems problematic, seems only partially applicable, when top judges in noble dream cases appeal to the Rule of Law, the second core notion is almost wholly absent. There seems very little concern with certainty, with shoring up settled expectations, with the 'known in advance' aspect of the ideal. In these noble dream type cases raising amorphously articulated human rights issues – think of same-sex marriage litigation in Iowa perhaps – the top judges rarely mention the benefits attaching to stability, certainty and predictability. Indeed, at least extra-judicially, such benefits are downplayed, even trivialized, by some top judges.

The third core notion, of being ruled by rules rather than men, takes on an odd quality from the Judge's Vantage. Returning to the question of where the constraining content of the Rule of Law ideal comes from in these noble dream cases, the answer appears largely to be that what limits the top judge's range of choices – from his perspective or vantage – is the opinions of other judges, including those in other jurisdictions. Actually, that is not quite right because the opinions of lawyers and law professors (including, again, those in other jurisdictions) will also constrain the top judges. The top judge will be no free agent in these noble dream cases. Or, rather, he will not see himself as a free agent. Yet the constraints will to a significant extent not be ruled based. Precedents and cases from other jurisdictions will in no way be binding on our top judge. At most they will be persuasive arguments. The same is true of the published articles and books of law professors and lawyers. And for our very top judge, sitting on the jurisdiction's highest court, even the earlier decisions of that same court will not be binding. If he wishes to focus wholly on what he thinks is the morally best (or, somewhat less expansively, the most in keeping with fundamental human rights) answer or outcome, he can. If he wishes to weigh other factors as well, he can do that too.

A briefer way to make the same point may be this: The more judges appeal (in noble dream cases) explicitly and overtly in their decisions to the Rule of Law ideal as some sort of crucial or decisive consideration, the less clear it is that they are referring to any of our three core notions. And I mean this as a claim from the Judge's Vantage. The top judges themselves do not seem to use the ideal as a proxy for being ruled by rules, not men, or for putting much weight on securing certainty of outcome. And as for narrowing the realm of allowable considerations that bear on the judges' decision making, that narrowing (though it occurs) does not work much through rules.

From the Judge's Vantage, the Rule of Law ideal never collapses into some shorthand proxy for Rule by Judges. It comes closest, though, in those relatively rare noble dream cases.

The Bad Man

Our amoral Bad Man is concerned with predicting outcomes. And as an intelligent, sophisticated operator he will observe that when the laid-down and case law rules have a substantial amount of specificity – tax laws and company laws could again serve as examples – the best way to predict what the judges will do is to predict that they will decide in line with what these rules dictate.

Of course our Bad Man will *not* have an unblemished predicting record when subscribing to this 'just bet on the rules being followed' adage. A few of his predictions will be wrong. It is just that this adage will deliver better long-term prediction results than any other alternative maxim. It will outperform 'bet based on the judge's party political preferences'; it will score better than 'bet based on the judge's sex, predominant racial characteristics, religious beliefs, class background, or fill in the group-based characteristic of your choice, making the difference'; it will beat 'bet based on the judge playing to popular opinion or to elite liberal opinion'.

Here, then, the Bad Man will be able to distinguish the Rule of Law ideal from Rule by Judges.

In noble dream cases, however, it is unlikely that the Bad Man will make such a distinction. Even if he is able to do so, he is unlikely to bother. From his vantage, in these highly moralized cases turning on the meaning and reach of indeterminate human rights claims, talk of the Rule of Law does not differ in practice from Rule by Judges.

True, our Bad Man will see that different judges reach different outcomes. And he will notice that some judges are more inclined to follow precedents than others. And he will see all the scope there is for cherry-picking precedents from overseas top national and international courts, possibly observing that top overseas courts frequently reach differing decisions on the debatable and contentious line-drawing exercises falling under the aegis of 'right to a fair trial' (e.g. Can the legislature

impose extra restrictions on cross-examinations of alleged rape victims?) or 'right
to free speech' (e.g. What limits can the legislature put on campaign finance
spending or attacking people's reputations or uttering words some find hateful?)
or any of the other enumerated rights. It will even register on our Bad Man that
judges make frequent reference to treaties, conventions and purportedly objective
or transcendent moral standards (though in disagreement-disguising generalities).
None of this will change his perception that in these noble dream cases the concept
of the Rule of Law is a shorthand or convenient abstraction for Rule by Judges.

The Concerned Citizen

Only in noble dream cases, where the law that applies to the litigated-fact situation
is very highly moralized, is there a question of eliding the Rule of Law concept with
Rule by Judges. From the Concerned Citizen's Vantage this elision is less likely to
be made than from the Bad Man's Vantage. To start, the Concerned Citizen is not
herself amoral. So when her moral judgments or sensibilities happen to align with
those of the majority of judges on the highest court – over whether precluding the
wearing of veils to school is a reasonable limit on the right to freedom of religion,
say, or whether this campaign finance regime does or does not impinge freedom
of speech or whether equality/equal protection guarantees extend to opening
up marriage to same-sex couples and so on and so forth – then it is unlikely to
seem to her that the answer was dictated to the judges by morality. The rules
that incorporated the vague, amorphous, highly moralized test, in other words,
are likely to be seen by our Concerned Citizen as indirectly dictating this outcome
which is in accord with her own moral judgment and sensibilities. And provided
judges' moral views – or more accurately stated, the moral views of the majority
of the judges on the top court – continue to mesh with hers to a high degree, our
Concerned Citizen will observe that there is much certainty and predictability as
regards the outcomes of these noble dream cases. It will not appear at all to her as
though the Rule of Law notion or ideal has collapsed into Rule by Judges.

However, when our Concerned Citizen finds her moral judgments and
sensibilities regularly to be in opposition to those of the top judges as regards how
these highly moralized noble dream cases ought to be decided, it will often not
appear to her as though the rule is dictating the outcomes. True, she will see that
the rule is incorporating an amorphous moral test. But it is the judges – or rather
the majority of them on the top court – with their moral sentiments and judgments
that differ and diverge from hers that she will often see as the immediate cause of
why the cases are being decided the way they are. She will be much of the same
view as our Bad Man once the judges' moral sentiments regularly differ from
hers.

For instance, the Concerned Citizen who believes abortion to be morally
wrong, even wicked, need not think it is a rule in the United States Constitution that
dictates a right to an abortion. She can more easily think it is the judges' differing
moral sensibilities or judgments that have created the entitlement. (And notice

here a clear difference between that and a United Kingdom-style legislatively laid-down, and more detailed, rule as regards access to abortions where it is clear that the judges are not the source of the disliked, or purportedly immoral, outcomes.) Other similar examples are plentiful. Consider how same-sex marriages were initially authorized by judges in Canada under their *Charter of Rights*. Or look at how the American and Canadian and New Zealand top judges have dealt with improperly obtained evidence.

At least sometimes, then, the Concerned Citizen will think that resolution of highly moralized noble dream cases takes place on a Rule by Judges basis. The United States is the most obvious jurisdiction in which large numbers of citizens seem to think this, and hence care (to the point of its occasionally outweighing all other vote-determining considerations) who in future will be appointed to that top court. Fewer Concerned Citizens in Canada, the United Kingdom, New Zealand and South Africa – or so it seems to me – have come to think that the resolution of noble dream cases is done on a Rule by Judges basis. But that may simply be a function of the length of time such jurisdictions have had instruments in place shifting significant last-word moral input to the judges.

Notice that whether the moral views of the majority of top judges do, or do not, generally differ from those of any particular Concerned Citizen – and so, for many, whether the core notions at the heart of the Rule of Law ideal do, or do not, appear to collapse into a perception of Rule by Judges in highly moralized cases – there can still be a fair amount of certainty and predictability vis-à-vis the likely outcome of these cases. Yes, certainty and predictability can be premised on the likelihood of point-of-application judges generally applying moderately specific rules to the facts in issue. That is undoubtedly true. But certainty and predictability can also be premised on the likelihood of judges with an X, Y and Z set of shared moral views deciding noble dream cases A, B and C in a certain way.

In fact, it is at least possible that *more* certainty can sometimes be generated by aiming for significant amounts of moral consensus amongst the top appointed judges than by operating via relatively specific rules. Even the Concerned Citizen who believes the judges' moral judgments and sentiments overwhelmingly to be wrong and distasteful can predict with a fair degree of certainty how they will decide when they exhibit the just-mentioned consensus of moral outlook. Indeed, that is why she wants new appointees on the bench.

This is not to say that each and every Concerned Citizen would prefer a top highest court on which all the judges shared her particular moral judgments and sentiments, or indeed shared her view of how best to interpret statutes (and, relatedly, constitutional provisions) or when to ignore *stare decisis* and overturn precedent. On a system-wide level one can make a case for the good consequences that flow from having a diversity of outlooks, of approaches to interpretation, of willingnesses to uphold settled precedents, and even of moral sensibilities represented on the top court. In fact, if there be benefits from having to confront and respond to opposing views and make explicit the pre-suppositions on which reliance is placed, then quite a strong case can be made for having a diversity of viewpoints, approaches and moral sensibilities represented on the top court. And the more that top court finds itself deciding highly moralized, noble dream type cases, the more the benefits of this sort of diversity may become evident to a Concerned Citizen.

Recall Lon Fuller's mock hypothetical, 'The Case of the Speluncean Explorers',[5] by way of illustration. Fuller there, after engineering things so that the relevant legal rule points one way and most people's moral judgment or sensibilities the other, provides the reader with the main approaches to statutory interpretation through the mouths of the fictitious Justices Foster, Keen and Handy. Not only is it impossible, on the basis of reading this article alone, to know which approach Fuller himself favoured, it also begins to dawn on the reader that a court with a Justice Foster *and* a Justice Keen *and* a Justice Handy might be preferable – as a whole – to one full of only Fosters or Keens or Handys.

Even the Concerned Citizen who came to share the Bad Man's opinion that the resolution of highly moralized noble dream cases was done on a Rule by Judges basis might nevertheless favour this diversity of sentiments and approaches and attitudes amongst the top judges. If so, it would come at the expense of the sort of predictability that follows solely from judicial homogeneity. Still, a series of 5–4 cases might make more evident the underlying Rule by Judges nature of resolving noble dream cases. For some Concerned Citizens, at least, making that more evident would be a further part of the countervailing attraction of aiming for judicial diversity or lack of homogeneity.

The Visiting Martian

The Visiting Martian would observe that people disagree, widely and regularly. They disagree about facts, about what has happened and will happen in the external, causal, empirical world. They disagree about which facts one needs to try to change and which facts one does not or cannot. They disagree about policies, about the actions that need to be taken to bring about change. They disagree about all sorts of 'ought' questions, about what ought to be the case. Facts, policies and morality: when it comes to these things there simply is widespread, observable dissensus and disagreement. Even within the subset of what the Visiting Martian takes to be smart, well-informed, reasonable and nice people there is the same disagreement and dissensus.

Given that thoroughgoing disagreement in society, the Visiting Martian sees law as a social institution the main job of which is to settle disputes. Law reduces the range and scope of factors that can be taken into account in deciding what one (an individual, a company, a government agency, the government itself) should do. It guides conduct by simplifying, by reducing the amount of information that has to be considered. By limiting what can be taken into account it produces more

---

5   See Lon Fuller, 'The Case of the Speluncean Explorers' (1949) 62 *Harvard Law Review* 616.

agreement than would be generated by some sort of 'do the right thing' injunction. And that in turn, given how difficult it otherwise would be to know what others are likely to do and to co-ordinate actions, increases predictability, the satisfying of expectations, and the level of citizens' certainty about what they are expected to do and about how those in power will decide.

All those guidance-performing and dispute-settling aspects of law, and how it can reduce errors, co-ordinate actions, speed up decision making and more, would be noted by our Visiting Martian, just as they have been pointed out by many others already. That law narrows or reduces the realm of relevant considerations, and so (at least if the legal rules are widely accepted as binding) the decision making costs, is no new insight. Our Visiting Martian will think it rather a trite observation.

Less trite, though, is the question of whether law that is highly moralized, that incorporates noble dream type amorphous moral standards or principles or tests, can achieve this settlement function. Or, rather, if it can achieve that function, is it solely because 'what law is' gets equated to 'what the judges say it is' by everyone save the judges themselves (or, maybe, by everyone save only the very top judges themselves)?

In any well-functioning Benevolent Legal System our Visiting Martian would answer 'yes' to both those questions. Were he pressed to explain this settlement *not* by means of a text but by means of a shared set of practices he might point to greater-than-in-the-population-at-large shared judicial attitudes as regards what is acceptable for them to do and to refer to, as well as simply what is morally right. A relative conformity of judicial outlook and approach means some portion of the certainty-enhancing and constrained decision making aspects of the Rule of Law filters through even in noble dream cases. The Visiting Martian could observe that Rule by Judges is not the same as Rule by *These* Judges Hearing *This* Case Today. He could observe that, while also conceding that from many vantages law can be bad, even when claiming to be good.

Concomitantly, he could return to Hart's point: Law works largely outside the courtroom. Cases that wind their way up to the United States Supreme Court or the United Kingdom's House of Lords (now Supreme Court too) are failures in the system. And having no democratic, 'let the numbers count' barrow to push himself, our Visiting Martian might wonder why it matters if the Rule of Law ideal does indeed collapse into Rule by Judges in a few noble dream cases.

Interpreting Constitutional (or Quasi-Constitutional) Instruments v. Rule by Judges

This section will pre-suppose at least a sketched-out conception of democracy. And the one I want to stipulate (though I would also be prepared to advocate and defend it) is a thin conception of democracy, one with relatively few – perhaps even the least possible number of – moral overlays. To put it differently, I want to stipulate a conception of democracy that is procedural rather than substantive, one that postpones much moral evaluation until later. In short, my stipulated conception of democracy is one in which it is possible to say 'this is a democracy, but a deficient or bad or wicked one'. I want to leave such notions as upholding individual rights or safeguarding the position of minorities or ensuring social justice outside of, and separate from, one's core conception of democracy.

Of course any argument about the best way of conceiving of democracy has these days to be made against the background that democracy is an 'essentially contested concept'.[6] It is a notion broad enough to encompass *both* the position of those who prefer a thin, procedural account *and* those who prefer a fat, substantive morally infused account. No one, or virtually no one, today professes to be against democracy. So any debate that collapses into an argument about the meaning of the word 'democracy' will not be terribly useful or instructive. Where a word and concept are expansive enough, and indeterminate enough, to encompass a range of senses, arguing about the meaning of the word becomes somewhat sterile. Not much is to be gained by heading down that road, however much there may be clear tactical and rhetorical advantages in positioning oneself on the side of democracy.

The concept of democracy, therefore, is a broad enough church to encompass both thin and fat, procedural and substantive, conceptions of democracy. That said, I want to stipulate a working account of a thin conception of democracy. 'Majority rules' or 'letting the numbers count' or 'rule *by* the people' seem to me to be good starting points, not least because they offer a position with which many people today disagree. Throughout the western world – in the law schools, the judiciary, the press, the intelligentsia, even in government – there are assuredly many people who are not supporters of unalloyed majoritarianism. They reject the view that the least bad procedure for resolving disagreements within a society, at least when it comes to rights, is to let the numbers count. For many of them, letting the numbers count or raw majoritarianism comes with too big a price tag; it is too likely to lead to the sacrifice of, say, individual rights or identifiable minority interests while making more likely still the dangers of what they often like to term 'the tyranny of the majority'.

They prefer a fat conception of democracy. They say something such as that:

> [w]e should, then, view democracy as a means for the collective pursuit of justice, enabling conflicts of interest to be resolved primarily on grounds of right rather than power and influence. Democratic deliberation should appeal to moral principles that facilitate agreement among people who seek the common good, instead of narrow self-interest, in order that the results can be accepted by everyone as amounting to a reasonable accommodation that treats all citizens as equally entitled to concern and respect.[7]

---

6   See W.B. Gallie, 'Essentially Contested Concepts' (1965) 56 *Proceedings of the Aristotelian Society* 167.

7   T.R.S. Allan, 'Common Law Constitutionalism and Freedom of Speech', in J. Beatson and T. Cripps (eds) *Freedom of Expression and Freedom of Information: Essays in*

Or, more directly, they say straight out that '[d]emocracy is not the same thing as majoritarianism'.[8]

So, according to one not uncommon account of what gets to count as democratic, a much more substantive, morally overlain account, majority rule alone will not suffice. Majority rule needs to be tempered by placing in the hands of the judiciary the power to ensure that legislation (passed on the basis of representative majoritarianism) can be struck down or declared incompatible or read down when it is held to be inconsistent with certain enumerated individual rights and when that inconsistency is held (again, by the judiciary) not to be reasonable or justifiable. On this sort of morally overlain account, democracy has at least two aspects – a head-counting, majoritarian aspect *and* a rights-respecting, morally good-outcomes aspect (where the latter is not determined by the former).

Substantive accounts of democracy such as these, however, discount fairly heavily the good consequences that can flow from adopting a thin conception of democracy.

Clarity

To start, a thin conception of democracy has the benefit of providing greater clarity than fatter, more substantive accounts. As less is rolled up into the concept it is, or should be, clearer to the disinterested observer whether the criteria for inclusion within the concept have been met.

In itself, this is an extremely modest consequentialist advantage. Indeed, to all but the categorizing political scientist or historian of political philosophy it may be too insignificant to tilt the debate between thin and fat one way or the other. And against this claimed greater clarity must be balanced the disadvantage involved in shifting to a different usage of the term – that is to say, for those who are used to understanding 'democracy' as including more than majoritarianism (and even as seeing themselves as part of a long tradition in doing so), any move to a thinner conception will, for them, carry a cost. This cost, for them, will need to be set against the claimed benefits of greater clarity.

Still, greater clarity of thought is not nothing. And as I will argue below, what goes hand in hand with the clearer, proceduralist conception of democracy is a postponement of moral evaluation, of assessing whether any particular system is deficient in terms of, say, upholding individual rights or protecting the position of minorities. That postponing of moral evaluation has much more evident consequentialist benefits. Or so I will argue next.

Honour of Sir David Williams (Oxford: Oxford University Press, 2000), pp. 23–4.

8 Christopher Eisgruber, *Constitutional Self-Government* (Cambridge, MA: Harvard University Press, 2001), p. 18. At p .62 Eisgruber says democracy is not the same thing as 'government by voters'.

Honesty

The thin, proceduralist conception of democracy leaves more scope than the fat, substantive conception for saying, and thinking, 'this is a democracy, but it is a wicked or bad or deficient one'. As noted above, it postpones more of the value judgments and moral evaluations until later. First you decide if it is a democracy (using the thin criteria) and *then* you decide how good or desirable a democracy it is (using criteria that would include some or all of those in a fat or substantive conception).

Why might that sort of deferral of the moral overlay judgments have good consequences? Here a main reason relates to honesty. The thin conception of democracy makes it harder for the observer or assessor to smuggle in his or her own moral sentiments. When the moral evaluations take place at some later stage they tend to be more in the open, more public, and more subject to being contested.

Take present-day Iraq, for example. In terms of upholding individual rights and protecting minority interests many of us could point to more than a few failings, to put it conservatively. On the thin conception of democracy, however, one first has to decide if enough people voted – and voted without fear and corruption – to pass some 'majority rules' or 'letting the numbers count' test. If one thinks it has passed this initial bare proceduralist test then one can, and should, go on to hold the government up to other tests. How are Kurds and Sunnis likely to fare? What of women? Will religious extremists pass distasteful, even reprehensible, laws?

Many of these later moral tests or assessments – on the desirability of Sharia law, say, or the need to pursue prosecutions against former Baathists – will be highly contentious. Indeed, as with deciding the range, scope and application of rights generally, we should expect that most of the time there will be disagreement and dissensus. And that disagreement will be between sincere, reasonable, not obviously stupid or evil, people.

The danger is that too much is apt to be left in the shadows if a judgment on the moral desirability of a government's policies is elided with – or wrapped up into – a comparatively straightforward claim about how that government was selected or came to take power (or perhaps, just as importantly, how the former government came to lose power and be tossed out). Under the thin conception one has less room to avoid confronting the debatable aspects of the moral issues in play and less scope to smuggle in one's own sentiments regarding those contentious issues under some such catch-all cry as 'democratic values'. It is harder to pretend, that is, that your moral sentiments are uncontentious and obviously right.

So a second potential good consequence of adopting the thin, proceduralist conception of democracy is that it is more likely to force moral evaluations – and relatedly their contestable, debatable nature – into the open. One's own moral sentiments are more likely to be exposed as not as widely shared, not as universal, as was assumed or hoped. Accordingly, the thin conception of democracy is more honest and transparent about the contested nature of claims regarding individual rights, social justice, minority protections, and the rest down in the Waldronian quagmire where high-level political and moral abstractions have to play out in practice.

Addressing Institutional Failings

A third consequentialist benefit attaching to the thin conception of democracy is that it focuses attention on the institutional arrangements that have to prop up or support the deceptively simple notion of 'majority rules' or 'letting the numbers count'. Quite obviously even the thin, bare proceduralist account of democracy leaves open a myriad possible ways to structure government. Choices include: federalist or unitary state; bicameralism or unicameralism; parliamentary or presidential system; constitutional monarchy or republic; fixed or floating election dates; proportional, preferential or first-past-the-post voting system; voluntary or compulsory voting; and more. Within the democratic world, even within the thin, proceduralist democratic world, there simply is no one, correct model of democracy.

To put it differently, even in stipulating a thin conception of democracy we would still need a body of theory that focuses directly on the justification and elaboration of voting systems, of boundary-drawing procedures or districting, of the funding of political campaigns, of media access and even – perhaps – of an overarching theory linking those all together. A thin conception of democracy will not diminish the demand for any of that. Indeed, it will make it more obvious. Hence, even if one is inclined, like me, to judge it best to postpone and so bring into the open moral evaluations related to upholding rights or safeguarding minorities or passing tolerably acceptable laws, there are still a large number of permutations and combinations available as regards how 'letting the numbers count' or 'rule by the people' can be brought into existence and justified.

Emerging Democracies

What about borderline cases, countries that might plausibly fit under the rubric of 'emerging democracies' or 'emerged but may now have lapsed democracies'? Here one might include Russia, Algeria, Zimbabwe, Hong Kong, Lebanon, the aforementioned Iraq, and others. And it is precisely here that stipulating the thin, proceduralist conception of democracy may be most informative, and hence useful. Some of these countries will fail to pass muster on the thin account of democracy. For instance, the voting process in Zimbabwe might be so tainted and full of intimidation, fraud, corruption, gerrymandering, control of the media and plain thuggery that no disinterested observer could say the election process reflected the adult voters' (or better still, would-be voters') duress-free preferences. The declared winner was on no plausible account the choice of the majority. The numbers did not count.

The thin account of democracy makes it clear why, say, Zimbabwe is not democratic. The fat, substantive account clouds the threshold issue. Is the country not democratic because the voters' preferences have been ignored, distorted and trammelled or is it because certain members of opposition parties and minority groups are shot, the rule of law attacked, individual rights grossly infringed and life expectancy has fallen from 63 years two decades ago to 33 today?

Another way to make this point is to claim that there is an independent value in knowing – or having a reasonable basis for believing – whether a majority of citizens' views have determined who gets to hold power. In a country such as Zimbabwe, where on neither a thin nor a fat account can democracy be said to hold sway, this may matter less. But what of Serbia, or Russia, or even Algeria? What of countries where the thin conception of democracy's threshold is arguably surpassed but the substantive account's threshold is not? The choice appears to boil down to classifying certain countries as morally deficient, rights-infringing democracies or as not counting them as democracies at all. (And for what it is worth, note the analogy here to the debate between natural law adherents and legal positivists, where much of the dispute is about little more than how to think about and describe the same thing.)

Or take the much, much rarer, obverse situation. Here we have a place where individual rights are fairly well respected, minorities safe, the rule of law in place and yet the majority clearly and evidently does not rule. Is Hong Kong today democratic? Was it so before the handover to China in 1997? Surely not, on anyone's account. Yet conceding that seems to me to go some way towards acknowledging that there are at least some benefits or advantages to adopting a thin conception of democracy. The fat conception of democracy must always embrace the thin, and then add on the moral overlays. Other than the tactical benefits of calling in aid a word with powerfully emotive connotations, though, what is lost in leaving that overlay till later and outside the confines of the concept of democracy?

Well-established Democracies

A fifth good consequence attendant upon adopting a proceduralist conception of democracy, and one related to the third point above, is that claims as to 'democratic failings' in what are patently well-established democratic countries have to relate to the process of determining majority intentions. Focus is forced onto gerrymandering in US House of Representatives' elections, over-representation of rural voters in Japan and Queensland, the power of political party leaders under the MMP voting system in New Zealand, postal voting in the UK, low voter turn-out pretty much everywhere, and many other issues related to how best to let the numbers count and measure what sort of government a majority of citizens want. That more narrowly defined focus on alleged procedural failings will be seen as consequentially beneficial if, like me, you think the moral overlay issues inherent in fat conceptions can be dealt with perfectly adequately in their own terms and outside the aegis of the concept of democracy.

Relatedly, what of supra-national entities like the European Union in which all the moral overlay concerns seem quite easily satisfied and yet the core-level issue of letting the numbers count and the majority ruling seems lacking. The EU, of course, is no Hong Kong. But then neither is it Switzerland, or Australia, or the United States where elected legislators have real power and parliament is the main law-making body. Talk of a 'democratic deficit' is very much warranted in the EU and it is solely focused on thin-conception concerns.

Liberalism and Democracy

It is at least arguable that a thin conception of democracy allows for a better understanding of the relationship between liberal values and letting the numbers count or majority rule. The claim would be that the thin conception's adherent would say that she is in a better position to assess, say, the ramifications of the election of a neo-fascist government in Austria or a neo-fascist coalition party in government in Italy. She can better separate the policies such parties espouse (which many would find distasteful and economically illiterate) from the way in which they came to have a share in government (which many would say is a good way of choosing governments). She can assert that 'this is a democratically elected government but it is one espousing some bad, evil, stupid and ignorant policies'.

Conversely, by adopting the thin conception of democracy one can consider the liberal credentials of, say, anti-hunt legislation in Britain or free-trade agreements without having to deny or ignore the clear 'rule by the people' mandate of those who enacted or entered into them. Relatedly, one is less apt to assume that a government that supports the free market is necessarily one that was selected by letting the numbers count.

Let us put away enumerating the potential good consequences of stipulating a thin account of democracy, one with relatively few moral overlays. This 'letting the numbers count' or 'rule by the people' or 'majority rules' conception is explicitly rejected by Amartya Sen, who argues that '[w]e must not identify democracy with majority rule'.[9] Sen prefers to build into his conception of democracy certain matters I want to leave outside that conception, matters such as 'the protection of liberties and freedoms [and] respect for legal entitlements'.[10]

For the consequentialist reasons given above I would not follow Sen; I would not build so many moral overlays into the conception of democracy. That said, a bare conception of democracy is not a skeletal one. Some moral overlay is needed to give life to the notion of 'letting the numbers count'. To put it differently, there is an element of the 'ought' involved in this notion, not just the 'is'. One needs to prescribe what *should* count as satisfying this test of majority rules. There is a range stretching from people raising their hands in the presence of men with

---

9   Amartya Sen, 'Democracy as a Universal Value' (1999) 10 *Journal of Democracy* No. 3, p. 8 (hereinafter 'Sen'). Another obvious proponent of a fat conception of democracy is Ronald Dworkin. See, *inter alia*, *Taking Rights Seriously* (London: Duckworth, 1977) and *Law's Empire* (Cambridge, MA: Belknap Press, 1986).

10   Sen, p. 9.

machine guns to voting by secret ballot but with the votes counted by unscrutinized henchmen to voting by secret ballot but in a state with only government-controlled news and swingeing defamation laws to voting by secret ballot in a state with a vigorously free press and no potential penalties (in terms of food distribution or roads being built) for living in a constituency that votes against the government. Somewhere along this range – and no doubt different people will draw the line at different places – the numbers stop really counting and who rules is not really being determined by the preferences of the majority. In this sense, Sen is clearly correct when he says that '[e]ven elections can be deeply defective if they occur without the different sides getting an adequate opportunity to present their cases, or without the electorate enjoying the freedom to obtain news and to consider the views of the competing protagonists'.[11]

The point is that even a thin conception of democracy – one focused on how governments are chosen rather than on what they decide to do once elected – cannot be a wholly emaciated conception. The notion of the majority choosing its government builds in a moral or normative component, a test of what does and does not count as an acceptable method of choosing; it builds in some John Ely-type questions or concerns.

More specifically, it raises other more complicated questions. Here one might point to issues about how the executive relates to the legislature and how both relate to the myriad bodies that implement law, and indeed interpret law. One might wonder, too, which decisions in large nation-states ought to be put separately to the voters – outside the regular process of voting for a legislature (and possibly executive). Different 'letting the numbers count' democracies can and will resolve these issues differently. Some resolutions will be preferred by some and others by others, with these various somes and others still falling within a thin 'letting the numbers count' conception. In addition, even the thin conception of democracy itself will have a core of settled meaning and a penumbra doubt – some real-life instances that clearly fall within the concept's ambit and some which are debatable, with arguments pointing both ways.

As I said above, then, 'letting the numbers count' or 'majority rules' is a deceptively simple notion. In fact, it requires some sort of moral overlay, some set of 'ought' judgments or criteria about the circumstances in which citizens can be said to have chosen their governments (and delegated some decisions to be taken for them), rather than having had it chosen for them. So to repeat, a thin conception of democracy cannot be a skeletal one. Confining how one thinks of democracy to issues of how legislatures and governments are chosen and relate to one another and the voter does not eliminate all the moral overlays. Nor does it eliminate contentious moral debates and the resulting dissensus about such things as voting systems, when referenda are needed, campaign finance rules, the merits of bicameralism or federalism or compulsory voting or any of the other matters connected to adding flesh to the notion of 'letting the numbers count'.

---

11   Sen, p. 9.

What counts as falling under the rubric of 'letting the numbers count', in other words, is a debatable evaluative matter. Hence thin conceptions of democracy do not and cannot eliminate all evaluative judgments and the resulting disagreement over these judgments.

Thin conceptions do, though, eliminate many other additional tiers of moral overlay, layers connected to the goodness or badness of the laws a government enacts or the things it does once elected, once the majority has ruled. Thin conceptions force these outer layers to be debated and discussed (and no doubt disagreed about) outside the confines of the concept of democracy. Proponents of thin conceptions of democracy think that a good thing, one that ought to be endorsed and followed.

At this point a critic who disliked my stipulating for a thin conception might well respond to me by saying something along the following lines:

> Your thin-conception-of-democracy argument looks to me to be irredeemably flawed. You concede that majoritarianism is not enough. You concede that some moral overlay is needed. But you do not say how much moral overlay is necessary. Drawing the line you want is harder than you think. You need to tell us how much overlay is needed as part of your thin conception, which protections and freedoms are related to ensuring the numbers count and which are related to after-the-fact-of-elections issues encompassed by claims to such things as justice or liberty or the common good. And I do not think you can tell us exactly where to draw that line, meaning your whole project is thrown into doubt.

That is a not unfair précis of what certain fat-conception-of-democracy adherents might at this point argue. They would focus on the difficulty thin-conception proponents would have in drawing any hard-and-fast distinctions between value judgments related to how governments are chosen so as to ensure the numbers really do count, on the one hand, and all the other value judgments, on the other hand, that are necessarily involved in governing, in deciding the scope of and reasonable limits on freedom of religion, say, or of search and seizure, or of immigration policy, or of how to spend society's limited resources on health, education and defence.

In general terms, such a critic is correct, of course, that drawing any hard-and-fast line between which value judgments relate to ensuring the numbers count and which do not is an inherently controversial one, an essentially contested one. As I have said already, it is one over which smart, reasonable, even nice people will disagree. Witness, for instance, the strong disagreements people have over voting systems and whether proportional or first-past-the-post or even preferential systems produce legislatures that better reflect (or reflect at all) majority sentiments.

However, such a critic is only correct in the most general sense. He or she demands that the proponent of a thin conception of democracy tell us exactly which rights and freedoms are aimed at ensuring the preferences of the majority have been translated into legislative reality. That demand for exactitude, however, is an unfair one in this sense.

Leave aside my point above that people will inevitably differ on when the numbers really have counted and that different weights and emphases will be put by different people on, say, respective campaign finance rules or access to media regulations or defamation regimes or even whether prisoners can vote. No, the unfairness of this criticism comes from demanding a level of preciseness or exactitude that the critic himself could not provide for his own, thick conception of democracy. After all, even for the proponent of a fat, substantive conception of democracy not all 'oughts' are related to what is or is not democratic. Even for him some claims for 'the protection of liberties and freedoms [and] respect for legal entitlements'[12] fall outside the aegis of his conception of democracy. The realm of living well and justly and fairly in social groups is not wholly subsumed by issues of what is or is not democratic, even for the most substantive and thick of conceptions.

So such a critic will have as difficult a time providing exactitude and precision in drawing his lines as will the thin-conception adherent; it is just that the difficulties will occur at different places.

To put it differently, this criticism assumes that there is no benefit in making a distinction between X and not-X unless the line between the two can be made crystal clear. I disagree. Thus, we can all differ over which writers to class as legal positivists without having to think there is therefore no use in distinguishing positivists from natural law adherents (or, indeed, in seeing the benefits of the two separate perspectives).

Stipulating a thin conception of democracy, then, has to be done in the full recognition that any two thin adherents could (and likely would) differ over where to draw various lines – just as any two thick-conception adherents could, and would. For both conceptions of democracy there will be, in Hartian terms, a core of settled meaning and a penumbra of doubt and uncertainty. Inside the penumbra of doubt people will simply disagree over whether some protection, rule or right does or does not contribute to letting the numbers count. Yet from recognizing that people will differ over where the thin conception of democracy ends it does not seem to me to follow that there is no value in seeking to postpone as much of the moral overlay as possible, in preferring the thin to the fat. Nor does it follow that most thick, morally overlain conceptions cannot be distinguished from most thin, morally exiguous conceptions. There can be a value to distinguishing between how governments ought to be chosen to ensure the majority has ruled and what governments ought to do once elected, even if at the margins – in the penumbra of doubt – there will be reasonable disagreement over where the one ends and the other begins. Thin conceptions of democracy eliminate many additional tiers of moral overlay, even if no definitive, exact line can be drawn to enclose such thin conceptions.

---

12   Sen, p. 9.

That is why I want to stipulate a thin conception of democracy. It is the one that I will use throughout the rest of this book (and, for that matter, have used in what has already been said).

With that stipulation out of the way, let us descend from the abstract ideal of Rule of Law talk to more down-to-earth matters.

In particular, the rest of this section will consider common law decision making of a certain sort. So we will be focused on a subset of Benevolent Legal Systems as a whole, namely those with a common law system.

Now such common law legal systems a century and a half ago, certainly in the United States and the United Kingdom, could be fairly characterized as having very modest amounts of legislation together with plenty of room for the judges (via the slow accretions of case law) to make or create the law of contract, of torts, of wills, of property and even of crimes. These judges, in other words, had plenty of law-making power. Common law adjudication back then, to a significant extent, meant law making in the absence of an enacted text.

Democracy, in my thin 'letting the numbers count' or 'majority rules' sense, changed all that. Statutes passed by a democratically elected legislature had a legitimacy much more obvious than wide open law making by unelected judges had. Or rather, that much greater legitimacy was a concomitant of the spreading idea that those with governing and law-making power should represent – and be accountable through regular elections to – the people. The idea of law being somehow 'out there' waiting to be discovered might be needed to justify the power held by judges 150 years ago; that century-and-a-half-old vintage of common law decision making might have required additional legitimacy-supporting props or diversions. But statute law emanating from a democratically elected legislature surely has no such need to justify the exercise of law-making power, at least no democratic need.

That means that even if we focus on 'the common law' in the sense of 'judge-made law' (and it had an older, different sense of 'the law common to all'), what that entails in terms of the extent of judicial power differs. Once the democratic era had arisen, judges are overwhelmingly interpreting enacted statutes; they are giving meaning to laid-down texts; they are *not* often creating law free from the constraints imposed by the legislature's enactment (which is not to deny that past cases, especially when combined with a hard-line *stare decisis* rule, can also impose constraints).

As Antonin Scalia points out, common law decision making in the democratic era – judge-made law that is based on interpreting, and even filling in the gaps, ambiguities and indeterminacies of, enacted statutes – much more easily overcomes the three seeming problems of retroactivity, of treating past cases as evidence of what some underlying, disembodied real law is, and of the slippery, highly contestable nature of specifying the holding or ratio of past cases. How? Well, where judges in a democratic-era system are overwhelmingly interpreting a legislatively laid-down text, the retroactive aspect or nature of their task only applies in so far as there is a gap in time between *a)* the dispute between the parties over meaning and *b)* the final decision as to meaning by the highest court. But as it is a laid-down text being interpreted, the parties cannot claim the law is being created or made up after the fact. The statute comes first, then the interpretation. But everyone is clear that it is the statute that is the source of the law. The top judges interpreting it are merely saying that the legislature's words always meant what they, the judges, are now authoritatively deciding they mean.

And as Hart pointed out, if the underlying grievance behind allegations of retroactivity relate to not knowing what the law is at the time you acted, then as regards any moderately specific statute this sort of grievance is massively reduced. At worst, your position falls into the penumbra of doubt or uncertainty as regards the meaning to be attributed to one or more provisions in this statute. Yet realizing that the laid-down statute is unclear, if you go to a lawyer and are told that it is a toss-up how the judges will decide – because no precedents are on point, the provision is a wholly new one, other parts of the statute point in opposite ways – then what is your actual grievance if you decide to roll the dice and litigate? Your grievance might be that statutes are not specific enough, but it is not that you were taken by surprise or that the law was changed after the fact. And compare that to the situation in which a party litigates because her lawyer tells her the words of the statute fall into the core of settled meaning because they are clear, dozens of past precedents all support that clear, unambiguous understanding of them and yet a majority of the judges on the top court decide the issue on the basis that attributing a different meaning to those words would, in their view, be more moral, just and in keeping with fundamental human rights. Only in the latter instance is retroactivity the core grievance, as opposed to an objection centred on this statute (and perhaps too many others) being too indeterminate, vague and amorphous to provide guidance and settle expectations.

Common law decision making in the pre-democratic era, when statutes were relatively scarce, has a much greater vulnerability to charges of 'retroactivity', and so a need for some sort of justificatory response that judges are merely discovering what was already somehow 'out there' and *not* making the law themselves, than does the interpreting-moderately-specific-statutes version of common law decision making.

The same goes for *stare decisis*. Why should we follow the reasoning of past cases? Before the democratic era, a strict reliance (at least in form, if not always in substance) on following past precedents could be seen as part of a wider background justificatory response to what might otherwise look like Rule by Judges, namely the response that past cases are evidence of what the 'out there' law is. Even on that understanding, one might think the jurisdiction's highest court ought to have some room to overrule past decisions, in order to allow for the fallibility of limited biological creatures (a category into which even judges fall). But disavow the notion that judges are simply 'finding' or 'discovering' a pre-existing law (even in Dworkin's sophisticated 'law as integrity' sense), and it becomes unclear why judges today who are making law should be hemmed in or constrained by the judges who in times past made law.

Or rather, the grounds for giving precedential weight to past decisions would have to be instrumental ones, encompassing factors such as furthering the goal of certainty for citizens, reducing the costs of continually reconsidering already-decided matters, and acknowledging that on many, many issues and questions a new set of judges will take the same view as the old set anyway. These sorts of instrumental or pragmatic grounds for adopting a doctrine of *stare decisis*, as it happens, apply at least as strongly in the democratic era of common law decision making. Indeed, justifying some sort of weak version of *stare decisis* on consequentialist grounds is easier (not harder but easier) against the backdrop of judges interpreting myriad and virtually all-encompassing democratically enacted statutes than it is in the earlier era of few statutes and plenty of untainted judge-made law. In the former case, judges can leave things as they are (on certainty grounds, say), knowing that the elected legislature can pass a statute to change them if it thinks it wise or politically expedient to do so or, indeed, if technological and social changes make such a move desirable. In the pre-democratic era, by contrast, almost always it will be the case that legal change will come from the judges, or it will not come at all. And that makes it extremely difficult always – or almost always – to opt for certainty over achieving justice or doing the right thing, at least in the absence of a rigid *stare decisis* rule justified at least nominally on the basis that judges are engaged in discovering the law that is 'out there' and whose decisions are evidence of what that law is.

The third seeming problem with common law decision making, the highly contestable nature of specifying what the ratio or holding of some past case is, matters much less in the democratic era. The statute is the law. The leading case merely gives an interpretation of that law. True, it is an authoritative and, barring statutory amendment, uncontestable ruling as to meaning. But any indeterminacy related to what the judges ruled the meaning of the statute to be still leaves the law there for all to see. When it is common law decision making of the older, pre-democratic sort, where the holding and ratio of the judges – what they say – *is* the law, then, indeterminacy seems far more worrying. If it becomes too pronounced, it can come close to a mild version of lawlessness.

All of that being accepted, here is the issue for the rest of this section. When we move from regular statutes to the realm of interpreting constitutions or quasi-constitutional instruments such as statutory bills of rights, are we heading forward to the past, as it were? Are the judges as unconstrained as they were in the pre-democratic era? Do the problems of retroactivity, of how to justify *stare decisis*, and of the relative indeterminacy of past case-law holdings take on their older, more virulent forms? Are we again in need of the idea that law is 'out there' to take attention away from the Rule by Judges aspect of this enterprise?

The Visiting Martian

From the disinterested observer's vantage, constitutional (and statutory) bills of rights, as well as many other provisions in a constitution, are expressed in vague and amorphous terms. 'Unreasonable search and seizure', 'due process', 'equal protection', 'right to free speech', 'equality' and much else of the same ilk are notions or concepts with a comparatively small core of settled meaning and correspondingly large penumbra of doubt and uncertainty. There is much indeterminacy.

Whenever the judges are called upon to interpret such terms or provisions our Visiting Martian might wonder if they are largely in the same position – the same relatively unconstrained-by-the-legislature position – as they were back in the pre-democratic era. Two factors will affect how the Visiting Martian answers that question, both contingent, empirical factors that could (and perhaps do) vary from jurisdiction to jurisdiction. The first regards interpretation. How are the words of the constitutional (or quasi-constitutional) provision read? Are they given the meaning they were widely understood to have at the time of adoption, or some other meaning? Relatedly, are the meanings of the words in these texts allowed to alter over time (perhaps to keep pace with current attitudes or values, as perceived by the judges), or is the meaning attributed to them more or less locked in?

The second regards the ability of the elected legislature to respond to authoritative judicial pronouncements as to meaning. Clearly, as regards constitutional provisions and entrenched bills of rights, there is no scope at all for the legislature to respond (absent a Canadian *Charter of Rights* section 33 notwithstanding clause-type provision, albeit one that has some practical likelihood of ever being used). Only by means of constitutional amendment can the meaning given by the judges be gainsaid. (So in that sense, if not others, the factors influencing how a judge ought to interpret a constitutional provision might differ from those affecting how she ought to interpret a statutory provision.) With statutory bills of rights, and other statutes described by the judges as quasi-constitutional enactments, this second issue is purely empirical. Yes, the legislature in theory retains a power to gainsay the meaning the judges have attributed to one of the amorphous, indeterminate provisions, but if the political cards are all stacked in such a way as to make using that power near-on impossible, then at some point the judges will know – for all practical purposes – that any interpretation they give the words cannot, or will not, be gainsaid or overruled by the legislature.

Much of this discussion I want to defer until Chapters 5 and 6, when we turn specifically to bills of rights. Here we can be much more narrowly focused. From the Visiting Martian's Vantage it can look as though interpreting constitutional (and quasi-constitutional) provisions is pretty similar to common law decision making in the pre-democratic era. Or rather, the more the words of the provision (say, 'equal protection') are given a meaning they were not understood to have at the time of adoption, and (relatedly) the more that attributed meaning is allowed to alter and change as time goes by, then the more the task of common law constitutional interpretation seems very similar to the older, pre-democratic form of common law. The same observation applies to quasi-constitutional interpretation to the extent that the legislature, in fact, never or almost never feels itself to be in a position politically to trump or gainsay the judges.

Given the extent to which 'living tree' or 'living constitution' or 'progressivist' or 'keeping pace with civilization' type approaches to constitutional interpretation are observably evident in common law Benevolent Legal Systems, our Visiting Martian would say that this sort of task can appear to collapse into a form of Rule by Judges. And that would resurrect the three problems of retroactivity, of why it is worth even sometimes being constrained by past judge-made law, and of the relative indeterminacy of that judge-made law.

In other words, the need for the natural law-type notion that law is somehow 'out there' waiting to be discovered – the very same notion mocked by Holmes and so widely seen as pure fantasy today, not least by many judges themselves – will be strongly felt when it comes to common law decision making as regards interpreting constitutional (and quite possibly quasi-constitutional) provisions. Without that background justification this sort of decision making (assuming some version of progressivist interpretation or other is used) will appear to the Visiting Martian to be highly retroactive. Indeed it will infringe one of the core procedural Rule of Law values, the aim of being able to know in advance what the rules are that affect you. It will also be likely to spur some judges – especially those who make the mistake of supposing that only through them will change come about – to discount concerns about certainty in favour of upholding their own views of what is in keeping with justice, fairness or rights-respecting conduct.

The Visiting Martian might well also observe how strikingly at odds with democracy this sort of common law law-making is.

The Judge

In moments of quiet contemplation many judges would concede that they – the judges – have a tendency to idealize their own system of common law decision making. Even the name 'common law' as opposed to 'judge-made law', has a tendency to obscure the retroactive and comparatively indeterminate aspects of this sort of law.

They might also allow that in the course of interpreting a bill of rights or a division-of-powers federal head of power in a constitution there is significantly more scope for them to consider political and moral principles than there is when interpreting most statutes. Some might even accept that what they are here doing looks remarkably like the older, pre-democratic-era form of common law decision making. They would accept, in other words, that whether the common law rules they are enunciating are subject to legislative override (one that can be, and on occasion is, used) is highly significant.

Asked for more clarity, some of our judges would admit that the term 'common law decision making' can be used to cover both the 'subject to legislative override' scenarios and the 'not so subject scenarios', and that the two are quite distinct in terms of their legitimacy, at least as regards democratic legitimacy. The latter calls for some sort of an additional justification in a way the former does not. And using the same term to describe both does not, without more, provide that justification.

Of course, for those judges who understand the concept of 'democracy' in terms much thicker and more substantive than those set out earlier in this section, there is more scope to avoid justification. Include within the concept of democracy a host of necessary rights not directly related to how a government is chosen, and specify that all those rights must be enforced, protected and upheld by the judiciary – not to mention weighed against one another by the judges, who can also say when reasonable limits on them will prevail – and you largely redefine away the problem. You eliminate the need for justification by defining your terms, just so.

You can also obscure the three problems with older, pre-democratic-era common law decision making by continuing to talk of the 'interpretation' of constitutional (and quasi-constitutional) provisions, even though what you are doing has little or nothing to do with a search for intended (or its proxy, originally understood) meaning. Calling the process of giving vague, amorphous terms what you think is their most moral meaning, or the meaning that is most in keeping with what you take to be their best background fit with everything else you know about the constitution, or the meaning you think is most in keeping with contemporary social values, is not interpretation in any sense that imposes constraints on the people doing the interpreting. Or rather, because that is not quite correct, any constraints inherent in *those sorts* of 'interpreting' are not coming from the words used or the intentions of those who carefully and deliberately chose those, as opposed to other, words. Nor are they coming from how those words were understood by the preponderance of people at the time of the adoption or entrenchment of this provision. Rather, any constraints there might be are coming from the internalized craft tradition of judging and from broader political and moral factors.

The same sort of obfuscating effects can be achieved by redefining other concepts, ones such as 'reasonableness', 'separation of powers' and 'justice' (not to mention 'Rule of Law').

Even with these obscuring or obfuscating or redefine-away-the-problems techniques available, however, from the Judge's Vantage the old-fashioned idea used to justify pre-democratic-era common law – that law is somehow 'out there' waiting to be discovered – can be an attractive one. It can apply to the sort of hyper common law that involves judges interpreting constitutional (and sometimes, too, quasi-constitutional) provisions. In fact, and this is somewhat ironic, from the Judge's Vantage this natural law-type notion of a disembodied law waiting to be discovered can be both mocked as pure fantasy and yet implicitly relied upon to justify the retroactive, indeterminate and anti-democratic aspects of what is being done.

Referring to, and Deferring to, Foreign Law

How does what might plausibly be described as Rule by Judges differ from, and how is it similar to, what may well eventuate, in part at least, in a Benevolent

Legal System where the notion of the Rule of Law is strongly emphasized or where common law constitutional (or quasi-constitutional) decision making is widespread? That has been the question thus far considered in this chapter. An issue which is tangential to that, and the one with which we will finish this chapter, has to do with the practice of referring to, and indeed on occasion deferring to, foreign law. Is that practice legitimate? Is it desirable?

Here I am going to assume those questions are being considered in a jurisdiction like the United States. Canada, Australia and New Zealand all have the complication of colonial ties to the United Kingdom having existed well within living memory. For all three their highest court was in London as recently as six decades, three decades and under one decade ago, respectively. Hence, though those formal ties exist no longer, the issue there of referring to, and on occasion deferring to, decisions of the top United Kingdom courts (and other parts of the former Empire) is more complex. And as for the United Kingdom itself, its membership of the European Union and the relationship of domestic and EU law compounds the complication. Similarly, jurisdictions such as South Africa whose constitutions make explicit provision for referring to, indeed direct the judges to consider, foreign law also complicate the issue.

I will not pursue any of those complications. Instead I want to consider the issue of justification for this practice of referring, and perhaps deferring, to foreign law in a more bare-bones way. But it will be a proffered justification other than one appealing to historical contingencies or explicit directions in a constitutional (or quasi-constitutional) provision.

In short, I want to consider a particular family of justifications that defends the appropriateness of citing or deferring to the law of nations, at least sometimes, including in controversial Bill of Rights cases before the Supreme Court such as whether the Eighth Amendment forbids the juvenile death penalty. What I have in mind are the sorts of justifications that defend that appropriateness on the basis that '[i]f these issues have been wrestled with in a number of other jurisdictions, then our commitment to the pursuit of justice should lead us to examine the end product of their labors for guidance ... the accumulated legal wisdom of mankind, embodied in *ius gentium*, may still have something to offer us'.[13]

Implicit, and sometimes explicit, in that sort of defence is the drawing of an analogy between the established body of scientific findings, on the one hand, and this notion of a law of nations or foreign law consensus. Here is how one defender of the analogy puts it:

> I have invoked the image of science and of scientific problem-solving several times to illustrate how a foreign law consensus may be relevant to U.S. legal decision making.[14]

---

13   Jeremy Waldron, 'Foreign Law and the Modern *Ius Gentium*' (2005) 119 *Harvard Law Review* 129, at p. 140.

14   *Ibid.*, p. 143.

> [A] consensus in either the law or the natural sciences can be wrong. In neither field, however, is there a sensible alternative to paying attention to the established body of findings to which others have contributed over the years.[15]

> It relies instead on the idea that solutions to certain kinds of problems in the law might get established in the way that scientific theories are established. They do not get established as infallible, they change over the years, and there are always outliers who refuse to accept them – some cranky, some whose reluctance leads eventually to progress.[16]

> [T]hat does not preclude turning to the legal consensus of civilized nations for assistance anymore than the American origin of an epidemic precludes Americans' turning to foreign scientists for guidance.[17]

Let us, therefore, consider this suggested analogy. My argument is that it is flawed and unpersuasive, or at least that it ought to be seen as such from the Visiting Martian's Vantage (and possibly even from the Judge's Vantage).

To begin this attack on that analogy, we will consider alternative medicine, then global warming and a few other examples before returning to the epidemic example. To what extent is it the case that it is some sort of widespread consensus – or rather a consensus of experts – that provides us with knowledge of and in the external, causal world? And is there anything lying behind that consensus – some sort of mind-independent, imposed reality – that is ultimately doing the work in the scientific realm, something not obviously underlying or propping up any legal consensus that may emerge when appealing to or citing foreign law?

Alternative Medicine

How would one assess the claims to respectability of the various sorts of alternative medicine treatments on offer, from homeopathy, acupuncture and echinacea to aromatherapy, magnetic resonance zones to anything with the word 'holistic' before it? A double-blind drug trial would seem to be a good starting point, at least where the suggested remedy can be given or not given with neither the patient nor doctor knowing if this is a placebo or the proffered remedy. Indeed, this sort of double-blind test of efficacy is the gold standard. No room is left for attributing causation and differential outcomes to social expectations, individual psychology, the placebo effect or the observed fact that most people, for most illnesses, simply get better on their own (whether they take nothing, a sugar pill or some unbelievably diluted addition to water).

---

15   *Ibid.*, p. 139.
16   *Ibid.*, p. 144.
17   *Ibid.*, p. 144.

Notice that nothing in this sort of double-blind trial is inconsistent with 'overlap, duplication, mutual elaboration, and the checking and rechecking of results that is characteristic of true science'.[18] Indeed we would expect such trials, and tests of efficacy generally, to make as sophisticated a use as possible of statistics, meta-analysis, computer modelling and attempts to control for more than one possible causal agent (not to mention sorting out causation from correlation).

We can happily concede all that. And yet, when we come to pass judgment on, say, the efficacy of echinacea or homeopathy, we need to be very clear just what it is we are checking and rechecking our results against. Is it against the opinions of all the professors of the Harvard University Faculty of Medicine? Is some consensus of their views (perhaps augmented by the views of medical professors at the universities of Oxford, Toronto and Melbourne), in and of itself, determinative of whether homeopathy or chemotherapy or antibiotics or echinacea can actually reverse the course of illnesses and make people better?

If anyone be inclined to answer 'yes' to this last query, stop and put yourself in the shoes of the Dean of Medicine at Harvard University. Against what does he or she assess effectiveness and check results? The whole edifice of science rests on the premise that the answer here is *not* just 'the consensus of views of the other expert doctors'. Penicillin does not save millions of lives just because a coterie of top doctors thinks it does. Homeopathy and echinacea are not worthless, no better than sugar pill idiocies, simply due to the fact that 99.9 per cent of top medical experts surveyed ticked the 'worthless' box. Penicillin would not stop working for no other reason than that the two (or five, or 13, or 25) most recently appointed medical professors at Harvard have now decided it will.

The point is a simple one, but one that can be left obscured by this analogy of law to science. Science rests on a belief that we all live in a material world; that there is an external, causal world of which we are a part; that Berkeley was wrong[19] and that Hume was right;[20] that there exists a mind-independent world out

---

18   *Ibid.*, pp. 138–9.

19   See George Berkeley, *A Treatise Concerning the Principles of Human Knowledge* (1710). Perhaps the correct term is not so much 'wrong' as 'weird' – thinking that the universe would disappear if God did not keep looking at it does not, strictly speaking, have implications for the scientific method or even, arguably, for the notion of causality. At least I think it doesn't.

20   David Hume, *A Treatise on Human Nature* (ed. L.A. Selby-Bigge, 2nd edn, rev. by P.H. Nidditch (Oxford: Oxford University Press, 1978; first published in 1739)). Hume began by conceding that we could not prove, in a deductive way, the existence of an external, causal world. All of our information comes from our senses. We have no direct contact with such a world. It is logically possible that such a world does not exist, that Berkeley is right. But no one believes that. We all naturally believe that such a mind-independent world exists. Any modern-day postmodernist English professor who purports to doubt it, or to adopt a radical anti-foundationalism, or to suggest all knowledge is, say, socially constructed, needs only to be shown to one's eighth-floor office window and asked to jump. He won't. As Hume argued, deep down, the self-proclaimed radical sceptic too believes in a mind-independent,

there that imposes outcomes on all us humans, no matter how we may have been socialized or inculcated.

In that sense, while it is true that science is not just a matter of idiosyncratic observations about energy or gravity, it is equally true that the whole scientific method and world-view (not to mention the general enlightenment way of thinking) starts from precisely those observations about our external, causal world. It is just those observations that are the basis of ever more sophisticated attempts to draw conclusions about how our world is structured and the cause-and-effect laws that govern it (independently of whatever we, or even Harvard professors, may happen to think).

Penicillin works because of a mind-independent truth about the way the world works and about the interactions of antibiotics with the human body.

Seen in that way, the consensus of experts in a particular scientific field still matters – but it matters in an indirect, evidential way because it is such a strong indication of what is likely to be true in the external, causal world. These people, who have spent their lives studying and testing the complex causal interactions, have far more expertise than we do. If a consensus of such experts in some scientific area believe that X is the case, then odds are overwhelming that X, in fact, is the case. Such experts are not infallible, of course. A seeming crank, every once in a while, will be proved correct. But she will be proved correct because her views are open to testing and potential falsifying and because, over time, the evidence builds up on her side (as it did with the expanding universe theory, say).

This is the only way to make sense of the claims to mind-independent truth that science makes. It is the only non-mysterious, non-mystical way to understand the presumptive force of any consensus of experts *in the realms of science*. It is the only basis for labelling much of alternative medicine as 'rubbish'.

What I think simply cannot be provided, and what one seems never to be offered, is any reason for any of us to believe that law is analogous to science in so far as what it is that underlies and supports a consensus of opinion in the two realms. More specifically, when American judges are pondering, say, whether the Eighth Amendment forbids the juvenile death penalty, and they look overseas and happen to note a consensus of legal opinion amongst western European and Canadian judges on that question, this analogy suggests that the legal consensus of those overseas judges somehow sits atop a body of mind-independent, imposed-on-humans truths (as it does in the scientific realm).

If it were otherwise, if the legal consensus of the European and Canadian judges did *not* rest on any mind-independent, same-cause-inevitably-leading-to-same-effect type testable truths,[21] then there would be at least some initial

---

external, causal world which imposes outcomes on all us humans however we may have been socialized or inculcated or whether we be male, female, rich, poor, etc.

21   However difficult and demanding of ingenuity and of familiarity with past results such testing might need to be – indeed however much it might amount to far, far more than mere idiosyncratic observations.

grounds for wondering why unelected American judges interpreting a Constitution which is next to impossible to change and whose decision in this area could not be overturned or reversed by statute should be paying heed to that foreign law consensus. Or at any rate, one might expect those who strongly value a democratic right to participate in social decision making, even to participate in decisions about the juvenile death penalty, to wonder this.

So we can see that this analogy, between a consensus in the natural sciences and a consensus in the law, can be made to carry a great deal of weight in defending the practice of referring to and even deferring to foreign law. The more any such foreign law consensus rests on moral sentiments (or, indeed, even on people's beliefs about some real, mind-independent moral truth where it is the case that they have no agreed method for getting at such claimed moral truths), the less such a consensus in law resembles a consensus in the natural sciences.

Global Warming and Other Examples

In the absence of the sort of empiricist world-view I have traced above, it is not at all clear why anyone, anywhere, would care in the least that a scientific consensus may be emerging as regards global warming (or indeed be motivated to challenge its underpinnings and assumptions or even know where to start in attempting to do so).

Here is another way to get at the same point, which is that consensus in the natural sciences is ultimately governed by – and open to being changed by – the imposed, mind-independent realities of the external, causal world. Imagine yourself on the eve of testing the first-ever atomic bomb or watching the first-ever attempt to fly a fixed-wing airplane. Some experts in physics, in chemistry, in advanced mathematics will think this atomic bomb will work. Other experts will not. A consensus may even have crystallized around one view or the other. But in no way will the answer to whether the bomb works or not depend upon that consensus. No, any such consensus is merely a good indication of how to wager if you are an educated layman. The same is true as regards whether that fixed-wing airplane will fly or not. The proof of the pudding will be in the eating.

One could go on and on and on in the same vein. Take stem cell research. Notice that the rights and wrongs of such research are independent of whether the fruits of such research – research into how the material world actually works and how to manipulate certain human cells so as to produce treatments that may cure or alleviate paralysis or Parkinson's disease or other ailments – will be successful. The scientific side of such research would ultimately be open to testing. It is the myriad interlinked causal relationships that exist in the material world, and the extent to which the researchers have understood those imposed relationships, that will determine whether this stem cell research achieves anything beneficial for human health.

By contrast, the rights and wrongs of such research do not look to be open to any such test or testing (or rather, that is the case unless one is a utilitarian or other consequentialist for whom the right thing to do is the thing that delivers the most cumulative happiness or satisfaction).[22] Once that absence of any imposed, mind-independent, empirical test is conceded, one might fairly ask the following: What does any consensus that may happen to develop around the rights and wrongs of such research represent? Is it something more than the view of some number of other people? If there be no underlying mind-independent truth that exists (or at least that can be known by any agreed procedures), then why should we pay heed to the consensus that has developed? Why should our unelected judges pay heed to the consensus view of some group of overseas unelected judges (and possibly lock us into that view) rather than paying heed to – or leaving this issue of stem cell research to be decided by – our elected representatives?

That last question ought to be an especially challenging one for those who are adverse to aristocratic elements in their social decision making procedures.

Epidemics Originating in America and the Juvenile Death Penalty

What about the specific example of an epidemic which originates in the US? Should that fact about its origins stop Americans from turning to foreign scientists for guidance? Of course not. One would be foolish not to consider and weigh up – and of course go on *to test* – any widespread views of scientists with knowledge of epidemics. Any such group's view can be checked and tested; the fact such a group of scientists might be foreigners is wholly irrelevant to whether their view proves able to withstand testing.

When we leave the realm of the natural sciences, though, and any consensus of opinion there, and turn to some consensus of opinion in the realm of law, we need to try to be quite specific about what we are checking and rechecking that consensus of opinion against. No longer will it be the Dean of Medicine of Harvard University or of Oxford University, some person or group whose opinion on the cause of an epidemic and on methods to end it can be tested against the mind-independent, imposed realities of the external, causal world. Now it will be the Chief Justice of the European Court of Human Rights, and the consensus view of those judges on the juvenile death penalty. Or maybe it will be the consensus view of the Canadian judges on same-sex marriage.[23] Or why not of the Irish judges on abortion[24] or the Turkish judges on girls wearing headscarves to school?[25]

---

22   In a sense, utilitarians dissolve their 'oughts' into 'ises', into questions about which actions are likely (given all we know at present about the world) to deliver best consequences. For them, moral rights and wrongs are a function of what does or does not happen in the external, causal world.

23   See *Halpern* v. *Canada (AG)* [2003] OJ No 2268 and *Barbeau* v. *British Columbia (AG)* 2003 BCCA 406.

24   See *AG* v. *X* (1992) IESC 1 and *Society for the Protection of the Unborn Child* v. *Grogan* [1997] IESC 4.

25   For a comprehensive discussion see, *Interim Report of the Special Rapporteur of the Commission on Human Rights on the elimination of all forms of intolerance and of*

In this legal realm we can ask the question we asked earlier of the realm of the natural sciences: Is some consensus of the top judges' views, in and of itself, determinative of whether that consensus is correct? This time, put yourself in the shoes of the Chief Justice rather than the Dean of Medicine. Against what does the Chief Justice assess effectiveness and check results? Is it something other than 'the consensus of views of other expert judges'?

Now in one sense the answer to that last question will be an obvious 'yes'. Judges swear to do justice 'according to law'. There are very few areas of law these days into which statutes do not intrude and have a decisive effect. In many areas, too, as in my mooted queries above, a country's constitution or bill of rights will be relevant. So it is not just the first-order moral opinion of the judge, or even the consensus moral opinion of the preponderance of judges (though in some bill of rights cases it can appear to come close to that). These opinions have to be rechecked against the legislature's statutes and the country's constitution and the consensus opinions of that jurisdiction's past judges. In law, any consensus of judges' opinions is always directed (at least purportedly) towards some law or some constitutional provision.

Yet this concession does not help to sustain the plausibility of the analogy. In law, it may well be that not only the policy views and principle judgments and rights-based opinions of judges matter; it may generally be that such views, judgments and opinions of legislators and of constitution makers matter too. But there is nothing mind-independent in any of that. When the Chief Justice checks and rechecks her results she is doing something qualitatively different to what the Dean of Medicine is doing when he checks and rechecks his against the mind-independent realities of the external, causal world. What he checks his results against is characteristic of true science. What the Chief Justice checks hers against is not.

That means that any attempt to harness for the realm of law the same sense of solid, objective, timeless knowledge that exists (and for good reason exists) in the realm of the natural sciences is *not* successful. If American judges ought to cite and consider and weigh the consensus of opinion of foreign judges, it cannot be because that consensus represents what it does in the natural sciences, namely the currently existing best understanding by us limited, biological humans of the underlying, mind-independent reality of our external causal world.[26]

---

discrimination based on religion or belief – Mission to Turkey, UN Doc A/55/280/Add.1. The leading United Kingdom case on headscarves in schools is *Begum, R (on the application of)* v. *Denbigh High School* [2006] UKHL 15.

26   That having been said, it is trite to say that current best understanding is not infallible. On occasion outliers prove correct. But such outliers do not suggest theories that involve discarding all the known laws of physics and more – they do not propose what amount to miracles. See David Hume's unsurpassed treatment of what would be needed to believe in miracles in section 10 of *Enquiries Concerning the Human Understanding and*

The realm of law is not analogous to the realm of the natural sciences in offering us humans that sort of indisputable knowledge; if it were, then refusals to at least consider or cite or weigh or be guided by any consensus that may have emerged in other civilized nations would appear to be perverse or xenophobic, if not downright irrational. But as I have argued, that analogy is highly flawed. The type of knowledge produced by the two is not analogous.

At the risk of belaboring the point, consider this assertion:

> Maybe we should not give weight to courts in Zimbabwe or the Sudan. By analogy we might not expect our public health officials to look to North Korea for guidance in their response to a possible avian flu epidemic.[27]

Yet dozens of countries around the world today (and no doubt a good many non-state organizations) *do* look for guidance to North Korea in the realm of scientific know-how. True, it is in the sub-realm of nuclear weapons production and atomic bomb making, not avian flu prevention. But the point remains. The scientific spirit does not depend on (indeed can be wholly divorced from) feelings of revulsion, abhorrence of Darfuresque slaughter, or disgust at Mugabean thuggery – all presumably factors in shying away from Zimbabwean and Sudanese case law precedents. In science, however, it is ultimately what works, what withstands duplication, what succeeds in harnessing the external, causal world to one's needs, that provides knowledge. So here again the two sorts of consensus appear quite distinct.

Without recourse to that flawed science analogy, the case for appealing to 'the law of nations' for guidance is significantly less straightforward. It may become dependent on a host of other factors, not least the ease with which the elected branches can respond to any decisions of the unelected judiciary that have been influenced by this accumulated legal wisdom of mankind. Whether it is the elected legislators or the unelected judges that have been so guided in their labours may matter too. In fact, one's underlying view of the relative role and competencies of the various branches of government, including as regards the deciding of questions of rights, may come into play once the realm of law is seen as importantly unlike the realm of the natural sciences.

Let me be more specific. When it comes to democratically elected legislators, or indeed elected members of the executive branch, arguments in favour of at least considering the law of nations or *ius gentium* or the accumulated wisdom of the world on rights and justice or a consensus in the law or however you want to put it, seem wholly uncontroversial. So if some group of elected representatives of the people come to the conclusion that there are serious problems with the way tort law operates in the field of, say, personal injuries – that it is an inefficient

Concerning the Principles of Morals (ed. L.A. Selby-Bigge, 3rd edn, rev. by P.H. Nidditch) (Oxford: Oxford University Press, 1975).

27   Jeremy Waldron, 'Foreign Law and the Modern *Ius Gentium*', p. 145.

way to compensate the injured because too big a slice of the compensation dollar currently goes to lawyers and insurers and the running of courts, that it unduly distorts behaviour by over-encouraging risk aversion, and that who is affected rests almost entirely on raw luck – then why should such legislators not look to New Zealand's no fault personal injury scheme or Canada's and Australia's and the United Kingdom's procedural rules that shift well over half of a defendant's legal costs onto the plaintiff when a lawsuit is unsuccessful? Other legal regimes can be considered, weighed, referred to, used to guide changes, or even completely and utterly deferred to. On what basis could anyone possibly object?

Remember, if the reforms that have been modelled on New Zealand's legal regime in this area, or the United Kingdom's, prove ultimately to be unpopular or unsuccessful, then they can be altered again or even changed back. We are mooting legislative reforms after all. Whatever amount of guidance, direction or instruction may have flowed from some overseas consensus, it will ultimately be the elected lawmakers here who will enact such changes, who will be held accountable by the voters for them, and who can always amend or appeal them using the exact same legislative procedural tools.

Concomitantly, when it comes to elected legislators referring to, indeed deferring to, foreign law models, there is simply no need at all to justify this copying on the basis of some purported analogy to the natural sciences – some hint or suggestion that New Zealand's no fault tort system happens to rest on a timeless, objective, mind-independent body of indisputable knowledge that is the product of testing, experimental duplication, possible falsification, and that got established in the way scientific theories are established. No, even where a majority of elected legislators are motivated to imitate or copy some foreign legal initiative on nothing much more than individual intuitions, that is appropriate.

In contesting claims about the role of any foreign law consensus, therefore, we need to be extremely clear about whether it is the judges or legislators who are being guided (or seeking guidance) in their labours. This initial distinction is crucial, as next to no one would contest the legitimacy of legislators being so influenced.

A second distinction can also be made. Perhaps it needs to be made. This is the distinction between judges deciding constitutional (and quasi-constitutional) cases and judges deciding non-constitutional cases. The key difference here is the ease with which the elected branches of government can respond to any decisions of the unelected judiciary that have been shaped or directed by this idea of the accumulated legal wisdom of mankind.

Unelected American judges interpreting, say, a Bill of Rights that is entrenched in a Constitution which is next to impossible to change effectively have the last word on such issues. Their view on whether to pay heed to some foreign law consensus cannot be reversed or overturned by statute; the elected legislators cannot gainsay them.

In all other areas of law where judges might wish to look to some foreign law consensus this is not the case. American judges who refer to, and perhaps even defer to, how Canadian and Irish courts – or even to how a more grandiose law of nations or consensus of civilized states – happen to treat litigants' claims under some statute or other can be met with a legislative response.

True, it can be difficult in a practical sense for an elected legislature to respond to every single court decision, not least because there is only so much political capital to draw upon, while so many issues are seen (by some) to warrant legislative action. And it is true, too, that the seemingly simple power of statutory interpretation (without any overt recourse to constitutional interpretation) should never be underestimated.

Nevertheless, this distinction between constitutional cases and other cases is a worthwhile one all the same. Only as regards the latter is the elected legislature left with (admittedly varying) room to put forward its view and ultimately prevail. As we have seen, almost no one objects to legislators' having scope to pay heed to some perceived consensus of civilized states. Where those same legislators are left in a reasonable position to respond to, and if need be to countermand, some use the judges have made of such a perceived consensus, the objections to it must surely be less powerful than when the legislators can do nothing and are impotent.

Or rather, that is a position and a distinction which seems to me to be one incumbent upon all those who place a high value on democracy to take. It should be comparatively easier for them to allow a role for the citation of foreign law in private law, for example, than it is in constitutional law.

In addition, for them and for all others considering this issue of appeals to foreign law, there is the further consideration that all resolutions of rights-based and other constitutional disputes will ultimately be on a procedural basis, not on a substantive basis (such as who writes the most morally wonderful opinion with the most references to John Stuart Mill). What is so attractive, then, about this particular procedure of resolving disputes by referring to, or deferring to, foreign law?

To start, there are no hard and fast rules governing the use of overseas precedents. Indeed, *there are no rules at all*. Nothing like the notion of *stare decisis* exists to help in choosing between the myriad overseas precedents on offer – nothing to guide the judges in determining when overseas decisions should be cited, which decisions should be cited, what weight particular decisions should be accorded, and so on.

Next, there is some evidence from overseas to suggest that the citation of overseas authority in rights-based litigation leads to a gradual ratchet-up effect, that on average, over time, this practice results in judges extending and broadening the ambit of various rights and the scope and range of their application.[28]

---

28   See James Allan, Grant Huscrott and Nessa Lynch, 'The Citation of Overseas Authority in Rights Litigation in New Zealand: How Much Bark? How Much Bite?' (2007) 11 *Otago Law Review* 433. In a study of reported *New Zealand Bill of Rights Act* cases at the Supreme Court and Court of Appeal level (from enactment in 1990 to April, 2006) in

In a different vein, there is a problem with comparative size or relative populations. The main common law jurisdictions of the United Kingdom, Canada, Australia and New Zealand have a *combined population* of just over a third of America's. These are likely to be some of the jurisdictions most often cited. Yet even were one a diehard internationalist, it is not obvious why a consensus of Canadian, British, Australian and New Zealand judges' views should count for any more than the views of Texan, Georgian, Floridian or even Californian judges.

Understood as a procedure for resolving reasonable disagreements over rights issues, this method of appealing to foreign law even raises the danger or prospect 'that a judge will invoke this theory opportunistically, picking and choosing the consensus he relies on, to reinforce conclusions that he wanted to reach anyway'.[29] In fact, I can see no reason why that sort of cherry-picking danger might not be seen as of crucial (perhaps determinative) significance or moment when it comes to assessing appeals to foreign law as a *procedure for resolving disagreement* (rather than as a science-like method for delivering solid, objective, timeless, mind-independent knowledge). Indeed, from the Visiting Martian's Vantage this may well appear to be the most likely outcome. A corollary of noting that cherry-picking danger, one our Visiting Martian would surely spot, is that such appeals to foreign law in constitutional interpretation cases will be less and less attractive the more committed one is to democratic decision making on these rights-related issues. To put it differently, we can expect this practice to appeal more from the Judge's Vantage than from the Concerned Citizen's. Indeed some Concerned Citizens might be expected to opt for or favour the interpretive approach that leaves the most scope for legislative decision making on these contentious issues – and it is hard to see how appeals to foreign law can be a part of any such interpretive approach.

One conclusion we can draw from this is that calls to refer to, and on occasion perhaps even to defer to, foreign law carry with them the potential for greater Rule by Judges outcomes. It is unlikely to be as potent a tool to achieve this as the emphasis on Rule of Law talk would be, and far less so than the scope provided by common law decision making in the context of interpreting a constitution or quasi-constitutional instrument. But neither will it be a wholly ineffective or worthless tool.

This chapter has looked at various ways in which an element of Rule by Judges might, from some vantages, be seen to operate in Benevolent Legal Systems. In the next two chapters we turn to consider how vantage affects one's assessment of the pros and cons of a bill of rights.

which reference was made to overseas precedents in interpreting the New Zealand Bill of Rights Act, the right at issue appears to be extended in some way or other in 40 per cent of all such cases (and it is extended four times more often than it is given an interpretation narrower than it had before the court's decision).

29   Jeremy Waldron, 'Foreign Law and the Modern *Ius Gentium*', p. 146.

Chapter 5
Bills of Rights – I

In this chapter and the next I turn to bills of rights.

I began this book with two chapters considering whether it is good or desirable to keep separate law and morality, posing and attempting to answer that question from various vantages and in the context of different sorts of legal systems. I then turned the focus onto judges for two chapters, again from various vantages but here overwhelmingly in the context of Benevolent Legal Systems. That focus raised issues such as the appointment of judges, how best to understand the concept of democracy, the desirability of referring to (and deferring to) foreign law, and the extent to which common law constitutionalism and the concept of the Rule of Law differ from Rule by Judges. Indeed, the issue of the likelihood of judges constraining themselves and being cautious and minimalist once broad moral standards have been incorporated into law was given most of a chapter of its own.

I said in the Introduction that this book would tackle three broad topics – the desirability of separating law and morality, judges and judging, and bills of rights – and that each was clearly related to the others. That is in part why the first two topics have already touched in passing on bills of rights. Yes, there are a number of ways in which moral tests can be incorporated into law. A regular statute can make reference to 'the best interests of the child', 'fairness', 'good faith bargaining' or any manner of value-oriented criteria. Judge-made case law (in its purer common law form or as a gloss on a statute) can equally make determinative such moral criteria. And of course there are all sorts of constitutional provisions that might incorporate a moral or normative test, provisions that are not part of an entrenched bill of rights. (For instance, think of heads of power federalism disputes and the need to determine, say, whether a legislative enactment falls under the aegis of 'trade and commerce' or 'external affairs'.) Conceding all that, it is nevertheless the case that for much of the world today – certainly for almost all Benevolent Legal Systems and arguably for some So-So Legal Systems as well – the most obvious way in which moral tests are blended or incorporated into law is by means of some sort of bill of rights. These instruments are, or can be, far reaching. Their effects can be great and next to impossible to overturn or countermand through the elected or popular branches of government. In a day-to-day sense, bills of rights not only are the most practical and potent manifestation of eliding law and morality, they also impact either squarely or tangentially on all of the issues related to judges and judging that were considered in the previous two chapters.

In this chapter and the next, therefore, bills of rights will be the central focus in their own right. The underlying issue will be whether and how vantage affects one's assessment of the pros and cons of a bill of rights. But that issue will be largely postponed until the next chapter. This one lays the groundwork for undertaking that assessment.

Why Rights at All?

A political or public morality – as distinct from a personal morality – offers a vision about the place of human beings in society, at a minimum, if not about their place in the whole of existence. Underlying such a vision is a particular view of human nature and some general sort of explanation of the way human beings live and think and feel. Any such comprehensive political morality will, amongst other things, also take some position on the status of evaluations, the normal meaning of moral language, the notions of good and bad, right and wrong, and the best way to organize society.

Some political moralities place no special importance on rights at all. Others take rights to be either fundamental or at least instrumentally important as means to other goals. Classical Marxism is an example of a political morality which tends to denigrate rights. For it, substantive equality is the general goal, to be achieved directly by making public the means of production, instilling class consciousness and eliminating exploitation of labour's surplus value. Formal rights merely stand in the way of classical Marxists achieving these ends. Purely goal-based or duty-based political moralities which see some event, quality, achievement or obligation as paramount will likewise often reject formal rights. If satisfying God's will or self-deduced and imposed imperatives or if achieving the betterment of the species be the aim, then why put in place procedural roadblocks like rights?

For the purposes of the present argument such views shall *not* be further discussed. Bills of rights clearly pre-suppose some sort of acceptance of rights and so, whatever be the reader's convictions, let us concentrate on political moralities which do afford at least instrumental importance to rights. I shall divide these into two categories, 'strong-rights theories' and 'weak-rights theories'. Before elaborating upon this distinction, though, it is worthwhile to step back and consider the concept of rights itself.

Analytically, it is true to say that the existence of a right pre-supposes the existence of a rule. Alternatively put, the existence of a right *is* the existence of a rule. This correlative nature of rights was first emphasized by W.N. Hohfeld. Thus, to the query, 'where do rights come from?' the analytical answer is straightforward – 'from a rule which imposes obligations on others (be they individuals, groups or institutions)'. In the *legal* realm, then one may find *legal* rights by finding *legal* rules, be they in statutory form (e.g. rules about theft or making valid wills), extracted from a line of cases (e.g. rules about negligence or *habeas corpus*), seen to have grown up from customary practices (e.g. rules governing the need for consideration in making an oral contract), or set out broadly and generally in a bill of rights for the judiciary to make more certain, specific and clear in the various cases that arise (e.g. whether advertising is to qualify as protected free speech).

However, in discussing political moralities we are talking at the level of first principles. At that level the correlative explanation of rights is of little value. It will not help to point to legal rules in defence of rights when the very point at issue is whether there *should be* these, or any other, legal rules in existence. A political morality, in offering a particular vision about humans in society, does not lie on the plane of what rules and rights *do exist*. Rather, it precedes that issue and looks to the very bases for claiming that some rules (and therefore rights) are desirable and others are not.

Weak-rights Theories

What I have dubbed as 'weak-rights theories' offer one possible defence of rights. Political moralities such as these are 'weak' because rights are not seen as good-in-themselves; rather, rights are conceived of as necessary evils. In order to achieve some other state of affairs it is judged necessary to establish rights (by enunciating rules). The starting premise here is *usually* (though not necessarily) an acceptance of non-cognitivism or moral scepticism or subjectivism, i.e., the conviction that objective or real or mind-independent values, however much one may feel one's own evaluations and tenets to be so, simply do not exist. On all questions of right and wrong, good and bad, there are no 'right answers', only more or less widely held beliefs and felt sentiments. According to this view we humans live in a world of conflicting interests, desires and needs, none of which is 'rationally right', 'true' or 'real'. At most one can say some such interests, desires and needs are vastly more popular and widespread than others, or that they have been genetically hard-wired into most of us, while perhaps arguing that that near-uniformity of outlook is enough.

From a starting point of scepticism about the mind-independent status of moral evaluations it is not terribly difficult to see the potential appeal of rights once one ponders the problem of what is to be done in such circumstances of competing interests and partial conflict. Surely some set of rules (and hence of attendant rights) is needed to resolve the diverging, and frequently incompatible, wishes of people living in the same society. No rights may be 'right in themselves', but something, anything, is likely to be better than nothing. From here one may make a Hobbesian appeal to the device of a social contract, one in which a sovereign is given absolute power in exchange for authoritatively resolving the myriad disputes, perhaps by establishing rules and rights. Alternatively, one may prefer the Humean variant of rejecting the need for an absolute political sovereign, positing the possibility that an equilibrium of the competing social interests would evolve at least partly by unplanned convention. Such a 'solution' need not be authoritarian.

Jeremy Bentham provides perhaps the most straightforward version of a weak-rights theory. He insists that only good consequences in terms of human happiness are to be aimed for directly. Thus freedom, justice, equality, what have you, are all desirable if and only if they tend, as measured by experience, to increase human happiness. This concentration on happiness-increasing consequences is the gist of the doctrine known as utilitarianism. It is often misunderstood, for, in keeping with what I take to be its core-level renunciation of moral realism, utilitarianism offers no answers to any problems. It merely demands that one look to consequences and aim for those which are likely to increase happiness. What they might be is open to dispute and disagreement. In a sense, utilitarianism's focus on consequences provides no more certainty than disputes about values and rights themselves. But there is one key difference. Utilitarianism shifts debate (admittedly on the basis of certain subjective preferences such as, firstly, what the membership of the group which is to count is to be – i.e., everyone now on the planet? future generations? only humans? – and secondly, that all such members' happiness is to count equally) *from* right and wrong, good and bad *to* likely consequences. The advantage of this is that in principle these consequences, *what will happen*, have objective, mind-independent answers, however much accurate prediction may be beyond the capacity of limited biological creatures such as human beings, though of course people need not agree on the desirability of any given set of likely future consequences.

One school of utilitarianism then argues that the best consequences are by and large or at any rate sometimes achieved by establishing rules. According to this school, aiming directly for best consequences in each circumstance, as it happens, achieves worse consequences, less happiness, than establishing relatively inflexible general rules to guide conduct. This rule-utilitarianism is most easily understood, I suspect, at the level of governmental action. Rather than allowing those with power to aim for best consequences in each instance, it is better to limit government by rules. In the long run, rule-bound governments will have happier citizens, says this argument. They will have a higher hit rate of achieving overall happiness than governments that shun rules. And of course a government whose conduct is fettered by rules is nothing more, from an alternate viewpoint, than a citizenry which has rights. It may even be that experience shows that some rights (and rules) lead to better consequences, as it happens, than others.

The point here is that with 'weak-rights theories' rights *are* valued, but in an instrumental way only. And from this sort of view of the world it is possible to offer a variety of more particular defences of rights (and the brief outline above in no way purports to be comprehensive). The question then arises of whether, on that general view of the world, it would be desirable to take a further step and make those legal rights part of a bill of rights. Would the weak-rights adherent who favours the establishment of certain legal rights like to see some of them implemented in the form of a full-blooded constitutionalized bill of rights, or even of a statutory version?

Strong-rights Theories

A much more vigorous vindication of rights begins from a quite polar premise, the idea that each human being simply has basic rights. Here we might think of

Kant or Nagel or Gewirth or Dworkin. Regardless of other aims, goals, duties, or even of fairly horrendous long-term consequences to the cumulative welfare of society, certain basic levels of treatment are mandated. Rights, on this view, are *not* mediately justified; they are good-in-themselves, come what may.

In other words, 'strong-rights theories' are political moralities which refuse to look behind the claim to rights. The basic currency of these moralities is rights themselves; they are the starting point. Adherents will not, or logically cannot, answer the question 'Why are rights good or desirable?' in terms of some other end – to do so would be to collapse one's political morality into a 'weak-rights theory'.

To say this and no more of 'strong-rights theories', however, would be to paint a grossly simplistic picture, if not a caricature, in which such theories seemed merely to proclaim some list of self-evident or rationally obvious rights. So injunctions on behalf of purportedly certain moral entitlements, claims or propositions – the bedrock supporting demands for rights – need a further purchase. As Jeremy Waldron says, 'No one now believes that the truth about rights is self-evident or that, if two people disagree about rights, one of them at least must be either corrupt or morally blind.'[1]

Many and varied are the offered theories that start with a fundamental attachment to rights and seek to provide that further purchase. Ronald Dworkin's is amongst the best known. Dworkin, or at least the early Dworkin, argues that there is always one best, right answer to questions of judicial interpretation. This is so because in any well-developed legal system one answer will always have weightier reasons in its favour than others. Judges have a duty, having recourse to the background political morality of their particular society, to find that 'right' answer. This means that one of the parties to a lawsuit has a right to a decision in her favour. In effect, Dworkin appears to be seeking to insulate epistemological questions from questions of ontology. Rights *can* be 'found' and 'discovered', on this understanding, independently of whether they really exist or not.

Rawlsians take a different tack, making use of a modernized social contract argument. Yet the very asking of what choices people behind a veil of ignorance would make in designing a political philosophy seems premised on the implicit acceptance of fundamental rights. And there are even theorists such as Alan Gewirth who argue that a 'supreme moral principle',[2] and therefore certain basic human rights, follows logically and deductively from the fact of beings being purposive agents (i.e., from the necessary conditions of *human* action).

Yet however varied 'strong-rights theories' might be in their defence of proclaimed fundamental rights, they all share one general feature. All such theories are broadly Kantian in conceiving of humans as autonomous, self-

---

1   Jeremy Waldron, 'A Right-Based Critique of Constitutional Rights' (1993) 13 *Oxford Journal of Legal Studies* 18, at p. 29.

2   See Alan Gewirth, 'The Epistemology of Human Rights' (1984) 1 *Social Philosophy and Policy* Issue 2, p. 12.

governing beings, entitled to respect and responsibility. We humans, they say in short, are thinking agents able to transcend our own personal interests and impose duties on ourselves related to how our actions will affect others. This makes us moral agents. Consequently, strong-rights theories in which individuals are comprehended as essentially bearers of rights cannot be said merely to make individualist pre-suppositions – this would be a distortion – but rather must be seen as making pre-suppositions about a particular type of individual. However, if this be the case, then the Waldronian question asks on what grounds is it desirable to disenfranchise the overwhelming majority of the population (in favour of a few select judges) on major social policy or on basic rights questions? Surely not on the basis of a distrust of others. But then what does a bill of rights do if not disenfranchise the non-judge on certain rights-related issues?

The point here is that the whole basis on which strong-rights political moralities rest seems also to require, perhaps demand, the additional right of all to participate in decision making. Or at least that is broadly the sort of line Waldron takes. His argument is that the link between this sort of view of humans and the desirability of widespread participation in decision making is obvious. However, while these strong-rights theories clearly lend support to participatory democracy they do not clearly seem to lend support to a full-blooded power of judicial review. One can therefore ask a similar question to the one asked above of the weak-rights adherent: Why would the Kantian strong-rights adherent who favours the establishment of certain legal rights like to see them in the form of a constitutionalized or statutory bill of rights?

To recap this section's claims, rights – if they are valued at all, and evidently they are so valued by most people on the planet today – can be prized on instrumental or intrinsic grounds, broadly speaking. They can be seen as goods because of their tendency (on average, over time) to lead on to or promote some desired state of affairs, perhaps outcomes exhibiting more liberty, equality, justice, fairness, happiness or what have you. This is weak-rights thinking according to which rights *are* valued, but only when (as an empirical generalization) they tend to have good consequences in terms of their likelihood of promoting or achieving some intrinsic good-in-itself. On the other hand, rights can be understood as goods-in-themselves, not requiring any instrumental appeal to the likely future consequences they will engender. This is strong-rights thinking, which shuns explicit or implicit consequentialist appeals in its defence of rights. Whatever the particular list of proffered rights, it will not be mediately justified.

Of course neither the strong nor the weak-rights adherent thinks any and all rights-based claims are in fact worthy of support. Only some rights are. That just about goes without saying, as does the observation that what will be put forward as the list of rights worthy of being protected and upheld will vary from person to person. It will be contestable and contested.

For my purposes in this chapter and the next I do not need to choose between consequentialist or instrumentalist or weak theories of rights on the one hand and non-consequentialist or Kantian or strong theories of rights on the other. It is enough to note, firstly, that any Visiting Martian who landed on earth today, early in the twenty-first century would observe that rights are now the dominant currency of political and indeed moral philosophy. He would likely also claim – as a matter of which of the two is more widely held, rather than the distinct issue of which of the two offers a more convincing or persuasive justification for rights – that much, if not most, of the aspirational, emotively powerful rights talk he heard on landing was premised on a strong-rights understanding. Put differently, the Visiting Martian would observe that the early twenty-first-century rights discourse largely, or overwhelmingly, rests on moral realist pre-suppositions (explicit or implicit) about the status of rights. Such strong-rights believers may be those who ground their understanding of rights in some sort of old-fashioned intuitionism or in born-again natural law thinking, or in its related Dworkinian cousin, or in purportedly logical connections between purposive human action and rights, or, perhaps most likely of all, they may simply think such groundings to be unnecessary, even distasteful.

Our Visiting Martian might even go so far as to suggest that a barely qualified absolutism is part of the attraction to many adherents.

Whether he went that far or not, he would certainly say this: Bills of rights, and rights themselves, play a significantly greater role in the operation of Benevolent Legal Systems (and possibly also of some other sorts of legal systems) than they did when Hart wrote *The Concept of Law* in 1961. Accordingly, if one's goal is to blend moral evaluations (to be made by some group or other) into law, then it is, as a practical matter and on the whole, easier to do so with a bill of rights in place than without.

Paternalism, Rights and Bills of Rights

The next step in laying the groundwork for an assessment of how vantage affects one's assessment of bills of rights has us consider the relationship of paternalism, rights and bills of rights.

At first glance many might think rights and paternalism have little to do with one another. Start with rights. Roughly speaking, 'legal rights are protections – protections against interference or uncooperativeness – conferred by legal norms'.[3] Similarly, moral rights are protection conferred by moral norms or rules. And in the realm of political morality, the realm in which rights are normally situated, those protections are overwhelmingly conferred on the individual. As even a perfunctory consideration of national bills of rights, international human rights documents or the concerns of groups such as Amnesty International or Human Rights Watch makes abundantly clear, group rights are the equivalent of a minor

---

3   Matthew Kramer, 'Also Among the Prophets: Some Rejoinders to Ronald Dworkin's Attacks on Legal Positivism' (1999) 12 *Canadian Journal of Law and Jurisprudence*, p. 76.

galaxy (albeit one expanding hyperbolically) in a universe dominated by concern for individual rights. It is the claims *of individuals* that rights overwhelmingly protect. It is *the individual* who is owed a duty (because of rights) not to have the free expression of his opinions interfered with, or not to have the free practice of her religion constrained, or not to be tortured, or – more contentiously – to be provided with fair wages, safe working conditions and an adequate standard of living. Rights everywhere are associated with the protection and claims *of individuals*, be they against the state, against persons or bodies acting in a public function or just against other individuals.

How are these claims attempted to be met? In almost all Benevolent Legal Systems it is in part by means of a bill of rights. In other words, today's Benevolent Legal Systems are ones (overwhelmingly, but not quite yet exclusively) in which rights seen to be the most fundamental ones have either been put into a constitutionalized or statutory bill of rights. Their protections of the individual have either been entrenched against mere legislative change or, as I will suggest below, that legislative route for change has been made near-on impossible in a practical, political sense. And the interpretation of these enumerated rights has been handed over to the judiciary to be interpreted, expanded, narrowed and applied – even altered and created *de novo* – as particular cases arise.

Now turn to paternalism. Something is described as paternalistic when it is imposed on others *for their benefit* (rather than the benefit of those doing the imposing). In the political context, then, when someone's (or some body's) liberty or scope for action is restricted on the basis of an argument about *this agent's own good*, we say the restriction was paternalistic. The defining test and characteristic is whether the action, restriction, limit or rule is motivated by a belief that it would be to the benefit of those so affected and limited.

Take the example of a government imposing speech restrictions on its citizens. Regulations that limited or foreclosed so-called 'hate speech' or which banned (only) pro-abortion expression would be unlikely to proceed from paternalistic motives. It is hard to see how in normal circumstances such restricting can be based upon a genuine concern *for the speakers*, rather than the listeners. (One obviously abnormal circumstance might be where the speaker's words were quite likely to lead to her inflaming the audience so much that she was, say, assaulted or killed. Banning her work then could be genuinely done on paternalistic grounds.) On the other hand, regulations disallowing the publication of how to make atomic weapons or limiting the amount of spending in election campaigns may plausibly be seen as paternalistic; these restrictions limit individuals' freedom of expression in pursuit of (what is thought to be) their own – and admittedly others' – good. Genuine concern *for the speakers* is one plausible motivation for such bans.

What motivates a paternalistic concern for others can vary, though, as these last two examples illustrate. One inducement to enacting paternalistic limits on people's freedom of action may be the realization that individuals sometimes find themselves in a Prisoner's Dilemma-type situation. The predicament may be such that performing certain individual actions would make everybody or nearly everybody worse off. Nevertheless, in this predicament people have an incentive to perform these actions unless assured that others will also abstain. In that situation a ban on those actions would be beneficial to almost all those upon whom it is imposed. Choices open to people are therefore restricted for their own good. Campaign finance limits can arguably be understood (at least partially) in this paternalistic way.

Notice that this first sort of paternalistic motive does *not* require those doing the imposing and restricting necessarily to believe the people governed by the restrictions cannot recognize what is good for them. It is in the nature of a Prisoner's Dilemma-type situation that in fact one *does* realize that uniform compliance with course A (which would be the result of an external rule limiting everyone's actions) would be preferable to uniform opting for course B (which is in everyone's self-interest in the absence of external constraints guaranteeing compliance). One realizes it but cannot effect it oneself. So paternalism in these sorts of situations does not really spring from a belief that the person or group imposing the limit knows what is good for some group of others better than they themselves do.

However, this first sort of paternalistic motive, where I impose something on you that I know you too think is for your benefit, is rather rare. Much more common is the out-and-out belief that we (the imposers of the restriction) know better than you (the group who will be so restricted) what is good *for you*. It is just as much in *your* long-term interest to be prevented from publishing the details of how to make an atomic bomb – even if you think otherwise. Paternalism generally originates in a belief about others' deficiencies: their incapacities to evaluate arguments; their lack of measured calmness and too-great emotionalism; their susceptibility to demagogues and populist appeals; and so on. It is this second sort of paternalism, by far the most common variety, that involves an attitude essentially hostile to the idea that each person knows what is best for himself (at the personal level), or that each generation knows what is best for itself (at the constitutional level).

Depending upon the particular factual circumstances and other people under consideration, we are all paternalists in this second, condescending sense. At some point each of us, even the most deferential-to-others liberal, is prepared to say she knows better than another what is good for that other. Sometimes we are even prepared to enforce that paternalistic assessment. It is all a question of where each of us draws the line. Jeremy Bentham thought the vast preponderance of individuals were, each one themselves, the best judges of their own happiness. However, he did *not* think *everyone* was the best such judge. Children and insane people are obvious counter-examples. Certainly when it comes to diet, television watching, wearing of seat-belts and myriad other matters it is not just the Sanctimonious Man, nor even the Concerned Citizen and Law Professor and Judge, but even the Bad Man, who thinks he knows what is better for his 6-year-old daughter than she herself does. They are all overtly paternalistic, in other words, and prepared to enforce their views over hers.

So paternalism, whatever the connotations of the word itself, is certainly not an indefensible notion in all circumstances, as applied to all others. Sometimes person X *will* know what is best for person Y better than person Y himself.

That said, the range of situations in which such paternalistic claims hold true (on average, over time) is highly contestable. Yes, they generally hold as regards children, the insane, possibly too the severely inebriated. But when it comes to the ordinary situation of normal adult and normal adult, the anti-paternalistic outlook is neither silly nor implausible. It runs something as follows.

Each of us is more likely to know what is best for ourselves better than any other person who could be identified in advance by some easily applicable rule – however intelligent, sensitive, socially attuned, psychologically perceptive, or well-read-up on social studies that other may be. Or put in political and social terms, even if I am not the best judge of what is optimal for me, the costs of the imposition by a paternalist who (for the sake of argument) *does* know what is best for me, will in most cases (save easily identifiable cases like children and the insane) more than cancel out the overall optimality of the paternalistic imposition. Jim wants to do X. There are experts out there who know Y is better for Jim. But the costs of imposing Y on Jim and preventing him from doing X are so high (in terms which include finding reliable experts with enough regularity, guarding against bureaucratic over-reach, allowing for Jim's anger and frustration in not having it his own way and in being treated this way, paying to administer the imposition process, and much more) that the imposition will be sub-optimal. This is because, while Y is more than X (*ex hypothesi*), Y minus Z (the costs) is less than X. So in most instances the best or most efficient rule is just to leave people to decide what is best for themselves.

The essence of paternalism then – that I know better than you what will further your welfare – is not always false nor indefensible. Rather, experience shows that, as a rule, it is highly contestable and sometimes, often or almost always (according to outlook) false. That means that if each adult (and each generation) *generally* knows what is best for herself (or itself) better than any practicable alternative, then the burden lies on the paternalist to show some particular situation is out of the ordinary.

We can now consider the relation between rights and paternalism, then bring in bills of rights. Provided one focuses on the *effects* of rights, their affording protections and guarantees and entitlements to the individual to protect his interests or scope to make autonomous decisions, then one is unlikely to link them to paternalism. However, if instead one asks about the *motives* for according rights to others, the link to paternalism is immediately more obvious. This link becomes even stronger if one thinks of an entrenched, constitutionalized bill of rights such as the American Bill of Rights or the Canadian Charter of Rights. One way of understanding such constitutionalized rights is in terms of the generation doing the entrenching thinking that it knows what is best for later generations – that is why the rights have to be entrenched or locked in and made more or less immune from ordinary democratic revision. If later generations of citizens were as much, or more, to be trusted, such locking in or entrenchment would make little sense. In fact it would appear to be counter-productive.

The same applies to statutory bills of rights to the extent that they will be, as a matter of fact, treated as quasi-constitutional enactments by the judges and other top officials. To the extent that judicial decisions as to the scope and effects of the statutorily enumerated rights, and their inter-relations, and what might allowably limit their reach, and more, are secure against legislative gainsaying and second-guessing – and for statutory bills of rights this will be a question of empirical fact and substance, not of constitutional form – to that extent are they, too, open to being justified on paternalistic grounds. If the judges' views virtually always prevail, and this is foreseeable, then again those who push for such an instrument can be understood as paternalists.

We can also tie in this connection, or potential connection, between paternalism, rights and bills of rights back to the first section of this chapter. We can do so as regards all those who support a bill of rights on 'Trust Judges More Than Elected Politicians' grounds. Such support might be voiced in various ways, or simply left unspoken but implicit. It might be part of a strong commitment to locking-things-in constitutionalism, in which democratic self-government is acknowledged not to be a pre-emptive value; it might be on division-of-powers type grounds or a checks-and-balances sort of thinking; it might be on institutional grounds premised on which branch of government can better protect against tyranny.

Whatever the specifics, and however one measures the competing abilities of unelected judges and elected politicians when it comes to shaping the scope, content and relative weight of rights, it is crucial that one realizes what one is doing in making this sort of 'Trust Judges More' argument. Quite simply, one is making the utilitarian, consequentialist case that judges better deliver the goods. Nothing more. If a set of high priests and clerics or of South American caudillos were as capable as judges, then they too should be entrusted with this power. It is results that count. But many people making these sorts of arguments will be strong-rights adherents, those who understand rights as goods-in-themselves. So the very people who made rights-based appeals focusing on the individual both fundamental and determinative before, now ignore *rights-based* appeals to individuals' right of participation (even in formulating and shaping rights themselves) or to the dignity, autonomy and self-governing nature of the individual. When it comes to how best to make certain rights legal and then uphold them, they *now* say, we are to restrict political participation to the select few who qualify as judges – we must opt for a bill of rights that ensures the vast majority's unvarying and continual exclusion from deliberation about so many rights – *because judges (for whatever institutional or personal reasons) are better at it than the rest of us.*

The irony of defending a non-utilitarian, non-subjective, non-contingent, strong version of rights while at the same time, on purely utilitarian grounds, leaving those same rights to be interpreted and shaped overwhelmingly by unelected judges, should be all too apparent. Those who take a weak-rights, instrumental view of rights can enjoy the incongruous spectacle; they can watch as democratic institutions are by-passed and diminished so that abortion and gun-control reforms in America and same-sex marriage reforms in Canada and extensions to the role of the military in Germany and much else besides can be sought (and frequently achieved) through the courts. They can watch this heightened trust that so many social activists, legal academics and no small number of ordinary citizens place in the judiciary and they can at least chuckle at the seeming irony of strong-rights adherents supporting bills of rights on weak or instrumental grounds.

Mapping a Blank Cheque

Imagine a provision in a bill of rights that read as follows:

> The duly elected, democratically chosen government shall be subject to whatever restrictions and limitations as are deemed reasonable and appropriate, from time to time, by a majority of judges of the highest court.[4]

This imagined provision makes several matters explicit. Firstly, it is clear that the judiciary is to have the last word. They are the ones who will decide what laws are reasonable and justifiable. In other words, a non-elective process is in place to scrutinize and – when it is felt appropriate – to over-ride what the elected legislature has done.

The second matter made explicit by our imagined provision is that the restrictions and limitations on what the elected legislature and government can do are fluid and evolving. The judges are to ensure that the legislature is held to a standard that 'keep[s] pace with civilization' and is 'progressive'; it is a 'living tree', 'constantly evolving' and keeping abreast of changing social values.

In other words, the limits on what the elected parliament can and cannot do will alter and vary over time, depending ultimately upon what the judges of the highest court consider to be reasonable and appropriate. The limits will *not* flow from some set of entitlements or rights that were negotiated about, haggled over, carefully drafted after much debate, and ultimately endorsed by referendum or by super-majority of legislators or by victory in an election campaign specifically fought on this issue.

No, all pretence is now gone when it comes to our imagined, hypothetical provision. Plainly and simply, this is about judicial oversight and judicial supremacy. It is *not* about locking in a set of protections against the 'danger of loss of political wisdom and morality'[5] or as a result of fear of 'the vicissitudes

---

4   This is a reworked version of the hypothetical provision mooted by Justice Antonin Scalia in 'Romancing the Constitution: Interpretation as Invention', in G. Huscroft and I. Brodie (eds) *Constitutionalism in the Charter Era* (Markham: LexisNexis, 2004), p. 341.

5   Larry Alexander (ed.), *Constitutionalism: Philosophical Foundations* (Cambridge: Cambridge University Press, 1998), p. 2.

of democratic politics'.[6] It is *not*, that is, about establishing a minimum level of protections – a floor – that remains constant and locked in with any additional levels of protections or entitlements coming through the normal statute-making legislative process or, very occasionally, by constitutional amendment.

On our imagined provision, the unelected judges are clearly not locked in. They may alter and update the legislature's shackles according to case law overseas or based on the latest international law strictures, or even according to their own senses of 'right reason' or perceptions of shifting social standards. What the judges say are the reasonable and appropriate standards can therefore alter without any constitutional amendment or statutory revision. In no way, then, is the judiciary locked in under our imagined, hypothetical bill of rights provision. Everyone else in society is, of course. For the rest of us, Concerned Citizens, Legislators, Law Professors, Bad Men and more, the only recourse against judicial decisions and limitations we disapprove of – *the only recourse* – is to seek to remove our imagined, hypothetical provision (to have it repealed or amended away) or, alternatively, to attempt to have more top judges appointed who share (we hope) our views. In every other way we, the 99.99 per cent of the rest of the voting population, really are locked in.

If the judges decide that free-speech concerns trump health and safety concerns in the context of tobacco,[7] it is the judges' view that would prevail. If they decide that it is reasonable and appropriate to foreclose the prevention of abortion,[8] their view would prevail. If they feel that a not-unlawful, good-faith police search of the house of a barrister's mother can nevertheless be unreasonable and give rise to a cause of action and monetary damages (notwithstanding a statutory immunity provision)[9] but that an unlawful police search of drug dealers' premises can all the same be reasonable,[10] again their view will win. The same goes for where to draw the line when it comes to whether legal recognition should be extended to same-sex marriage,[11] what campaign finance rules are acceptable,[12] and how to balance an accused drink-driver's access to legal counsel against potential road and highway deaths.[13]

---

6   *Ibid.*, p. 8.

7   See *RJR MacDonald Inc* v. *Canada* (1995) 127 DLR (4th) 1.

8   See *Roe* v. *Wade* 410 U.S. 113.

9   See Simpson v. Attorney-General [Baigent's Case] [1994] 3 NZLR 667.

10   See *R* v. *Grayson and Taylor* [1997] 1 NZLR 399. This finding meant there was no basis for seeking to exclude the discovered evidence.

11   See *Halpern* v. *Canada* (2003) (Ont. C.A.) and *Goodridge* v. *Department of Public Health* 440 Mass. 309, 798 N.E.2d 941, 948 (Mass. 3003).

12   In Canada see, *inter alia*, *Harper* v. *Canada (Attorney General)* [2004] 1 S.C.R. 827 or *Libman and Equality Party* v. *Attorney General of Quebec* [1997] 3 SCR 569. In Australia see *Australian Capital Television* v. *Commonwealth* (1992) 177 CLR 106, the start of the so-called 'implied rights' cases. In the United States see *Citizens United* v. *Federal Election Commission* 130 S.Ct. 876 (2010).

13   See *Ministry of Transport* v. *Noort* [1992] 3 NZLR 260; *R* v. *Elias* 2005 SCC 37.

The point is that my hypothetical bill of rights provision is a powerful one indeed. Let us just note that, as worded, it makes plain a third matter too that is occasionally missed or glossed over, namely that when judges of the highest court disagree about what is or is not reasonable they resolve their disagreement by voting. Five votes beat four or four beat three. The quality of moral reasoning or the substantive worth of a point of view or the number of references to Mill or Milton or the European Court of Human Rights is in no way determinative. Judges resolve their disputes by letting the numbers count, full stop.

Having set out this imaginary provision, and having made clear that it gives the judges the last word while bringing with it an ever-changing (but judicially determined) set of standards as to what counts as reasonable, with the judges voting amongst themselves when they disagree, I want now to consider just how fanciful this provision is. To what extent does the substance of my imagined hypothetical accord with the underlying position of judges in various common law democracies? What sort of set-up is farthest away from it and hence most constraining of judges, and what sort least constraining and most similar to, this imagined bill of rights provision?

Before we move to that descriptive mapping task, however, let me return to the hypothetical briefly to deal with a potential objection. In my imagined, hypothetical provision I have deliberately made no mention of rights. Surely an astute objector might balk and say that judges operating or interpreting a bill of rights can only limit the duly elected legislature and government to the extent that rights allow. It is not 'whatever restrictions the judges deem reasonable' that checks the scope for action of the elected branches but rather 'whatever restrictions *flowing from rights* the judges deem reasonable'.

Let us acknowledge the objection and see what follows. Our imagined provision now reads as before save that 'flowing from rights' is inserted after the word 'limitations'. How constraining is that, by itself? Notice that every example I gave above from real-life cases – about where to draw the line when it comes to free speech, privacy, search and seizure, equality and access to a lawyer – was decided under the aegis of rights. In other words, the restrictions and limitations on a democratically elected legislature that might plausibly be thought to flow from rights are myriad indeed. Nor need this be overly surprising, once it is remembered that although the rights in a bill of rights are sold up in the Olympian heights of consensus-achieving, disagreement-finessing moral abstractions – hands up all those against free speech? – they play out down in the quagmire of detail, of drawing debatable and contested lines about defamation, campaign finance rules, hate speech provisions, and much more. Down in the quagmire of social-policy line drawing there is not just plenty of disagreement between intelligent, reasonable people, there are also no uniformly agreed boundaries to the reach of these rights.

So while it is true that in theory the realm of all limitations deemed reasonable by judges is a bigger one than the realm of all such limitations *flowing from rights*, in practice the latter realm seems plenty big enough. True, the particular list of enumerated rights may matter and may expand that realm further still. For instance, if there are social and economic rights included, then the scope plausibly to second-guess the elected branches in areas of, say, health and education and housing is magnified. But even where social and economic rights are not explicitly included, this may not constrain the judges over long where the method of interpretation adopted is an evolving, progressive, fluid, 'keeping pace with civilization' one.

As a result, a redrafted version of our imagined hypothetical – one circumscribing the judges' powers of review to what 'flows from rights' or to what 'flows from this particular set of rights' – might be virtually as potent as my initial version. Whether it will be depends significantly on how the judges themselves choose to interpret the bill of rights, as a 'living document' or, say, as a floor-level set of protections tied to the original intentions of the enactors (or, analogously, to the original understandings of those when it was first passed or adopted).

With that potential objection at least flagged, we can turn now to the descriptive task of charting or mapping what sort of arrangements look closest to my imagined provision (and so impose the fewest constraints on the unelected judiciary) and what sort look farthest away from it (and so impose the most constraints).

Recall that under my imagined bill of rights provision three things are made explicit: 1) judges get the last word; 2) the restrictions they impose evolve and alter as the judges' views of what is reasonable and appropriate alter; and 3) when the judges disagree they vote amongst themselves.

I want now to try to map or chart this onto the array of constitutional arrangements in various common law democracies spanning from those producing results least like what my imagined hypothetical provision produces to those whose results look most like it.

At the far end of the spectrum, the end least like what my imagined hypothetical produces, is the pure parliamentary sovereignty with no bill of rights at all. Here we have an unwritten constitution where the rule of recognition, the ultimate test of legal validity, gives no quarter to unelected judges to second-guess or gainsay the statutes passed by the elected legislature. This is the United Kingdom before entry into Europe in 1973 and more so before the Human Rights Act of 1998, its statutory bill of rights. This is New Zealand before its New Zealand Bill of Rights Act 1990, its statutory bill of rights.

Judges here are far more constrained than under my imagined hypothetical. Most obviously, they do not have the last word; the elected legislature does. This may be justified on the anti-paternalistic basis that each generation should be left to decide fundamental moral issues for itself, including issues about rights. So on democratic grounds one can defend the lack of a written constitution locking in future generations and the absence of a bill of rights handing much social line-drawing power over to an unelected judiciary.

Of course some may posit a sort of common law constitutionalism, a power inherent in the judiciary to second-guess the elected branches even in the absence of a bill of rights. If judges' deference to statutes is self-imposed, they will argue, then that deference can lapse when the judges themselves think it right to lapse.

On this way of thinking, legislative supremacy, oddly enough, rests on a sort of judicial supremacy. It also rests on that very large 'if' at the start of the last sentence but one, the notion that judges are deferential solely because *they* choose to be, that the social fact of legislative supremacy depends on them alone and not also on the views of other top officials in society – politicians, bureaucrats, police, the press. It may even be thought that the notions of common law rights and common law constitutionalism are both historically inapt and prescriptively undesirable, too much of a bootstraps operation benefiting too obviously the people doing the bootstrapping.

Even so, even without such grandiose common law pretensions, judges in a pure parliamentary sovereignty jurisdiction, as point-of-application interpreters of the parliament's statutes, would still have the power to give meaning to the words used. They would have the power of interpretation. And this power should never be underestimated. There are a variety of statutory interpretation techniques that give primacy to rights, or at least to rights valued by judges. But this arrangement looks nothing like the three-pronged effect of my imagined provision. Judges here are far more constrained. Indeed, they are ultimately constrained by the moral and political and rights-based choices of the elected legislators.

Moving along our spectrum, inwards from parliamentary sovereignties with no bill of rights, what we would encounter next, as we move from most constraints on the judiciary to least, is the jurisdiction with a written constitution but no bill of rights. This will probably be a federal system. The reasons for having the written constitution will flow from what the federalist bargain requires, not least dividing up powers between the centre and regions. Here we have Canada before 1982 and Australia today, now arguably the only country in the Western world without some kind of national bill of rights – be it a constitutionalized or statutory model, the incorporation (in justiciable form) of the European Convention on Human Rights into domestic law, or simply a series of Basic Laws which amount to more or less the same thing.

Judges in such bill of rights-free federations are overwhelmingly restricted to the role of umpires. Save for rights implied into the written Constitution and a few other matters related to federalism, it is true that one of the legislatures – the particular state legislature or the Commonwealth Parliament – has the judicially unrestrained power to do whatever is attempting to be done. Accordingly, judges have only somewhat more room to manoeuvre – are still very much constrained, if marginally less so – than in the pure parliamentary sovereignty of 1970s New Zealand and Britain; they do not have the last word; there may be the additional scope for them to say a disliked statute was in an area properly belonging to the other level of federal government, but that is about it.

Hence we are still a considerable distance away from anything that resembles the role of judges under my imagined provision. Let us therefore continue our mapping exercise and move further still towards the least-constrained judges' end of the spectrum.

What comes next is debatable. It might be those parliamentary sovereignty jurisdictions with their newly enacted statutory bills of rights *or* it might in some circumstances be a jurisdiction with an entrenched, constitutionalized bill of rights. Whichever comes next, notice that there is a big gap between the Australia-like set-up with no bill of rights at all and whatever you think comes next. My imagined jurisdiction with its extremely powerful judges is considerably closer to hand, wherever we find our next stop. I shall argue in the next section below that even if it is only a statutory bill of rights that the judges have to operate, those same judges can move a considerable distance towards having the *de facto* last word on a significant number of moral and political disputes that arise in society. In other words, even the jurisdiction with only a statutory bill of rights can – not necessarily will, but can or might – begin to resemble one that had adopted my imaginary or hypothetical provision, one in which unelected judges subjected the democratically elected legislature and government to whatever limitations they, from time to time, deemed reasonable.

For that to be plausible it must be the case that judicial review under a statutory bill of rights has the potential to collapse into strong judicial review of the American or Canadian sort. But let us here simply note that possibility and defer any assessments of its plausibility until the next section of this chapter.

There is another possibility as we continue this most-to-least constrained judges mapping exercise. Surprisingly, perhaps, we might next arrive at a jurisdiction with an entrenched, constitutionalized bill of rights where the judges operating that instrument are nevertheless moderately constrained. True, we still will have travelled a noticeable distance along that spectrum of ever less constrained judges. But we will remain some distance away from what judges would be like under my imagined bill of rights provision.

How can that be? After all, at first sight my imagined hypothetical bill of rights provision is a thinly disguised description of the judiciary in places with an entrenched, justiciable, constitutionalized bill of rights. Think of Canada's Supreme Court today and ask yourself how life for it under the 1982 *Charter of Rights and Freedoms* is any different from what it would be under my imagined provision. Do the Canadian unelected judges have the last word on a host of moral and political issues – what Ronald Dworkin described as 'intractable, controversial and profound questions of political morality'?[14] Undoubtedly they do.

Do these same Canadian judges today adopt an evolutionary, living-tree approach to constitutional and *Charter of Rights* interpretation, 'updating' the restrictions they impose on the elected branches? Again, they undoubtedly do.

And when these same judges disagree about how the *Charter*'s set of vague, amorphous rights guarantees are to play out down in the quagmire of detail – where to draw the line when it comes to campaign finance rules, hate speech provisions, tobacco advertising, how long those accused of serious criminal offences should

---

14 Ronald Dworkin, *Freedom's Law: The Moral Reading of the American Constitution* (Cambridge, MA: Harvard University Press, 1996), p. 74.

be kept waiting for trial before being released, the permissibility of abortions, the rewriting of a province's human rights legislation to add a new ground, same sex-marriage, who can vote, bans on private health insurance, and, yes, even whether the pay of their judicial brethren can be frozen – do the judges of the Supreme Court of Canada resolve their differences by voting, by 'letting the numbers count' (however much such a procedure may be sneered at by them in others' hands)? Of course they do.

So the imaginary, hypothetical bill of rights provision with which I began looks to be a thinly disguised account of the role of judges under a constitutionalized bill of rights. Or rather, it looks a lot like the role of judges in Canada today or in the US during, say, the 1960s and 1970s (or even the 1920s or 1930s).

However, that outcome is not pre-ordained. Judges operating a US or Canadian-style constitutionalized bill of rights will always be more powerful and less constrained than the judges of a pure parliamentary sovereignty or of an Australian-style bill of rights-free federation. We will always find them a good way along our spectrum. But a good way along need not be all the way along. There is the possibility of self-imposed constraint. The judges might possibly limit themselves.

Here is where a particular notion of constitutionalism and of the interpretation of constitutions comes in.

For judges working under an entrenched, justiciable, constitutionalized bill of rights, one outcome – the Canadian one, as I have just indicated – is to end up with something next to indistinguishable from what flows from my imagined, hypothetical provision. If that collapse is to be avoided, and notice that the actual wording of the particular protected rights can never by itself guarantee to stop the collapse – think of how procedural due process (however phrased) is always vulnerable to collapsing into substantive due process – then we need the judges to constrain themselves.

This takes us into the realm of constitutional interpretation. We are now in the realm of last-gasp efforts to avoid outcomes like those under my hypothetical provision. To make that effort, start with this set of assumptions. Firstly, written constitutions are about locking things in, a division of powers, say, or a set of specified rights. We choose to adopt a constitution, rather than to shun constitutionalism and leave each generation to decide such matters for itself, because we decide that 'risking rigidity rather than risking security' is the better bet.

Notice that this is not an uncontentious way of understanding constitutions and constitutionalism. Another possibility, one that happens to underpin or at least coexist with my hypothetical provision, is to understand a constitution as 'a statement of our most important values and the vehicle through which these values are created and crystallized'. In other words, on this second possibility, constitutions are in part an amorphous, indeterminate list of society's values – a list that will need changing and altering as society advances and grows in accord with rather Whiggish pre-suppositions and with more concern given to getting the upgrades right than to who effects them.

Ex hypothesi, however, we are here rejecting that second possible justification in favour of the desire to lock some set of arrangements in place, to make them harder to change than an ordinary statute. That goes for a constitutionalized bill of rights too.

Hence our second assumption. The bill of rights that has been adopted locks in a particular set of protections that the people – at some point in the past – have decided to make unusually hard to remove or alter or change. It gives us a new floor level of locked-in protections above which matters are to be decided in the same way as in a pure parliamentary sovereignty – by voting and by majority rule.

I want to be explicit about this. On these two assumptions we openly and emphatically reject the second prong of my imagined hypothetical, the part about the unelected judges updating the scope, ambit and application of rights, from time to time, in order to keep pace with civilization and abreast of changing social values. Nor is this rejection of the second prong an obviously unattractive stance, since it is clear that the locked-in rights are overwhelmingly a floor, not a ceiling. If some one-century-old or two-century-old locked-in bill of rights does not protect same-sex marriage or access to abortion or prisoner voting entitlements, nothing, anywhere, prevents the elected legislature from doing so by means of an ordinary statute. There is no need to amend the constitution to give extra protections. The locked-in rights hardly ever constitute a ceiling or restriction on further liberalizations. So if access to abortion is not extended or same sex-marriage not enacted, one's gravamen on this hypothesis is with the elected legislature and one's effort for change is focused on the political process – a state of affairs known as democracy in my Chapter 4 sense.

On our two assumptions, then, what you have is one area or sub-set in which some catalogue of rights has coverage and another area or sub-set in which it does not, in which we effectively have parliamentary sovereignty.

For the purposes of this mapping exercise, the point is that this locked-in view of constitutionalism can at least in theory give us a sort of halfway house between pure parliamentary sovereignty on the one hand and my imagined hypothetical on the other. It offers the prospect of driving down the middle between pure parliamentary sovereignty on one side, and what can at times come close to a full-blooded judicial supremacy or kritarchy of the sort my imagined hypothetical was meant to convey on the other.

That said, the desirability or otherwise of this locking-things-in possibility is distinct from its practicality and sustainability. The attempt to avoid inflating, indeed constantly inflating, the range and scope of whatever set of rights happens to have been adopted in one's bill of rights requires judges to impose constraints on themselves. As we saw in Chapter 3, and for the further reasons I shall now trace out, it is far from clear that we can be overly optimistic about judges limiting their role in the way this particular view of constitutionalism and constitutional interpretation requires.

Recall where we are on our spectrum. This is *not* the pure parliamentary sovereignty jurisdiction, nor is it the Australia-style federation lacking a bill of rights. No, we are now considering a place like Canada or the US with an entrenched, constitutionalized, justiciable bill of rights. The external constraints on the judiciary that come from lacking a bill of rights – from having a rule of recognition which gives the final word over social and political matters, including rights-related matters, to some set or other of elected legislators by means of properly enacted statutes – do not exist.

Where then can we find constraints on the judiciary? The short answer is that there simply are no practical external constraints, that all constraints are self-imposed and internal to the judges. Without doubt our unelected judges will be inclined to shy away from certain issues, perhaps those related to threats to the realm or to election results or to extremely polarizing issues like who can marry. Or perhaps not. Whether they do or not, however, will not be dictated by the rule of recognition, by anything external to their own views of what constitutes proper bill of rights' interpretation. Each judge will constrain himself or herself from removing issues from democratic deliberation and resolution to the extent that he or she believes appropriate.

The possibility I have just mooted is an approach that calls for an internally imposed external constraint, in other words, to adopt a version of originalism when it comes to constitutional interpretation. Hence the judges accept that their constitution with its bill of rights was adopted to lock in a floor level of protections. Changes above that floor level must come via statute; changes below it via constitutional amendment. And once the rights in a bill of rights are understood as a set of fairly definite locked-in protections – *not* as something that grows and mutates in accord with the judge's personal moral convictions or her account of society's present-day moral convictions or her sense of what a moral phrase (e.g., 'unreasonable searches', 'due process', 'cruel and unusual punishment', 'freedom of expression') should mean – then that requires recourse to some sort of external evidence of what others thought these guarantees meant, of what was being locked in.

Originalism, either of the sort that looks to original intent or of the sort that looks to original understanding, is a sort of internally imposed external constraint. It is not unlike the person who believes there are no mind-independent, transcendent moral values but who nevertheless seeks to avoid raw subjectivism, 'sympathy and antipathy', by opting for the external, inter-subjective standards generated by utilitarianism. Similarly here, the judge adopts originalism because he thinks it proper to do so; but once adopted this sort of bill of rights interpretation requires him to give the particular provision or right the meaning intended by those who enshrined it or as it would have been understood at the time. So, for instance, capital punishment is left for the elected legislature to consider and possibly eliminate because the external evidence is taken to be clear that in the late eighteenth century virtually no one considered it to be a cruel and unusual punishment. A particular judge today may herself think capital punishment wrong, even gravely immoral, but the floor-level protection against unusual and cruel punishments – she thinks – is not to be extended by her and her judicial colleagues. She constrains herself, but she does so on the basis of external evidence of what the locked-in set of rights were taken to mean at the time of adoption. Such a judge might here also point out what was briefly alluded to in Chapter 3, namely that when it comes to interpreting constitutions and their bills of rights the 'plain meaning' approach to interpretation provides almost no constraints in and of itself. What do the words 'right to free speech' tell the judge about where to draw the line when it comes to hate speech provisions, campaign finance rules or defamation laws? And what does the plain meaning of 'cruel and unusual punishment', without more, tell the judge about the acceptability of capital punishment?

I noted a moment ago that this sort of commitment to an internally imposed external constraint – to some version of originalism – may not be sustainable as a matter of empirical fact. Not the least of the difficulties will be that many judges, our Visiting Martian might say, probably most of them once a bill of rights is in place, will find the temptations of fixing what they perceive to be moral wrongs too great to be resisted. Indeed, such was the message of Chapter 3. Relatedly, there is the evident appeal to many judges of 'progressive' or 'living tree' interpretation, of the second prong of my imagined hypothetical. This is abundantly plain from the fact that it is now uncontested orthodoxy in the Canadian Supreme Court and probably the majority position in the US Supreme Court.

At a more philosophical level, and I raised this briefly in Chapter 3, there is also the possibility that originalism itself demands my prong two. This may seem paradoxical, but it is not. The claim here is that in using abstract moral terms, in having a bill of rights at all really, the founders intended judges to apply their own moral beliefs and so to have the restrictions such rights impose on the elected branches as fluid and evolving ones. In other words, the claim is that that was their intention or that was the understanding at the time. A commitment to originalism, in other words, may end up being a commitment to Dworkinian interpretive methods rather than any sort of Sirens-like tying oneself to the mast and locking in a set of floor-level protections.

What the actual intentions of the founders were, of course, is a question of empirical fact, as is what the understanding of the terms was at the time of adoption. Historical evidence may, or may not, be sparse. (If it is, that is a further problem.) In one jurisdiction the evidence, such as it is, might point in the Dworkinian direction; in another it might not.

These potential difficulties, together with the obvious fact that only an exiguous number of judges (outside, perhaps, Australia, and the US) prefer a commitment to the non-Dworkinian sort of originalism, must give anyone pause and make him or her wonder how many eggs to put in this basket of relying on the judges to constrain themselves.

If, however, judges do make that commitment, and putting that conditional 'if' in as bold a font as you like, it nevertheless follows that our jurisdiction with a constitutionalized bill of rights can be slotted in on our spectrum somewhere after the Australia-like set-up but somewhere well before jurisdictions with our imagined provision and possibly even before jurisdictions with a statutory bill of rights.

Put differently, it is the second prong of my imagined bill of rights provision – the one explicitly empowering judges to update and amend what the rights mean and the limits they place on democratic decision making – that makes the difference when it comes to our mapping exercise.

To sum up this descriptive exercise, the absence of a bill of rights makes all the difference. Any Benevolent Legal System common law jurisdiction of the sort we are looking at that has such an instrument, whatever its form, will have less constrained judges than those without one. But once a bill of rights is opted for, it may not even follow that statutory models will necessarily leave judges more constrained than constitutional models.

That just about concludes this descriptive mapping exercise. We have moved from the 1970s New Zealand or UK end of the spectrum, past Australia today, noted a large chunk of uninhabited terrain, then passed either a mooted locking-things-in US or the statutory bill of rights jurisdictions of New Zealand and the UK, arriving at the far, least-constrained end of the spectrum with the US and finally, some further ways on, Canada.

Here, at this far end of the spectrum, the reality is all but exactly the same as in my mooted hypothetical – the judges have the last word; the restrictions they impose on democratic decision making evolve, alter, mutate (pick your favourite verb) in conjunction with those same judges' shifting senses or perceptions of what is reasonable or appropriate or morally acceptable; and when those same judges disagree amongst themselves they resort to the purely procedural decision-making rule of voting and majority rules (albeit only amongst themselves).

Here, at this far end, it turns out that my imagined bill of rights provision simply makes explicit what is more or less the status quo in Canada, what is widespread orthodoxy in the US law schools and amongst many of its judges, and possibly even where it is that the statutory bill of rights regimes seem intent on approaching. Only Australia can say it looks nothing like what my imagined provision reaps.

My imagined provision was not really imaginary at all.

Just how Weak or Enervated Are Statutory Bills of Rights?

To conclude this groundwork-laying chapter we have one last stop. We need to consider if, and how much, it matters whether the bill of rights in our jurisdiction is a statutory one rather than a constitutional one. To put it differently, does judicial review under a statutory bill of rights have the potential to collapse into strong judicial review of the American or Canadian sort?

Some might object at this point that Canada itself, though it has a constitutionalized bill of rights, does not really have US-style strong judicial review. Such an objection would point to the section 33 notwithstanding clause in their *Charter of Rights*. Such an objection would assert that this clause gives the elected legislature the ability to gainsay decisions of the Supreme Court of Canada as to rulings about the scope of rights, how they inter-relate and when limits on them are or are not reasonable.

The weakness in such an objection is not simply that this section 33 clause does not apply to all of the enumerated rights but only to some of them. (Namely, it applies solely to sections 2 and 7–15 of the *Charter of Rights*.) Nor is it just that section 33 operates only for a five-year period, subject to renewal, after which the judges' view prevails (making their view of how the rights in Canada's *Charter of Rights* ought to play out the default position in two senses, not just one). Nor is it simply that section 33 applies only prospectively, the Supreme Court judges themselves having read in a further narrowing of the provision's scope, holding that it cannot be used to over-ride already-decided matters but only prospectively.[15] No, the weakness in such an objection's trying to claim that Canada has a more democratically balanced or weaker form of judicial review than does the United States is also that this section 33 has not been used once – not one single time – by the federal parliament in all the years since the *Charter of Rights'* adoption back in 1982. (Nor has there been a single significant use of the clause at the provincial level, save in Quebec.) As Grant Huscroft and Jeffrey Goldsworthy convincingly argue, this may be attributable, in part, to the wording of section 33. This wording implies that there is a power in the elected legislature to over-ride the *Charter of Rights* itself, rather than saying that the elected legislature has a power to over-ride disputed and debatable judicial interpretations of the *Charter of Rights* – the point being that the actual wording makes any response by the legislature much more politically difficult than would a wording that did not beg the question *by assuming* that judges' views are a better indication of what the *Charter of Rights* does or does not require than are the views of elected legislators.

More bluntly put, this section 33 is framed in what some would describe as a biased, pro-judges way that leaves the elected legislature with the option to say 'those may be people's rights but we are going to take them away', but not with the option to say 'the judicial view this time on what is rights-respecting is misguided and we are substituting our rights-respecting view'. And as the facts clearly indicate, the former option – the only one accorded the legislature – proves next to impossible to use, at least thus far in time.

There is even a further claim that might be made as regards Canada's section 33 notwithstanding clause. It is a more contestable one. It argues that section 33 in practice, and paradoxically, has the unintended effect of freeing up the Canadian judges to be even more activist – even more prepared to use their own moral views to second-guess the legislature's line drawing – than they would without the 'cover' provided by such a clause. American judges know they have the last word and that this cannot be disguised. In Canada, judges can point to section 33 to escape this conclusion, and they can do so even while knowing that the practical chances of its actually being used are (at present, at least) barely above zero.

Whether section 33 be an unintended amplifier of strong judicial review, or not, the potential objection that Canada does not really have US-style strong judicial review seems far fetched.

---

15   See *Ford* v. *Quebec (Attorney General)* [1988] 2 SCR 712 at paragraph [36].

A much more plausible claim, on the face of things, involves leaving constitutionalized bills of rights and turning to statutory models, arguing that statutory bills of rights can limit judges' power more than constitutionalized versions. So how credible is it to assert that that plausible-looking claim – as a matter of empirical fact – turns out to be false and that *prima facie* weak judicial review under a statutory bill of rights will collapse into a strong judicial review not all that different to the American or Canadian sort?

To trace out an answer to that question it is important to pause for a moment and realize where the main potential lies for transmogrifying weak judicial review (under a statutory bill of rights) into something that looks not unrecognizably like strong judicial review. That potential lies in reading-down provisions, which both the New Zealand and United Kingdom statutory models contain. The New Zealand version, section 6, reads:

> Whenever an enactment *can be given a meaning* that is consistent with the rights and freedoms contained in this Bill of Rights, that meaning *shall be preferred* to any other meaning. (Italics mine)

The UK version, section 3(1), reads to start:

> So far as *it is possible to do so*, primary legislation and subordinate legislation *must be read* and given effect in a way which is compatible with Convention rights. (Italics mine)

Leave aside the somewhat scholastic – and in all likelihood moot or otiose – question of whether 'can be given' is more, or less, commanding than 'so far as is possible', and whether 'shall' is more, or less, peremptory than 'must'. The potential danger with reading-down provisions such as these is that just about any statutory language – however clear in wording and intent – might possibly be given (by the judges) some other meaning or reading. In other words, there is not all that much beyond the wit of man when it comes to being directed to give the words of a statute a meaning you, the point-of-application interpreter, think more moral and more in keeping with what you believe to be fundamental human rights. What you 'can' do, what it is 'possible' to do, may prove to be a very great deal indeed. It may come close to what the disinterested observer, our Visiting Martian, would characterize as an out-and-out re-writing or re-drafting of some offending statute.

These reading-down provisions appear largely to leave it to the unelected judges to constrain themselves, to decide how far they can go in reading 'black' to mean 'white' while keeping a straight face. The farther they go, of course – the straighter the faces they can keep – the more this exercise in statutory interpretation under the aegis of the bill of rights' reading down provision begins to collapse into an exercise in re-drafting statutes to make them read as the judges would prefer them to read (or, more punctiliously put, as those unelected judges happen to believe is in keeping with how rather abstract, indeterminate rights guarantees should play out down in the quagmire of social-policy line drawing).

There is at least the chance, then, that a particular set of judges in a particular jurisdiction would choose to keep a particularly straight set of faces. At that point there would seem not to be all that much difference between openly striking down a statute (for its claimed inconsistency with a constitutionalized bill of rights) and rewriting that same statute (to be consistent and compatible with a statutory bill of rights). True, in the latter case the legislature can respond with even clearer words indicating its intention. But those new, clearer, amended words would also have to be read by the judges as consistent and compatible with the bill of rights, if possible. (Moreover, reading down analyses can encourage judges to use global jurisprudence as a kind of smorgasbord, picking here and there what they need to reach the conclusion they want.)

This game of bluff will no doubt stop short of the level of political support needed to amend a constitution, but it will go far past what is normally required to pass a statute. It has the potential to make a statutory bill of rights regime look a good deal like a jurisdiction with my imagined provision from the last section.

Consider the United Kingdom's statutory bill of rights and the case of *Ghaidan* v. *Mendoza*.[16] In that case the House of Lords (Lord Millett dissenting) held that the section 3 reading down provision in the *Human Rights Act* (their statutory bill of rights) enabled a court to depart from the unambiguous meaning that a piece of legislation would otherwise bear. (That is their characterization, by the way, not mine). Lord Nicholls of Birkenhead made the claim in these words:

> It is now generally accepted that the application of s. 3 does not depend upon the presence of ambiguity in the legislation being interpreted. Even if, construed according to the ordinary principles of interpretation, the meaning of the legislation admits of no doubt, s. 3 may none the less require the legislation to be given a different meaning ... Section 3 may require the court to ... depart from the intention of the Parliament which enacted the legislation ... It is also apt to require a court to read in words which change the meaning of the enacted legislation, so as to make it convention-compliant [meaning bill of rights compliant].[17]

Lord Steyn's view was that the reading down provision applies even if there is no ambiguity. 'The word "possible" in s. 3(1) is used in a different and much stronger sense'.[18] He suggested in clear terms that the interpretation adopted need not even be a reasonable one.[19]

---

16   [2004] 3 All ER 411.
17   *Ibid.*, paras. [29], [30] and [32].
18   *Ibid.*, para. [44].
19   *Ibid.*

And just to give you the full flavour of the potential power of these reading down provisions, it is crucial to realize that in reaching this result their Lordships overruled one of their own House of Lords authorities – a case on the meaning of exactly this same statutory provision, an authority only five years old, and one that had held the meaning to be clear.[20] Even more to the point, this *Ghaidan* approach has been affirmed repeatedly;[21] it is no outlier; the top judges in the United Kingdom with this comparatively new statutory bill of rights now in place see themselves operating under a 'new legal order'[22] – one in which their views on a host of political and moral line-drawing exercises are significantly more influential than before.

So the danger is that reading down provisions such as these throw open the possibility of 'Alice in Wonderland' judicial interpretations; they confer an 'interpretation on steroids' power on the unelected judges. Although there is no power to invalidate or strike down legislation, the judges can potentially accomplish just as much by re-writing it, by saying that seen through the prism (that is, their own prism) of human rights, 'near black' means 'near white'. They can make bill of rights sceptics half long for the honesty of judges (under constitutionalized bills of rights) who strike down legislation rather than gut it of the meaning everyone knows it was intended to have (rule-of-law values notwithstanding).

Yet that is not the only tool given to judges by a statutory bill of rights. In the absence of any power to strike down legislation (as per constitutionalized bills of rights as in the US and Canada), and assuming (optimistically perhaps) that the judges will not go too far down the *Ghaidan* reading down path, there is also a power to issue declarations of incompatibility[23] – to declare that the court is satisfied that the statutory provision under consideration is incompatible with one or more of the rights in the enacted bill of rights. It is precisely these judicial declarations that are supposed to give rise to all the benefits proponents of statutory bills of rights predict. The claim is that there will be some sort of dialogue and that the legislature – on learning that one of its statutes has attracted one of these judicial declarations – will ponder it and will then reflect on how best to accomplish its aims while at the same time attempting to uphold the various enunciated human rights, or at least limiting them only to an extent that is reasonable and justifiable.

---

20   See *Fitzpatrick* v. *Sterling Housing Association Ltd.* [2001] 1 AC 27.

21   *Ghaidan*'s interpretive approach has been affirmed in *National Westminster Bank* v. *Spectrum Plus* [2005] UKHL 41; *Secretary of State for Work and Pensions* v. *M* [2006] UKHL 11; *Countryside Alliance and others* v. *Attorney General* [2007] UKHL 52 and *P & Ors, Re (Northern Ireland)* [2008] UKHL 38, *inter alia*. That said, there have been moments of uncertainty. See, for example, Lord Bingham in *Secretary of State for the Home Department* v. *MB* [2007] UKHL 46, at para. [44] and Lord Hope in *Doherty & Ors* v. *Birmingham City Council* [2008] UKHL 57.

22   *Jackson* v. *Attorney-General* [2006] 1 AC 262 at para [102] *per* Lord Steyn.

23   This is section 4 (2) in the United Kingdom's statutory bill of rights. In New Zealand the judges simply gave themselves an equivalent power on no statutory warrant. See *Moonen* v. *Film & Literature Board of Review* [2000] 2 NZLR 9.

That is the claim. However, that claim is only remotely plausible where the elected legislature is left in a position in which it feels it can, on occasion at least, disagree with and overrule the unelected judges on how the substantive enumerated rights in the bill of rights ought to play out and what limits on them are reasonable. Recall that these rights are pitched up in the Olympian heights of moral abstractions (for example, 'the right to freedom of expression', 'to life', 'to freedom of religion') in terms that in themselves do *not* resolve difficult policy decisions down in the quagmire of detail – decisions related to where to draw the line when it comes to campaign finance rules, hate speech provisions, euthanasia regimes, what devout religious adherents can wear to school and much, much more. In brief, the rights in a bill of rights are in no way self-executing. Nor is the determination of what may or may not constitute a reasonable and justifiable limit on these rights self-evident.

As an empirical matter, then, what has been happening in the United Kingdom under the provision in its statutory bill of rights allowing the judges to make declarations of incompatibility? What, in fact, happens there after the judges issue them? Does the elected legislature ever dispute what almost always amounts to a highly debatable line-drawing call, one over which sincere, reasonable, well-informed, even nice people can and do disagree?

The answer is 'no'. According to Francesca Klug and Keir Starmer, writing in 2005, '[i]n *every case* where remedial action had not been taken before the [judicial] declaration was made, the government responded by repealing, amending or committing to repeal or amend, the relevant provision'.[24] In other words, after every single judicial declaration of incompatibility in the UK, every single one of them, the elected legislature deferred to the unelected judges. That remains the case as of writing in 2010, with over two dozen such judicial declarations having now been issued, and deferred to once appeals were completed.

One reason for this legislative reticence to stand up to these judicial declarations, a reason mirroring the one given above as regards the non-use of section 33 in Canada, is that here too the Declaration power is structured so as to make the judges' views on rights (including what limits on them are and are not reasonable) not only authoritative but incontestable, leaving Parliament with just a 'we are going to take your rights away' option, one that significantly mischaracterizes what is generally in dispute between the judges and legislators (or rather, to be more precise, between the majority of judges and the majority of legislators).

By now there is at least some scope for thinking statutory bills of rights offer the possibility of a substantive outcome that collapses into a version of strong

---

24 Francesca Klug and Keir Starmer, 'Standing Back from the *Human Rights Act*: How Effective Is It Five Years On?' [2005] *Public Law* 716, 721 (emphasis added) (citations omitted). To the same effect see too 'Monitoring the Government's Response to Human Rights Judgments: Annual Report 2008', A Report by a Standing Committee of the House of Lords and House of Commons. Note, for what it is worth, that in both instances the lack of any legislative gainsaying is presumed to be a good thing.

judicial review. In form, it is true, the judges operating a statutory bill of rights cannot strike down statutes. They can, however, do what would look to the Visiting Martian to be something akin to re-writing or re-drafting them – to make them say what the judges think is more in keeping with one (or more) of the enumerated rights. On top of that, the judges in the United Kingdom can issue declarations of incompatibility which, in practice, always prevail.

For the purposes of the next chapter that is probably sufficient. I could go on to examine the New Zealand experience as well or to look at the indirect ways in which judges' views on rights issues prevail under statutory bills of rights – not least through the need for legislators to make statements when introducing Bills into the legislature as to their compatibility with the bill of rights, and how this requirement has collapsed into a form of government lawyers guessing what the judges will think by sifting through past decisions and overseas cases, with virtually no evidence of this requirement's prodding legislators to think for themselves more about rights-related aspects of Bills. However, just how great a collapse of weak judicial review into strong judicial review has taken place in the United Kingdom and New Zealand need not concern us. It may well be that weak-form judicial review under a statutory bill of rights is ultimately unstable, and that the judges will either (in the absence of any strong resistance from other officials) collapse it into a variant of strong judicial review or (where there is such resistance or a lack of judicial desire to push for such a collapse) the statutory bill of rights will make little or not over-much impact on the extent of parliamentary sovereignty that existed before the bill of rights.

In the next chapter we will just be assuming that to some significant extent strong judicial review has been created by the bill of rights, whether it be a constitutionalized or statutory one. So, having set out in this chapter the weak-rights and strong-rights bases that can sustain such instruments and their enumerated rights together with their possible connection to paternalism, and having mapped out the range of powers they might confer on unelected judges (whether via an entrenched, constitutionalized form or via a statutory form), we can now proceed to the issue of how vantage affects one's assessment of the pros and cons of a bill of rights.

That will require a separate chapter of its own.

Chapter 6

Bills of Rights – II

The Law Professor

In considering how vantage affects one's assessment of the merits or desirability of a bill of rights, let us start with the Law Professor. This is a seemingly unusual starting point, I know. Yet if we are seeking a vantage that tends to be favourably disposed towards bills of rights and strong judicial review – and in this chapter the latter will be assumed to encompass both what flows from a US or Canadian-style constitutionalized version and what flows from a UK-style statutory version – then this is certainly one of them.

A more obvious starting point in looking for a broadly favourable vantage might be thought to be the judiciary. After all, to the extent that a bill of rights shifts social policy line-drawing powers to any group of officials, it is to the unelected judges. They, not law professors, will be the ones deciding contentious issues such as who can marry, whether capital punishment or anti-abortion regimes can be enacted, what limits on free expression or religious observances are allowable, the permitted procedures to be used by the police and by those who determine which people can and cannot lawfully enter the country, and much else too. When an instrument transfers decision making powers over all those sorts of questions to a particular group of people, that same group of people might be assumed to think such an instrument desirable, maybe even necessary. Of course such a claim would be based on a generalization of what the preponderance, or even the vast preponderance, of individual judges might be predicted likely to think about bills of rights. There will obviously be outliers, as there would in any group. But as far as generalizations go, when we look at the top judges in the United States, the United Kingdom, Canada, South Africa, New Zealand – and probably even in Australia too, despite that country's virtually uniquely not having a national-level bill of rights – this is a very safe one to make indeed. Judges in common law Benevolent Legal Systems overwhelmingly tend to be favourably disposed towards bills of rights.

So why start with law professors? In part it is because the Judge's Vantage is so exceptional. Unlike any other vantage one might adopt, from the Judge's Vantage it is possible to use a bill of rights to blend one's own personal moral judgments or evaluations into the determination of what counts as a valid law. Yes, that possibility is a circumscribed one. On the Hartian understanding it is restricted to those cases that fall outside the core of settled meaning of the bill of rights and into its penumbra of doubt; these cases are the inevitable 'failures in the system' and in any well-functioning legal system they will be far from pervasive, though with bills of rights they will be more frequent than without. Meanwhile, perhaps even more so on the Dworkinian understanding, the judge has recourse to his own personal moral judgments or evaluations; they will be needed to construct the best background fit of the settled legal materials, of the metaphorical first nine chapters of the chain novel, and so will come into play only in a second-order sense rather than in a more straightforward, first-order search for the best moral answer; and appeal to them may be restricted to deciding Hard Cases as opposed to Easy Cases, though it is arguable (persuasively so in my view) that all cases are potentially Hard Cases on the Dworkinian understanding and to decide which are which one must first construct that morally laden best background fit. This is more obviously so when interpreting a bill of rights.

On either view, judges may only sometimes, not always, be able to elide their own personal moral judgments or evaluations into the determination of what counts as law. And as I have noted in earlier chapters, judges on all but the jurisdiction's highest court will also be constrained by the prospect of a potentially successful appeal. That prospect will vary based on a host of factors, but the general perception that the judge has simply substituted his or her own moral preferences for the established law of the land will be one of them (though it may not, alone, be enough).

Even a judge on the highest court, as I have said, must be in the majority on a case in order for it possibly to transpire that her personal moral judgments and evaluations get made part of what becomes valid law.

Those qualifications, and possibly more, notwithstanding, it remains true that judges – and only judges – are in a position different to all others. As point-of-application interpreters, their moral views (if only sometimes) on what the bill of rights means – including on its reach, whether to interpret as a 'living document' or by recourse to some version of originalism, how the enumerated rights relate to one another, and more – will be authoritative. They will determine what is held to be valid law. For no other vantage is that the case.

That wholly unique vantage is not the best place to begin in assessing a bill of rights. Any vantage outside of that of the authoritative operator of such instruments would be better, as a starting point. And this is reinforced by the doubts raised in Chapter 3 above, namely that even the bill of rights-disliking appointee to the highest court will find it difficult on occasion not to use the bill of rights to gainsay the elected legislature. One need not add to that some sort of overly reductionist claim framed in terms of judges' being the main beneficiaries of such instruments, in some zero-sum division of powers or public choice-theory sense. It suffices, and is more plausible, to postpone adopting the Judge's Vantage simply because so few people in society ever get to hold that vantage, as a matter of fact.

Once we opt to postpone adopting the Judge's Vantage, but wish nevertheless to start with a vantage that tends to be solidly in favour of bills of rights, then that of the Law Professor is the obvious choice.

And favourable to bills of rights that Law Professor's Vantage undoubtedly is. Limiting our consideration to common law Benevolent Legal Systems, my own inexact, based-on-personal-experiences-only sense is that support for these instruments within the legal academy is overwhelming. It is by no means universal. Supporters and proponents, though, vastly outnumber sceptics and opponents. Take any top English-language law journal and count up the articles over the past decade or two or three that are explicitly or implicitly in favour of bills of rights, then count those opposed. I doubt you could find a single law journal where articles opposing these instruments outnumber – or come close to outnumbering – the number of those in favour.

In Canada, there is very, very little opposition by law professors to their *Charter of Rights*, and what little there is falls almost wholly into the category of 'the judges aren't doing enough for the groups we happen to think are deserving of decisions going in their favour'. It is a sort of opposition, in other words, contingent upon the bill of rights' results that happen to flow from the top court. Change those results enough, and the opposition evaporates.

If Canadian law professors (and probably those in South Africa too) be the strongest bill of rights supporters in terms of a supporter-to-sceptic ratio, that same ratio would not be all that much lower in the United States, the United Kingdom, New Zealand and probably even Australia. True, in those other jurisdictions there are opponents on democratic legitimacy grounds, not simply on 'the outcomes are disappointing us' grounds. And there are more of these dissenters, proportionally. But they are still a clear minority. So in that sense, bills of rights are seen as desirable from the Law Professor's Vantage.

Before moving to assess bills of rights from this vantage, let me concede that there is a certain irony involved in rejecting the Judge's Vantage for the Law Professor's as our first point of reference. That irony flows from the fact that so many legal academics implicitly adopt the Judge's Vantage in their writings. After telling the reader what the judges did decide – and you will notice how this is the rule and being told what the legislators did decide is the exception – they move on to tell the reader what the judges should have decided and how they should have decided it. When it comes to writing about bills of rights this implicit 'put yourself in the shoes of the judge' or appeal-court-itis is even more pronounced.

That said, the Law Professor is never in a position to ensure her recommendations are acted upon. At best, she can hope to catch the eye of some actual judge who might act upon them. In terms of bringing about some sort of change from the status quo, therefore, the most obvious intended audience of those who implicitly adopt the Judge's Vantage is judges themselves.

Not all writing, of course, aims to bring about judicially driven change. Other motives might exist on their own or in conjunction with this one. For instance, for those Law Professors attempting to legitimize or justify the status quo, the implicit adoption of the Judge's Vantage in discussions of how cases (including bill of rights cases) ought to be decided seems to me to be compatible with an intended audience of Concerned Citizens. Any message along the lines of 'here is how judges do decide and here is how they should and you can see the gap between them is fairly small' or 'judges will get these sort of decisions right more often than any other proposed decision maker' can be delivered from the Judge's Vantage but intended for the Concerned Citizen. Indeed, it can even be incestuously intended mainly for other Law Professors.

On top of that, and as O.W. Holmes noted over a century ago, law schools in the common law world overwhelmingly teach their subjects by implicitly asking students to adopt the Judge's Vantage. Students read, digest, parse and critique countless cases. Rarely, or certainly comparatively rarely, do they do the same with statutes. With bills of rights, of course, the written text is short; it is articulated using relatively vague, amorphous, indeterminate terms in the language of rights; it is pitched up in the Olympian heights of disagreement-finessing moral abstractions but its practical effects come only after the judges apply it down in the quagmire of social-policy line drawing. So in teaching courses on bills of rights it is not at all surprising that Law Professors generally do so, implicitly, from the Judge's Vantage. Yes, such instruments could be studied from the Visiting Martian's Vantage, the Concerned Citizen's, even the Legislator's. But such is infrequently the case, as a matter of fact.

To recap, Law Professors regularly, at a minimum, adopt some sort of ersatz or implicit Judge's Vantage and just as regularly have their students do so. And yes, there is a certain irony in beginning our vantage-specific assessment of bills of rights there, rather than with the actual Judge's Vantage. Such a charge, however, is not an overly serious one and so, for the reasons already given, we will begin our assessment of bills of rights from this vantage.

As argued in Chapter 5, bills of rights incorporate a moral test, at the point-of-application, into the determination of what counts as law. They allow the point-of-application interpreters scope to strike down or to re-write statutes judged by them to be inconsistent with one or more of the moral standards (expressed in the language of rights) they enunciate. This transmogrification of politics into law plays into the strengths of the Law Professor. When the questions of the permissible extent of abortion or the acceptability of same-sex marriage or the wisest limits to put on free speech are posed as political questions and decided democratically, meaning by letting the numbers count, the Law Professor has no special expertise. He may be better read, or more articulate, than average and this may allow him to sway the votes of some fellow citizens. But the same can be said of many others, the preponderance of whom will not be Law Professors.

Adopt a bill of rights, however, and the Law Professor does have a special expertise. First off, he understands the new decision making procedures better than almost all other citizens. Secondly, given that the laid-down words of the bill of rights are sufficiently amorphous and indeterminate that they themselves will rarely be determinative or preclude either party from prevailing in court, the judges will regularly look to past decisions for guidance. Law Professors will know the content of these past decisions far better than Concerned Citizens or even Legislators. Relatedly, this lack of guidance from the bare words of the bill of rights itself makes it likely that judges may sometimes seek the opinions of other non-judges. This is far more likely to be the opinions of Law Professors (and other lawyers) than anyone else.

In addition, bills of rights are likely to be attractive to all those Law Professors who are moral objectivists or moral realists on the question of the status of moral evaluations. These are people who say there are objective moral values – moral rights and wrongs whose status as such does not depend on what other people, or even oneself, happen to think or feel. In other words, right and wrong, moral goodness and moral badness, duty and obligation, have a non-relative, 'higher' pedigree, independent of the beliefs and sentiments that happen to exist. Hence for the moral realist Law Professor there is more to support such claims as 'slavery is evil', 'human freedom and autonomy are good' or 'racial vilification is wicked' than that most people (or the speaker) happen to feel that way, or that they have undesirable long-term consequences. There is some further mind-independent quality which makes some moral claims true and others false.

Moral sceptics and noncognitivists deny this and so reject the purchase moral realism or moral objectivism purports to provide. Sceptics assert that moral values – right and wrong, good and bad, moral truth and moral falsehood – are tied to nothing more than the contingent and observably varying responses of human beings. Neither do mind-independent values exist nor is there some logical relation between humans and values. Or so say moral sceptics. According to them, the relation depends on the way humans happen to be constructed. This not only varies over time, place, culture and rank but could conceivably have been otherwise.

Now my suggestion is that those Law Professors who are moral realists or moral objectivists will be more inclined to support a bill of rights – an instrument that increases the moral input at the point-of-application – than will the moral sceptics amongst them.

For the moral sceptics living in a Benevolent Legal System the case against a bill of rights is reasonably straightforward. In a world where mind-independent moral facts simply do not exist, where evaluations of right and wrong are in effect personal sentiments (albeit sentiments that have been largely shaped by the social norms of the community into which one happens to have been born or that have been hard-wired into us by evolution), a judge's moral views seem unlikely to be any better than anyone else's. Wishing judges to have an enhanced bill of rights role would therefore have to rest on something else, a checks-and-balances claim perhaps or an ersatz upper house analogy.

So one probable attraction of the anti-bill of rights position for the moral sceptic Law Professor is that it better restricts social-policy making and moral input into decision making to elected politicians. Judges' moral and political views are made comparatively impotent. Political and moral preferences are fought about openly in the give-and-take, compromise-filled world of electoral politics. For one who believes there are no objective, mind-independent values, this prospect of majority preferences' prevailing may prove very appealing. Letting the numbers count, when it is sentiments versus sentiments, will be attractive to many.

It is of course not impossible that a particular moral sceptic Law Professor could believe that judges' moral and political views, when implemented, *will* produce better consequences for society than those of elected politicians. There is nothing inconsistent in holding to this belief and to the tenets of moral scepticism. On this view, judges' moral views are not more 'right' or more 'valid' or more 'true' than anyone else's, rather their views simply tend to lead to more social utility or welfare (just as having a social system of constraints on action – *any* system – leads to more welfare than one without constraints). The reasons that can be given for thinking that judges' views generally lead to better social consequences include such assertions as:

1. Judges are better educated on average than the population at large;
2. Judges are less susceptible to lobbying and special-interest groups;
3. Judges must decide in a written, reasoned way open to scrutiny;
4. The judiciary's powers are much less prone to abuse than the executive's or legislature's;
5. Judges are there to protect minorities and any errors on the side of such groups are a price the majority has to pay to live in a pluralistic society.

Such consequentialist claims are highly debatable, of course. And whether convincing or unconvincing, they ignore other similarly focused assertions, such as the consequentialist claim that not having a bill of rights will lead to a greater certainty of outcome (though, admittedly, that is more obviously a benefit from the Concerned Citizen's Vantage than the Law Professor's).

Let us put the moral sceptic Law Professor to one side, however, and ask the more interesting question of whether the moral realist Law Professor will find it easier to support a bill of rights. Above, I ventured the opinion that this is plausible. In a world in which, *ex hypothesi*, there *are* objective moral values and hence certain moral evaluations *do* have the status of truth, permitting and indeed encouraging judges to appeal to and rely on the moral considerations in a bill of rights in making their decisions seems neither problematical nor dangerous. If there are right moral answers then judges should find them. Knowing this, we may not worry as much that a lack of predictability will infect the legal system. Nor might we worry greatly that power is being exercised by unelected, and so seemingly illegitimate players in the system. After all, if there be right and true mind-independent moral answers then surely what matters is finding those answers, not the extent of the popular mandate of the finders. In sum, it seems the moral objectivist could be quite at home with a bill of rights and its effects on the judiciary–legislature relationship.

Against that instinctive sort of linking of moral realism or moral objectivism and support for a bill of rights there is a counter-argument of the type Jeremy Waldron has made. Waldron attempts to explode the apparent connection between moral realist presuppositions and support for greater point-of-application moral input. His basic argument rests on three main pillars.

Firstly, the fact there are 'true', 'right' values (*ex hypothesi*) does not mean any particular person knows what they are. Each moral objectivist Law Professor has only his or her own moral beliefs, his or her own opinions about what is mind-independently right. What he or she does not have is a method or way to determine which beliefs are in fact the 'right', 'true' ones – or rather there is no such method that those with differing moral beliefs will accept as the correct method for determining these mind-independently right moral answers.

That being so, says Waldron, the moral realist's or moral objectivist's value opinions (about what she thinks is a true, right, mind-independent value) are no less arbitrary than the moral sceptic's value opinions (which he thinks have the status of being simply sentiments, attitudes or feelings). Combine that with a second, archetypal Waldronian claim that moral disagreement and moral dissensus are inescapable facts of social life, and the Law Professor comes back to the question of why support a bill of rights that will enable judges' moral views to prevail far more frequently than they would without a bill of rights.

Having come this far, Waldron's counter-argument finishes with a third pillar – pointing out that even if moral realism be true, that truth does not reduce the dangers of increased moral decision making by judges that a bill of rights will foster, nourish and accentuate. That truth makes no difference to the predictability of judicial decisions that involve a moral element. (We predict judges' future decisions from their past ones and this is true whether a specific judge thinks she is expressing a moral attitude or enunciating a belief about a moral fact.) That truth does not affect how judges act in terms of the sort of reasoned decisions they provide. (The sceptic who merely announces her attitude is no more dangerous than the objectivist who simply states his belief and that he knows the fair, just etc. outcome when he sees it. Nor does anything prevent the sceptic from giving reasons for an outcome which stem from a general attitude, say repugnance at suffering, and which work step by step towards a result, perhaps an acquittal for stealing bread.) Finally, that truth adds nothing to the legitimacy of a select few unelected judges making moral as opposed to legal decisions. (The moral objectivist has to say that judges' *beliefs* about what is morally right are better than elected legislators' *beliefs*. The sceptic has to say that judges' moral *preferences* are better than elected legislators' moral *preferences*. The former is every bit as difficult as the latter. And, Waldron notes, it is an error, a fallacy even, to attempt to avoid the difficulty by comparing judges' *beliefs* with legislators' *preferences*. Like must be weighed against like and somehow it must be argued that judges are elevated, superior moral deliberators.)

That, in brief, is the Waldronian counter-argument against the *prima facie* sense that moral realist Law Professors will find it easier to support a bill of rights than their moral sceptic colleagues. The truth of moral objectivity or moral scepticism is irrelevant, argues Waldron, to the choice between lots of judicial moral input under a bill of rights or significantly less such input without one.

This Waldronian counter-argument attempting to explode the apparent connection between moral realist or moral objectivist pre-suppositions and support for greater point-of-application moral input is a strong one. All three pillars on which he rests that counter-argument seem to me to be correct. Having conceded that, there is nevertheless a side to this question that Waldron overlooks, one that may well make it easier for the moral realist Law Professor to support a bill of rights.

Recall the gist of Waldron's counter-argument. *A)* First-order moral disagreement is pervasive, regardless of people's second-order (i.e., objectivist versus sceptical) views. *B)* There is no way to determine whose first-order views are the right ones, even assuming the objectivist be correct and there is in fact some such thing as a right moral view. Consequently, given widespread moral dissensus and no method of resolving such conflicts by discovering 'right' answers, *C)* the attraction of 'letting the numbers count' as a way of resolving disputes should be equally strong for objectivist and sceptic alike.

If one accepts the premises *A)* and *B)*, conclusion *C)* is a very persuasive one. Mind you, *C)* does *not* follow necessarily from *A)* and *B)*, but then Waldron never claims it does. Even the sceptic can favour handing moral decision-making and dispute-resolving powers to an elite group of moral guardians, *provided the sceptic also thinks these guardians do a better job – in consequentialist terms – of resolving them, even after allowing for the greater uncertainty of case-by-case resolutions.* Nevertheless, all Waldron claims is that there is *as much* reason for objectivists to dislike handing this sort of bill of rights power to judges (to be moral guardians) as there is for sceptics. And that being so, the corollary is also true that the objectivist too must defend such a delegation to the judiciary solely in terms of the superior moral skills or decision making of judges. 'Far from all of us being equal, legally trained judges are in fact better able to decide *moral* issues than the rest of us', she must say.

Very, very few people I know of, Law Professors included, be they sceptic or objectivist, are prepared to make that claim, at least openly. This is why conclusion *C)*, although not deductively mandated, is an extremely attractive one to draw from premises *A)* and *B)*. At this point I agree completely with Waldron. However, his conclusion rests on the two premises. Although premise *A)* seems to me indisputable, premise *B)* is different. I do not mean that Waldron is wrong about premise *B)*. Rather, I think that there is more than one vantage from which to assess premise *B)*. Waldron, however, implicitly assumes there is but one vantage. Let me elaborate. Waldron, in arguing that there is no way to determine whose moral views are the right ones, adopts the Visiting Martian's Vantage. From that vantage it is doubtlessly true that moral objectivists are unable to demonstrate the truth of their judgments. The Visiting Martian makes that assessment after considering all the various and diverse participants' views and noting their inability to offer to those who disagree anything in the way of a method for approaching and resolving moral disputes.

But suppose that instead of adopting that vantage we take up the moral realist Law Professor's Vantage. From this vantage do there not appear to be right answers? Does not such a participant in the system operate on the assumption there are right answers? And, having sincerely tried to find them, does not this person suppose that his views *are*, for all intents, the right ones (at least until he can be convinced to change his mind)? Dworkin certainly thinks so. Indeed Dworkin demands that we adopt something like such a participant-in-the-system's vantage.

With this point about differing perspectives in mind, if we now look again at premise *B)*, but this time from the moral realist Law Professor's Vantage, it is no longer clear that knowledge of the right answer is elusive. It depends upon whether, as a participating interpreter with a stake in the system, I think *my answer* is the right answer. That in turn will frequently be affected, it seems to me, by whether I accept moral objectivism or moral scepticism. If I am of the latter inclination, and do not think there is any such thing as 'right' or 'true' moral values, I can hardly ascribe rightness to my own views and so would accept *B)*. If I am an objectivist, however, I certainly can. I need only believe that others, who hold contrary moral views, are wrong. My inability to convince most or all of them of the correctness of my views may *a)* turn me into a moral sceptic; it may *b)* lead me, as Waldron urges, to append 'this is only my opinion about what is mind-independently right' after my moral views; or it may *c)* lead me to think others, for whatever reason, simply cannot see the 'right' and 'true' mind-independent moral answer. From the perspective of a moral objectivist (including a moral objectivist Law Professor) who believes there are 'right' and 'true' moral answers, neither the aspostasy of *a)* nor the agnosticism of *b)* is required. In fact, *c)* is much the more likely outcome in psychological terms.

Let me stress that I am *not* arguing that the truth of moral views is in fact self-certifying – i.e., if our Law Professor honestly believes values A–Z are the true, right ones on all the best evidence at hand, then that is enough to make values A–Z true. Of course not! I am trying instead to make the more subtle point about how the vantage one adopts influences the propensity one has to favour letting judges make moral decisions, especially under a bill of rights. Once one takes up a standpoint like that of our Law Professor, the psychology of anyone who happens also to accept moral objectivism *can*, and probably often does, undermine Waldron's premise *B)*. It makes it easier to think there are right views which *are* knowable.

This alone, however, though partially undermining premise *B)*, is not enough to show that a moral objectivist will find it harder than a moral sceptic to reject a bill of rights and so to keep relatively low judges' moral input. Consider the reply to me of the person who says: 'I agree that a moral objectivist, as you argue, is more likely to think *her* moral views are correct and right. But I fail to see why she would think *judges'* moral views are likely to be correct.' And I agree with this response to the extent that no necessary connection can be drawn between the two. The tendency of moral objectivists to equate their own moral opinions with the 'right' moral answers need not make those same moral objectivists sympathetic to high degrees of moral decision making by judges. But as far as moral realist *Law Professors* are concerned, and as an empirical generalization, I think it is likely to have that effect.

To start, the believer in 'right' moral answers – those, most usually, that concur with his own opinions – optimistically may well assume that judges will agree with his views. This applies to Law Professor and Concerned Citizen alike, though it may be more warranted as regards the former. The pervasive generality and indefiniteness of the language of bills of rights which hides both the inevitable conflicts between competing rights and even the non-absolute character of rights may make this easier to do. Added to that is the possible influence of a Dworkin-like belief that 'right' answers should, and eventually will, be found.

The interest the actors in a legal system have in speaking as though there are and always were, correct answers to legal disputes may also play a small role in making attractive to the moral objectivist Law Professor the 'legalizing' of moral disputes.

For my present purposes I go no further than this. I say that from a participating interpreter's standpoint such as that of the Law Professor, where one believes in 'right' moral answers one will tend to think those answers are knowable and that they correspond with one's own opinions. As well, given a shared training and working culture, one may be more inclined to assume judges will reach those same conclusions. In short, the psychology of the moral objectivist – and especially of the Law Professor moral objectivist – will make it easier for her to be more insouciant about high degrees of moral decision making by judges than for the moral sceptic. This moral objectivist Law Professor is more likely to support a bill of rights, in other words.

This follows from changing the perspective from which one considers Waldron's premise *B)*. Abandon the Visiting Martian's Vantage for that of the Law Professor. Then ask if there is a way to know which views are the morally right ones. The moral objectivist Law Professor, it seems to me, is more likely to answer 'yes' (and assume they align with her own views), more likely to be optimistic about judges reaching those 'right' conclusions, and hence more likely to endorse the widespread power of moral decision making by judges that comes with a bill of rights.

There are other reasons for the Law Professor to look favourably on bills of rights. For instance, these instruments, with their capacity for a relatively unchecked incorporation of morality into law, significantly increase the number of what Dworkin calls 'Hard Cases'. In Hartian terms, bills of rights increase the open texture or relative penumbra of doubt of a legal system; they expand the discretionary moral (and for that matter broader policy or economic efficiency) input of the judges. And that means that any Law Professor seeking to construct a theory of law out of a theory of adjudication will be better off. As a matter of empirical fact, having a bill of rights in place will make that Law Professor's adjudication-centred theory a more plausible and convincing one than it would be without a bill of rights. His professional standing will be improved.

The flip side of that is this. For those Law Professors who advise on, or themselves take, cases that go to court, bills of rights give them more scope to appeal to their own personal morality as lawyers. True, in formulating how best to argue their case they will have to distinguish judges' morality from their own; the lawyer is not in the judges' unique position of sometimes being able to blend their views of what is morally best into what is, or becomes, law. But more indirectly, by expanding the penumbra of doubt, bills of rights increase the range of plausible arguments judges might find attractive. In coarser terms, the Law Professor/Lawyer has more room to fashion arguments in line with his own moral sentiments or judgments under a bill of rights.

And in terms of raw professional self-interest, it is extremely hard to see how a bill of rights will not be advantageous to most Law Professors. There will be books to write; there will be blogs to run; there will be seemingly endless conferences to organize, speak at and attend. True, such opportunities will create a niche market for the anti-bill of rights Law Professor. But it will be a considerably smaller and more circumscribed one, attractive mostly to contrarians.

Some small number of Law Professors will even say, openly and in clear terms, that they favour bills of rights because for them democratic decision making is not any sort of pre-eminent value. Perhaps some in this group think putting in place some sort of ersatz, aristocratic UK-style House of Lords (but staffed with judges) will be desirable to check the actions of those who need to seek regular re-election. Or perhaps some have a 'lock things in' view of constitutions and bills of rights which they think ought to be interpreted on the basis of some version or other of originalism – in other words they have views more or less in sympathy with the ones described in the third section of Chapter 5 – so that democratic decision making will be unfettered save where the locked-in, interpreted according to originalism, bill of rights applies. Either way, these provide other bases on which Law Professors can be favourably disposed to bills of rights, and suffice to conclude this section.

The Bad Man

When a bill of rights is newly introduced into a Benevolent Legal System its effects will be felt in four possible areas. It will affect criminal procedure; it will bear on civil actions for money against the government or public bodies or persons or bodies performing a public function or duty pursuant to law; it will influence how statutes and (for entrenched bills of rights) constitutional provisions are interpreted; and it will affect, too, the common law or judge-made law in areas such as tort law and even contract law. (These so-called horizontal or citizen–citizen effects of a bill of rights will vary significantly from jurisdiction to jurisdiction, from those where the effects are massive to those where they are slight.)

In general terms, the criminal procedure effects will be the first to be felt and noticed. The bill of rights will be used by the judges to affect what the police must do as regards informing suspects about entitlements to call a lawyer; to affect how long accused can be held before trial; to affect search and seizure rules; to affect when evidence that has been obtained improperly will be admissible in court; and more. Almost all of these changes will be to the advantage of those suspected or accused of criminal offences.

From the amoral Bad Man's Vantage all these criminal procedure effects of a bill of rights, as they apply to him personally, will therefore be highly desirable. They will make it less likely (than it would be without a bill of rights) that he will be convicted and punished for any of the close-to-the-line activities he opts to do after weighing up the potential benefits of those activities against the potential legal (but not moral) costs. Indeed the increased procedural legal protections now afforded him – and the better the lawyer he can employ, the greater these are likely to be in practice – will change the calculations he makes. They will move where he draws the line between 'give this close-to-the-line activity a go' and 'refrain from giving it a go'. His optimal legal position, as an amoral user of that system, will in this sense be improved once a bill of rights is in place.

However, there will also be a downside from the Bad Man's Vantage with the introduction of a bill of rights. There will be more uncertainty as to outcomes; the moral tests in the language of rights introduced by the bill of rights will increase the legal system's penumbra of doubt or uncertainty (if you prefer to see law in Hartian terms) or the number of Hard Cases (if you move to a Dworkinian analysis). Of course this greater uncertainty will not bother the Bad Man because he has some theoretical attachment to Rule of Law values. When it comes to the criminal law's application to the Bad Man himself, this greater uncertainty will not bother him at all. Any doubt caused by the bill of rights as to whether a penal law applies to him or not will be a doubt in his favour. From the Bad Man's Vantage that sort of self-interested uncertainty will be seen as a positive or desirable effect of having a bill of rights.

Other sorts of uncertainty, though, will be seen as pejorative or undesirable from the Bad Man's Vantage. To start, bill of rights-driven criminal procedure changes that benefit others and so make convicting them more uncertain will not obviously appeal to the Bad Man. His position here is analogous to that of the Free Rider. The Free Rider does *not* want the system of social rules and restraints to break down. He is no revolutionary and still less an anarchist. Rather, he wants everyone else to be constrained by, and comply with, the network of reciprocal social rules while he evades some, most or all of them (and without being seen by others to evade them too). Similarly, the Bad Man can regret the changes wrought to criminal procedures as they apply to all others, while welcoming them in his own case.

That, however, may be of trifling concern to the Bad Man. From his vantage the significant downside of a bill of rights has to do with the uncertainty it generates as to the meaning and status of all other statutes. Will the US or Canadian-style constitutionalized bill of rights be used to strike down statute X or Y? Will the UK or New Zealand-style statutory bill of rights be used to rewrite or redraft statute A or B? Uncertainty here will make more difficult and risky the amoral calculations of the Bad Man.

And here is an irony. H.L.A. Hart in *The Concept of Law* observed that all legal systems will have to strike a balance between certainty in the application of laws and flexibility at their point-of-application. With a bill of rights that balance shifts in favour of greater flexibility at the point-of-application at the expense of certainty. And the irony in that is that the Bad Man – the person motivated only by law not by any moral concerns – will have as much cause to regret that shift as anyone. In some respects the Bad Man will have more cause than anyone else. Unlike all others, he acts only based on his legal position and so the Bad Man ought to place an extremely high premium on knowing exactly where he stands.

If we strip away the veil here, and treat the Bad Man's Vantage as largely corresponding with that of the office lawyer, we will see the same tension. On the one hand, the office lawyer will support the bill of rights in so far as it aids her to defend her client against these criminal charges. On the other hand, the office lawyer will disapprove of its uncertainty-enhancing effects when it comes to advising clients before they act – and not just as regards the criminal law but equally administrative law, tort law, commercial law, constitutional law and more. The big difference will be that the Lawyer's Vantage does not align perfectly with the Bad Man's; as I noted in the Introduction to this book there is no 1:1 correlation. And where the two vantages diverge – which amounts to that space where the Lawyer's own morality *and* her own self-interest come into play – a bill of rights will look even more attractive. Her professional self-interest will almost always be furthered by the adoption of a bill of rights. Meanwhile her political and moral outlook is just as likely as the Law Professor's to trust judges more than politicians, to see law in terms of adjudicating tough cases, and to prefer transmogrifying political line-drawing disputes into legal, or pseudo-legal, ones.

The Legislator

Why might the Legislator be favourably disposed towards a bill of rights? After all, the advent of one will result in fewer social line-drawing powers for the elected legislature and more for the unelected judiciary. Only up in the Olympian heights of amorphous and indeterminate moral abstractions – the enunciating of a right, say, to freedom of speech or against unreasonable searches and seizures or to equal protection of the laws or to freedom of religion – will the morality of the Legislator (or maker or amender of the Constitution) prevail. When society's moral disagreements and moral dissensus can no longer be finessed by such abstractions, and a specific line needs to be drawn down in the quagmire of detailing acceptable campaign finance rules or police practices or what religious practices will and will not be tolerated, the default assumption will be that under a bill of rights it is the judges' morality (in the sense of how best to interpret the instrument, which will for some judges encompass the issue of what is its best moral understanding) that will prevail. From the Legislator's Vantage, why might that be attractive?

One possibility is that the Legislator, on a few morally charged issues, might want to insulate himself against the voters, and perhaps even against himself. In some situations he might trust the unelected judges with life tenure more than he trusts himself – or assuming that the Legislator would not forsake what he felt was the morally correct course of action but calculates that the voters would abandon him for that at the next election, then he trusts the judges more than the voters. A bill of rights, on that reckoning, could be supported by the Legislator as a form of pre-emptively tying himself to the mast, Ulysses-like, against the occasional Siren-song blandishments that might arise.

In a jurisdiction debating whether to adopt or enact a bill of rights, this possibility is not far fetched. That said, it will probably be a minority viewpoint amongst most Legislators, most of the time. Concomitantly, some other Legislators will be moral realists or moral objectivists whose thinking follows that traced out above as regards Law Professors. Either these Legislators will fail to realize that a bill of rights is not self-interpreting and self-executing and hence not automatically able to produce the morally right answers, though few could for long be under this illusion, or they will calculate that the unelected judges will have a better hit rate when it comes to delivering the morally right outcomes than would the legislature of which they are a part.

Again, though, I suspect that most Legislators, most of the time, will be against adopting or enacting a bill of rights before one happens already to be in place. That sort of empirical claim is wholly consistent with the evident fact that the last half century has seen virtually all Benevolent Legal Systems (Australia notwithstanding) introduce some version or other of a bill of rights. Legislatures, and so the majority of legislators, have at some point in time either enacted a statutory bill of rights or, by voting in favour, been part of the amending process that led to incorporating one into the Constitution. (And one cannot help but wonder about the causal relevance of the fact that Australia's constitutional amendment process cannot bypass the voters, that change requires the approval of the people in a referendum rather than simply of national and state legislators.)

Sufficient support for a bill of rights to be introduced needs only to be found once. These instruments are virtually impossible, as a matter of empirical fact, ever to repeal or amend away once incorporated into the Constitution or enacted as a statute. Indeed, within the realm of Benevolent Legal Systems I do not think there is a single instance of this ever happening. In that sense, once a jurisdiction has a bill of rights, the Legislator supports it, or at least is unwilling to take the steps needed to try to remove it. Moreover, once in place, the bill of rights can come in handy. From the Legislator's Vantage it can allow him to duck difficult and unpopular issues. So the Legislator can vote for a flag-burning criminal law knowing full well that the judges will almost certainly interpret the bill of rights to strike down or re-write such a law. The Legislator can do this even were it the case that without a bill of rights he would vote against such a law.

This sort of legislative abdication of making difficult moral decisions comes with any instrument that takes final responsibility (in theory or in practice) for such decisions away from the people and their elected representatives. Of the entire set of legislative decisions made with a bill of rights in place, this is the subset of those decisions that would not have been made had there not been a bill of rights. No one can know for certain how large this subset is, but it would be remarkable to suppose it is an empty one. It would be almost as remarkable to imagine that such inevitable abdications did not give rise to any bad long-term consequences related to the weakening of an involved and active citizenry living in a participatory democracy.

We can finish this section with a short digression. It relates to the requirement in statutory bills of rights, and sometimes in entrenched versions in Westminster systems, for the person introducing a Bill into the legislature (or her proxy) to make a statement as to whether the Bill is, or is not, compatible with the bill of rights. From the Legislator's Vantage this appears at first sight to involve at least some members of the legislative (and most times also the executive) branch in thinking about the range, scope and limits of the bill of rights and in debating them all. If that first impression were correct, this sort of provision would be attractive from the Legislator's Vantage. However, the attractions of such statements of compatibility provisions from the Legislator's Vantage will vary directly with the extent to which this first impression is borne out by experience. Hence, the more it is the actual legislators themselves who debate, ponder, reflect on and ultimately decide based on their own opinions whether the Bill is compatible with the bill of rights, the more such provisions will appear attractive to the Legislator.

Conversely, the more it is that those introducing Bills into the legislature have in-house civil servant lawyers who scour the law reports to determine what judges in the jurisdiction are likely to think – and if it is a new point for this jurisdiction, then what overseas judges are likely to think, so that in reality the legislators themselves do very little thinking on their own about the desirable reach of and limits on the enumerated rights – then the less such provisions hold much appeal from the Legislator's Vantage. My view is that the evidence to date from Benevolent Legal Systems with these types of provisions points fairly convincingly this latter, unappealing-to-legislators way.

The Concerned Citizen

As bills of rights increase the scope for moral input at the point-of-application (namely by the unelected judges), then for all the reasons given in the second section of Chapter 2 above, one might expect these instruments to appear least attractive from the Concerned Citizen's Vantage. From that vantage the consequentialist benefits of democratic decision making are far more likely to be apparent than from the Judge's Vantage or Law Professor's or Lawyer's.

Just as clear from the Concerned Citizen's Vantage is that democratic decision making procedures and institutions will make it more difficult to portray as wicked or dumb those who disagree with you on such fundamental social issues as capital punishment, same-sex marriage, abortion and euthanasia than would be the case were a bill of rights in place with judges settling these and a host of other line-drawing disputes. The machinery of legislative decision making is not only significantly more prone to compromise than is judicial decision making, with more capacity to weigh the wider social effects of these decisions and to consider a wider array of relevant evidence: it is also more legitimate. Or rather, legislative decision making is comparatively more legitimate, provided that you start from the premise that all citizens ought to be given a more-or-less equal say in deciding society's important issues, especially the highly controversial ones evoking the most disagreement and dissensus. And that premise, in turn, will be most widely supported from the Concerned Citizen's Vantage.

Another way to make the same claim is to say that process – how decisions are to be made – will be given more weight from the Concerned Citizen's Vantage than from almost any other. In balancing *1)* trying to reach the best possible decision and *2)* trying to use the most democratically legitimate process to make decisions, it will be from the Concerned Citizen's Vantage that *2)* is most heavily weighted against *1)*. Again, as I argued in more detail in the second section of Chapter 2 above, there are benefits or good consequences or republican-values pay-offs flowing from *2)*.

That means that if a particular Concerned Citizen believes that the social line-drawing decisions made by the judges under a bill of rights reach preferable or more optimal or better outcomes more often than they would have been reached without a bill of rights in place – that judges have a higher hit rate on at least some rights-related issues than elected legislators – that Concerned Citizen might still favour democratic decision making without a bill of rights. It would depend on how much better or more optimal the hit rate of the unelected judges was. If there were not much in it – perhaps the judges get around to allowing abortion or same-sex marriage a decade earlier than the legislature – then this Concerned Citizen would say the long-term benefits associated with *2)* more than counter-balance the slightly better hit rate that a bill of rights regime produces (from his perspective) as regards *1)*. Only a significantly better set of decisions over a sustained period of time would push this Concerned Citizen into the pro-bill of rights camp.

A first analogy here might be to making a decision as to when your 14-year-old son should study. You could decide or he could decide for himself. You would probably make a better decision, but the process of leaving him to decide for himself might look – to him – to be a better method of going about making this decision. The force of this analogy, however, might in part rest on the assumption that leaving your son to make this decision (and other similar ones) will have good long-term consequences for him *as far as these sorts of decisions are concerned*. Any short-term blunders he makes, by procrastinating and going to the movies when he should be preparing for the science exam, will be more than offset by the improvements to his decision making as he learns from his mistakes. In other words, on this analogy one opts to go with the decision making procedure that produces worse short-term results, but one opts this way solely because one calculates that this procedure will eventually result in an improved hit rate, one that may ultimately even be better than you could achieve (for him).

That would be equivalent to saying something along the lines of 'we ought to forswear a bill of rights, because even though the judges will produce slightly better decisions in the short term, we the voting public will learn from our mistakes and our hit rate on these controversial rights issues will eventually equal, if not surpass, that of the judges'. This is simply a long-term consequentialist argument being used to trump a short-term consequentialist argument. Where the decisions reached are not overwhelmingly better – do not have an overwhelmingly higher hit rate – when made by you (or by the judges), then go with a better decision making procedure (namely, let your son or the elected legislature decide) because that procedure will eventually lift the hit rate to one that equals or surpasses yours (and the judges').

The trouble with this first analogy, whereby the *2)* 'how' issue trumps the *1)* best-outcomes issue unless the disparity in competing hit rates is significant, is that it rests on the belief that eventually the decision making results without a bill of rights will equal or surpass those made with one. And that, I think, is an unnecessary constraint or limitation or assumption. I think a particular Concerned Citizen might justifiably opt for no bill of rights even where she believes the unelected judges using the bill of rights will have a marginally superior hit rate deciding some sorts of contentious rights issues into the foreseeable future.

So a second analogy might be to a sports team. Let us say it is a basketball team. And the issue that needs deciding is who will be the captain. Let us suppose, for the purposes of the analogy, that you as coach will be marginally better at deciding this than would the twelve players, voting amongst themselves. Your choice would outperform the choice the players made whenever the two choices differed, which of course would not be always and might well be fairly infrequently. Your choice of captain would show slightly better leadership skills and – everything else being equal – better skills related to helping the team win than would the choice for captain of the players themselves. There would not be much in it. But your choice, on average, over time, would be the better choice.

Even assuming or supposing all that, the better alternative might be to let the players choose their captain. And the reason for that is that everything else might not be equal. The 'how to choose' question can affect the performance of the players. They might play better for their sub-optimal captain simply because they had a hand in picking him. We can suppose that the players might never have quite as good a hit rate at choosing their captain as would you, the coach. So in terms of deciding that number *1)* best-outcomes issue, by supposition the process that lets the players vote will be slightly poorer on average than one whereby you, the coach, decide. And yet the good consequences in other areas relevant to the team, but not limited to this 'who should be captain?' question, will more than compensate for this marginally poorer performance in captain choosing. The team will simply play harder for their captain, even with his marginally poorer leadership skills, and that harder play will more than compensate for their captain's slightly poorer captaincy skills.

Applying this second analogy to whether or not to opt for a bill of rights, and considering it from the Concerned Citizen's Vantage, a particular Concerned Citizen might well argue that in her view judges slightly outperformed the legislature in reaching preferable or better or more optimal answers as regards at least some sorts of rights issues, but that the costs of this undemocratic (in the letting the numbers count sense) form of decision making were significant in areas not limited solely to these rights issues. Opting for a system that placed resolution of these particular questions in the hands of an unelected and democratically unaccountable judiciary had bad system-wide consequences; people started casting their votes on the basis of whom the respective parties or candidates were likely to nominate to sit on the top courts; people voted less frequently, at any rate those people who cared most about those rights issues that were now ultimately in the hands of the judges interpreting the bill of rights; people became more and more cynical about their elected representatives but perhaps (due to the differing levels of scrutiny and publicity applied to judges and legislators) without anything like the same cynicism as regards their judges; people channelled their political efforts into hard-to-win constitutional amendments to gainsay the judges, into attacking the judges themselves as well as the legitimacy of what the judges were doing, and into devising possible legislative end-runs around the judges' rulings. In short, the overall performance of, and commitment to, democratic self-government declined even while the yearly quota of debatable, contentious social policy line-drawing decisions falling under the aegis of the bill of rights were being marginally better resolved by the unelected judges.

In my opinion, any argument along those lines is plausible. I do not agree with those writers who think that the question of 'who produces the best outcomes, the judges interpreting a bill of rights to decide some set of rights issues or the elected legislature deciding them without a bill of rights' can be wholly insulated against, or uninfected by, or made independent of the 'which decision-making process is the more legitimate one with the better social consequences related to that type of decision-making' question.

Whether one agrees with that claim or not, there will certainly be Concerned Citizens who hold the more forceful view that, on the specific issue of who better decides rights issues of the sort falling under the aegis of a bill of rights, it is the elected legislature. When it comes to society's difficult, contentious, highly disputed moral line-drawing exercises of the sort bills of rights leave the judges to decide, they will say that better outcomes would be generated *as regards resolving these issues themselves* by letting the numbers count. The legislature will outperform the judges; it will have a better hit rate. So for these Concerned Citizens opposition to a bill of rights will be more straightforward. Not only on considerations related to *2)* – to what decision-making procedure is most legitimate and preferable – but on those related to *1)* as well – to who better decides rights questions – will the legislature outscore the judiciary from these Concerned Citizens' Vantages.

In addition, the Concerned Citizen's Vantage is perhaps the best one from which to grasp the point made in the third section of Chapter 2 above. That point was that if one's support for a bill of rights rests on the benefits and protections that such an instrument is thought to provide in extreme situations – as a guarantor or safety check against possible actions by the elected branches that would be seen, in calmer times, as heavy handed and even morally odious – then it needs to be understood that the bill of rights will also have effects when times are not extreme. Where judges can use a bill of rights to infuse their particularized moral views into the determination of whether to strike down a statute or to re-write it, they can also do so when times are good and the statute under consideration was enacted in regular circumstances not overshadowed by fear of terrorists or looming war or moral panic, where reasonable, regular citizens simply disagreed about where to draw debatable, contentious social-policy lines.

The Concerned Citizen, in other words, may well be the one most likely to conclude that a bill of rights ought to be chosen or forsworn *not* on the basis of the extreme situation. For him, the greater risk is not of the elected branches' grossly over-reacting but of the unelected judges' becoming overly powerful under a bill of rights in the normal, non-extreme situations. It is easier for this Concerned Citizen's Vantage to focus on these many regular situations than it would be for the Judge's, Lawyer's, Law Professor's, Sanctimonious Man's or any other participant's vantage in the system. For all of them it will be more tempting than for the Concerned Citizen's to focus on the extreme situation, to ignore or heavily discount the effects of bills of rights in ordinary, day-to-day situations, to forget just how difficult and unlikely it will be for judges actually to stand up to the elected branches in those rare instances when times really are bleak, and to overlook the possibility that even without a bill of rights some few judges in these extreme situations might just lie, cheat and instil their own moral views into law anyway.

Hence that is another reason for thinking a bill of rights is likely to appear least attractive from the Concerned Citizen's Vantage. And of course when the law is highly moralized, as is more likely with a bill of rights than without, then it is simply harder to know what the law requires of one. It is not only the Bad Man who wants to know what is required of him by the law. The Concerned Citizen does too.

Of course not all Concerned Citizens will oppose bills of rights. As with the Law Professor above, some will be moral realists or moral objectivists who think judges' moral views more closely align with the mind-independently right answers (and presumably with their own moral views) than do those of legislators – though my hunch is that thinking highly of judges' moral perspicacity in this way is probably more widespread amongst Law Professors and Lawyers than it is amongst Concerned Citizens.

Some other Concerned Citizens will support bills of rights because they think flexibility at the point-of-application is generally of more importance than certainty of outcome. Others will do so because for them locking in certain entitlements or protections counts for more than democratic decision making. (These others will presumably take a moderately optimistic view of the chances of sufficient numbers of judges adopting originalist interpretive approaches to the bill of rights as opposed to 'living document' or 'keeping pace with civilization' approaches.) Others still will make a raw, self-interested calculation that the judges interpreting a bill of rights are more likely to decide their way – to satisfy more of their first-order moral and political preferences on issues including affirmative action, abortion, acceptable police and criminal procedures, same-sex marriage, limits on speech and more – than would the elected legislators. And others again will be proponents of bills of rights because their focus stays up in the Olympian heights of moral abstractions and rarely travels down to the point where these instruments stop finessing disagreement and no longer appear to be self-enforcing and self-interpreting.

All these, and more, are possible grounds for supporting a bill of rights from the vantage of the Concerned Citizen. Yet, conceding them all, it still remains the case that a bill of rights will appear least attractive from the Concerned Citizen's Vantage. It is from that vantage that the increased moral input afforded to judges by bills of rights is seen to be the most unpalatable, the most productive of bad long-term consequences, and the most illegitimate in procedural decision-making terms.

The Judge

I argued in Chapter 2 that the consequences of minimizing moral input by judges at the point-of-application will generally look worst from the Judge's Vantage. Put in terms of whether or not to opt for a bill of rights, the case *against* one of these instruments will generally appear least persuasive when considered from the Judge's Vantage.

As the operator of the bill of rights – the one who will decide on a case-by-case basis what the appropriate scope of the enumerated rights will be, how competing rights will be balanced against one another, what limits on them will be held reasonable, when non-rights-based concerns will be ruled of sufficient importance to trump the enumerated rights, whether the practical reach of the rights will be allowed to expand over time, and more – it is from this vantage that its attractions can be expected to be most keenly felt. From the Judge's Vantage, unlike from any other, it is possible to use a bill of rights to blend one's own moral judgments or evaluations into the authoritative determination of what counts as valid law. In such a unique, and privileged, position it would be quite surprising if bills of rights were not more favourably viewed (by and large, and allowing for the inevitable judicial outlier, sceptic and contrarian every once in a while) from the Judge's Vantage than from any other.

If you have to trust someone's moral instincts and judgments in extreme situations or in highly contentious disputes, it is easiest to trust your own. If an instrument offers more than otherwise scope to its point-of-application interpreters to infuse their own moral views into law and so on occasion to decide morally controversially social issues, then that instrument will generally be most readily defended and appear most attractive from that same point-of-application vantage.

If there can be too much moral input into law by unelected judges, that realization will be least apparent to the judges themselves.

For these reasons, together with those given in the second section of Chapter 2, I think it safe to assert, as a generalization, that bills of rights will appear most attractive from the Judge's Vantage. Conversely, the consequential benefits of going some way towards puncturing puffed-up judicial moral windbags – by not putting in place a bill of rights – will be least apparent from the Judge's Vantage.

Accordingly, the more one is asked (implicitly or explicitly) to situate himself in the Judge's shoes and adopt the Judge's Vantage, the more support we can expect there to be for a bill of rights. This will be true despite the reality that very few Concerned Citizens, and for that matter few Lawyers or Law Professors, ever get to adopt this judicial vantage in fact and become real-life judges themselves, to say nothing of their chances of becoming judges on the highest court in the jurisdiction.

Nor is the goal of limiting judicial power a goal that is likely to be at the forefront of the Judge's concerns. As a matter of empirical fact, few of today's judges in Benevolent Legal Systems are going to be Benthamites; few of them will think it important to minimize judges' last-word moral input, though on occasion those who do not may nevertheless think it expedient to make a gesture in this direction. And few of them will dwell over-much on when, how frequently, and why Concerned Citizens' moral judgments and evaluations differ from theirs, yet again making it easier to support a bill of rights from the Judge's Vantage.

The Visiting Martian

The Visiting Martian, asked for his observations on the effects of a bill of rights in a Benevolent Legal System, might well begin by pointing out how these instruments are likely to be interpreted. Outside of the United States it is almost certain to be the case that the bill of rights will be treated by the interpreting judges as a 'living document' or on the basis of a similar sort of metaphor that suggests that the meaning of the enumerated rights can shift, alter, update and expand to keep pace with changing social mores or values. Of course the Visiting Martian would go on to point out that any such metaphor tends to obscure the fact that it is the unelected judges who will be changing, updating and expanding the meaning of the bill of rights. The document, be it considered living or dead, cannot interpret itself. And as a matter of observable fact the judges interpreting the bill of rights – not just if it be an entrenched, constitutionalized one but even if it be a statutory version – will adopt an approach that is less constrained by the intentions of those who framed it (or, alternatively, by the understandings of those alive when it was framed) than would be the case with regular statutes.

In fact, even in the United States this sort of 'living document' approach to interpreting the bill of rights is likely to prevail, though our Visiting Martian will concede that in that jurisdiction the matter is not yet settled and continues to be debated by the highest judges. As a corollary to this observation of how bills of rights at present will be interpreted, and putting the United States to one side for the moment, the Visiting Martian would go on to say that there is little, if any, empirical basis for thinking the bill of rights will be interpreted as locking in a floor-level set of protections above which legislative sovereignty and democratic decision making will decide society's contested moral issues (along the lines sketched out in the third section of the last chapter). Hence those who support a bill of rights on this locking-things-in basis, with its concomitant prospect of a moderately constrained judiciary, are most likely to be found in the United States.

Our Visiting Martian might here observe a certain irony. The irony is that interpretation by appeal to some version or other of originalism – to intentions and/or understandings at the time of adoption – is more likely when the judges are deciding division of powers disputes in federal systems than when those same judges (in the same Benevolent Legal Systems) are deciding bills of rights disputes. To decide which level of government has which powers the judges will look to the original intentions of the framers or understandings of the citizens then alive more often – noticeably more often – than when those same judges are deciding the meaning, reach and limits of the rights in the bill of rights.

The Visiting Martian's point has to do with how interpreting bills of rights – more than any other sort of interpretation – appears to involve a severing of *1)* the attributing of meaning from *2)* the search for the intentions of those who framed and adopted the words now being given a meaning by the judges. This severing, or comparatively greater severing, of meaning from intentions when it comes to bills of rights interpretation can be contrasted to what happens with regular statutory interpretation.

When courts are asked to interpret the meaning of some regular statutory provision, their starting point is the words that have been used by the legislature. That much, at least, is uncontroversial. Of course there is then a variety of ways those statutory words can be understood. For instance, they might be treated literally, with appeal to the dictionary when uncertainty arises. Or they might be given their plain or ordinary meaning in society, with recourse to extrinsic aids to construction (such as the legislative record and materials) *precluded* except in cases of ambiguity or of absurdity. Or they might be understood broadly and liberally against the specific background criterion of the statute's governing purpose. This purposive approach to interpretation, in turn, may or may not also include wide-open access to the legislative history of the enactment under consideration.

In all of these possible approaches to statutory interpretation there is an implicit acceptance that the legislature's authority to pass the statute under consideration is legitimate. (Leave to one side instances of statutes' potentially being ruled unconstitutional and illegitimate.) That assumed or presupposed or accepted legitimacy is the reason the judges are interpreting the statute and not the proclamations of a king or the commands of a dictator or the orders of an oligarchy (or, indeed, the provisions of a constitution). The legislature is taken to be the legitimate source of this type of law.

It is a short step from accepting that legitimacy of the legislature to interpreting its enactments with regard to the enactors' intentions. All the various approaches to statutory interpretation mooted above can, with different degrees of emphasis, be understood as paying regard to the enactors' intentions. Consider again my examples, though in the opposite order.

To start, a purposive approach to regular statutory interpretation that permits, even encourages, the judge to consult the legislative history of the enactment being interpreted clearly places great weight on the enactors' intentions. Why else would one care about the speeches and comments of legislators?

The same is true, despite initial impressions, of a purposive approach that is combined with quite restricted access to the legislative history. After all, it is people that have purposes, not words on paper. To seek the purpose of a regular statutory provision is, directly or indirectly, to attribute an intention and purpose to its drafters, sponsors and enactors. The fact that access to the legislative history is restricted, at the same time as the purpose of the statutory provision is sought, is best understood in pragmatic terms. Firstly, it is generally the case that the normal, plain meaning of words coincides with their intended meaning. Secondly, it is time-consuming and often wasteful to allow lawyers and judges to look behind the normal, plain meaning of the statutory words. Thirdly, and relatedly, there are good civic grounds (from the point of view of regular citizens reading statutes and expecting to comprehend them and what they lay down) for usually interpreting statutes at face value, without forcing readers to have to refer to hard-to-obtain records of legislative debates. Fourthly, there is the further utilitarian advantage that restricting access to the legislative history encourages the legislature to pass statutes that are clearer and better drafted, while concomitantly eliminating most of the worth of self-serving speeches about the enactment's purpose during the law-making process. In other words, there is a pragmatic case for restricting wide-open access to a statute's legislative history. This is true *even though* one is (sincerely) attempting to give the statutory provision the meaning most in accord with the statute's overall purpose. Bluntly put, some bargains to discover that purpose come at too high a price and are not worth making. Nevertheless, enactors' intentions still remain central to this approach to statutory interpretation.

On its face, by contrast, the plain or ordinary meaning approach to statutory interpretation – where the judge gives the words in the statute their standard meaning in the community – seems to pay scant, if any, attention to the enactors' intentions (either directly, or indirectly by first concerning itself with the statute's governing purpose). *Prima facie*, what matters on this approach is the likely response of the reader to the particular statutory provision, *not* the intentions of its enactors.

Yet the first-glance impression is not as conclusive as it seems. For one thing, as I mentioned above, the ordinary, standard meaning of words in the community often (arguably overwhelmingly) coincides with their intended meaning. It would be odd indeed for legislators regularly to use words intending them to be understood in an abnormal, unusual way. Another indication that enactors' intentions count for something even here is that the plain meaning approach is often accompanied by an exception – where the language used is ambiguous, according to its standard meaning, recourse is allowed to extrinsic aids to construction, including legislative materials.

So enactors' intentions count when interpreting regular statutes even under the plain meaning approach. True, those intentions do not count for quite as much, or anyway as directly and immediately, as they do under a purposive approach. Still, any attempt to justify the adoption of a plain meaning approach to interpreting regular statutes would probably have to do so in terms related to the upholding of enactors' intentions. It would start by claiming that the most important aspect of statutory interpretation is applying the statute as written, *not* re-making it to meet its underlying purpose or to mesh with the enactors' intentions. In those (probably quite few) instances where there is divergence (or evidence of divergence) between the clear, ordinary meaning of the regular statute's words and what it is likely the enactors intended, applying the former, *not* the latter, actually is the best way to reinforce the dominance of the legislature and so in the long run give most weight to enactors' interactions.

In other words, the claim on behalf of a plain meaning approach is that, in the mid to long term, legislative pre-eminence is best protected by according statutory words their plain and ordinary meaning. The claim seems counter-intuitive because it is easy to suppose that the best way to ensure the legislature's dominance (and the judiciary's deference) is to have statutes interpreted in the light of the enactors' intentions. But this supposition is far from sure. For one thing, a vigorous and rigorous judicial policy of always, or nearly always, according statutory words their plain and ordinary meaning (when these are relatively clear) will quite quickly encourage the legislature to pass statutes in which its intentions are expressed in clear words having their plain, ordinary meaning. This will only be true over time, however. There will be specific cases that arise in which the legislators' intentions *can* be inferred from extrinsic aids with a very high degree of likelihood. Moreover, that intention will very occasionally be distinct and different from what the words actually used in the statute – given their plain, ordinary meaning – happen to indicate. Yet even allowing for that, the best way to ensure legislative pre-eminence may be by means of the plain or ordinary meaning approach. This is because a rule that demands that the judges apply the plain, ordinary words when they are clear (and their application not patently absurd) may end up being a stronger constraint on judicial room to manoeuvre or discretion than would be one telling them to search for enactors' intentions.

So even the plain meaning approach to interpreting regular statutes is probably most convincingly justified or defended in terms of its long-term effects in upholding enactors' intentions. And if that is correct then all approaches to interpreting regular statutes look to pay a fair degree of heed to the enactors' intentions.

The Visiting Martian's point about interpreting bills of rights is not just that a plain meaning approach to them, as compared to regular statutes, would far less frequently result in clear outcomes, though he could well assert that too (while belabouring the point and noting the significant amounts of discretion such a plain meaning approach to vague, amorphous instruments like bills of rights in effect hands to the judges). Instead, his point is that, in contrast to regular statutes – where the approach to interpretation can be linked quite strongly in either a short-term or a long-term way to a search for intentions – the way bills of rights are generally interpreted makes the connection to intentions far more tenuous. Any version of progressivist interpretation or living document interpretation will dilute the connection to the intentions of the framers to little more than a version of 'they wanted us, the judges, to use or apply our own moral judgments and evaluations. They wanted us to update, alter and expand the meaning to be given to the enumerated rights.'

The Visiting Martian will be adamant that when judges in Benevolent Legal Systems are asked to interpret their bill of rights, those judges have more leeway, more scope to rely on their own moral intuitions, than they do in interpreting the vast preponderance of other regular statutes (and even than they do in interpreting division of powers federalism disputes, though here it is a much closer call). This is true whether their bill of rights is a constitutionalized or statutory model.

Our Visiting Martian might make three other main observations. First off, he might note that tyranny is tyranny and that it is not at all clear that a purported 'tyranny of the majority' is a more awful or frightening prospect than a purported 'tyranny of the minority'. In fact, from the Visiting Martian's Vantage the historical evidence would conclusively point the other way. Tyrannies of the minority are, on average, vastly worse in terms of slaughtering citizens, crushing civil liberties, exhibiting intolerant tendencies, impoverishing the country, or in just about any other terms or criteria one cares to name.

That being the case, any instrument designed specifically to forestall the likelihood of a tyranny of the majority – and bills of rights are not uncommonly defended on just this general sort of ground – ought also to be measured in terms of its effects on the prospects of bringing about a tyranny of the minority. Does the bill of rights make less likely a tyranny of the majority by an amount greater than its proclivity for making more likely a tyranny of the minority? And ought we to weigh the two admittedly distant threats equally, or ought the tyranny of the minority to be seen as the one that is likely to bring with it worse consequences for virtually everyone, and so be the one against which greater protections are needed?

Our Visiting Martian's second observation would relate to one effect of a bill of rights on some – not all, but some – judges. And that effect, to put it in an unkindly way, is to turn the Judge into the Sanctimonious Man.

In Chapter 3 we considered what might result from the appointment to the highest court of someone who thought it desirable to keep to a minimum moral input at the point-of-application. Even our bill of rights sceptic appointee might well find his views changing as far as the desirability of there being scope to infuse *his* own moral views into law, at least on occasion. More to the point here, we saw that such doubters about the desirability of more than minimal moral input by the judges would be unlikely often to be appointed to the highest court.

The preponderance of appointees to the highest court would be supporters of bills of rights and supporters of a fair degree of moral input at the point-of-application, or rather of there being legitimate scope for such moral input, should the judges think it appropriate. Amongst this sort of cohort of likely judicial appointees our Visiting Martian would observe that a certain sub-set of them would, over time, draw ever less of a distinction between their own moral views and the moral views that in some external (i.e., mind-independent, moral realist) or inter-subjective (i.e., utilitarian, consequentialist) sense really are best. They would lose too much modesty. They would begin to resemble, in their professional capacity, the Sanctimonious Man. And some of this our Visiting Martian would put down to the bill of rights.

Nor would the Visiting Martian find it difficult to provide instances of this. Hence, by way of example, he might point to Canada and decisions by the top judges there related to prisoner voting entitlements.[1] These cases would be singled out by the Visiting Martian *not* because the majority of the Supreme Court of Canada judges twice overruled the elected federal parliament there on whether convicted and incarcerated prisoners must in all cases be allowed to vote, the latter time after nation-wide Select Committee hearings had been undertaken and a milder, compromise regime put in place. From the Visiting Martian's Vantage this sort of judicial last word is the intended and expected effect of adopting a bill of rights. No, these cases would be singled out because of several comments by the Chief Justice of Canada in the latter *Sauve* decision. In that second case, writing the 5–4 majority decision, and responding to the dissenting judgment's point that plenty of Benevolent Legal Systems – including Australia, the United Kingdom, the United States, New Zealand and more – put limits on prisoner voting entitlements, the Chief Justice referred obliquely to these countries where the rule was different from the one she thought morally preferable as 'self-proclaimed democracies'.[2]

From the Visiting Martian's Vantage that sort of staggering self-assuredness, that sort of forthright self-righteousness, looks much the same as what one would expect to hear from the Sanctimonious Man. Certainly the Visiting Martian would not expect any sort of similar judgment to be passed openly, and in writing, by the democratically elected leader of a Benevolent Legal System.

The Visiting Martian might even go on, in similar vein and again to illustrate this same potential effect of a bill of rights, and quote this same Chief Justice's views in

---

1   See *Sauve* v. *Canada (Attorney General)* [1993] 2 SCR 438 and *Sauve* v. *Canada (Chief Electoral Officer)* [2002] 3 SCR 519.

2   *Sauve* v. *Canada (Chief Electoral Officer)* [2002] 3 SCR 519, at para. [41], referring to the countries discussed in Justice Gonthier's dissent in paras [125], [130] and [131].

this same case about the notion of a bill of rights giving rise to some sort of dialogue between the elected and unelected branches of government:

> Finally, the fact that the challenged denial of the right to vote followed judicial rejection of an even more comprehensive denial, does not mean that the Court should defer to Parliament as part of a 'dialogue'. Parliament must ensure that whatever law it passes, at whatever stage of the process, conforms to the Constitution. The healthy and important promotion of a dialogue between legislature and the courts should not be debased to a rule of 'if at first you don't succeed, try, try, again'.[3]

From the Visiting Martian's Vantage there is more than a trace of sanctimoniousness in this, and in plenty of other judicial decisions under bills of rights throughout the Benevolent Legal System world.

The last main observation our Visiting Martian might make as regards bills of rights is more of a question, and one he cannot answer in any convincing way. The question he might ask is this: 'Who has more incentive to comply with the vague and amorphous values embodied in a bill of rights, the unelected judges or the elected legislators?' The difficulty is that smart, reasonable, well-intentioned people will disagree about the scope of the enumerated rights, their inter-relationship, what limits on them are reasonable, and all the other issues that a bill of rights raises. From the Visiting Martian's Vantage, disagreement and dissensus over how to resolve the sort of moral issues that a bill of rights makes legal, and puts into the hands of the judges, is inevitable. However much a bill of rights might be framed in terms that attempt to finesse disagreement, its application in the cases that day-after-day come before the highest courts will be highly contentious. The disagreement will be as much about the right moral answer as it is about the right legal answer.

That means that our Visiting Martian's question, at least in part, collapses into the query 'Who has more incentive to be moral?' Benthamite incentives framed in terms of accountability to voters might point one way. Independence from the need to win re-election might point the other. But neither is determinative. What first needs answering is which potential outcomes are, in fact, the moral ones. And from the Visiting Martian's Vantage that cannot be answered. Indeed it cannot even be determined from that vantage if there are any such mind-independent moral answers.

Bills of Rights in Non-Benevolent Legal Systems

This last section can be short, and it can be short for obvious reasons. The former Soviet Union had a bill of rights, one as emotively stirring as any. It did nothing. Unless the point-of-application judges have real decision making powers, the bill of rights will have no effects other than as politically desirable window dressing.

---

3   *Ibid.*, para. [17].

In Wicked Legal Systems, where the judges do not even have the power to interpret the law as written – to give it its plain meaning – there will be no power for judges to infuse their moral views into law by using the bill of rights. At any rate, any effects of a bill of rights in such a legal system will be vanishingly slight.

In Theocratic Legal Systems things are more complicated. If the enumerated rights in any bill of rights in one of these jurisdictions can be aligned with entitlements or guarantees thought (by many, or at least by many clerics) to issue from God himself, then the bill of rights will not be ignored. On the other hand, what will be motivating or causing the point-of-application judges' decisions will ultimately be the set of divine commands or guidelines believed to exist, not the bill of rights itself. To the extent of any overlap, though, the bill of rights might appear to be determinative (as a shorthand proxy, drafted by limited biological creatures, of God's essentially unfathomable edicts). Otherwise it will fall into the window-dressing category as well.

Bills of rights in So-So Legal Systems will have effectiveness to the extent that judges in that jurisdiction have real decision making independence from the Party, leader, government, monarch, what have you. Any cataloguing exercise for one of these systems would find that many answers to questions about the benevolence of that jurisdiction's political and legal system fall into the penumbra of doubt. There are factors pointing towards benevolence, and others pointing away from it. That is why it has been classified as a So-So Legal System. In much the same way, any bills of rights in such So-So Legal Systems will work partly as those in Benevolent Legal System's work, and partly they will just be window dressing.

Finally, and this is something of a digression, there is what we can call the 'Hong Kong possibility'. This is the jurisdiction with an independent judiciary, a desirable range of civil liberties, even a functioning and effective bill of rights, but no democracy. The striking thing about this possibility is how exceptionally rare it is. The relationship between *a)* jurisdictions with liberal, tolerant rights protections (whether with, or even without, a bill of rights) and *b)* jurisdictions with real 'letting the numbers count' democratic decision making is that *a)* virtually always comes with *b)* (and certainly does so more than *a)* comes without *b)*). To put it more bluntly, only democracies will protect rights (save for the Hong Kong exception), though any particular democracy may not do so. To put it differently again, *a)* implies *b)* but *b)* does not always imply *a)*. In fact our Visiting Martian would be hard pressed to name a second example of the 'Hong Kong possibility', itself a creature of historical circumstances unlikely to be mimicked any time soon.

A brief way to précis this last section is to say that bills of rights are really only of interest, and concern, in Benevolent Legal Systems. The controversies they engender about over-powerful judges and the counter-majoritarian difficulty only arise in Benevolent Legal Systems.

Concerned Citizens in non-Benevolent Legal Systems have more pressing concerns.

Chapter 7
Concluding Remarks and Dialogue

In the almost half century since H.L.A. Hart wrote *The Concept of Law* much thinking and writing about law – though by no means all, as some of his more conceptual followers make clear – has been done (implicitly or explicitly) from the Judge's Vantage. Too much perhaps.

Of course this complaint is not a new one. Or even one that post-dates Hart. O.W. Holmes voiced the same grievance over a hundred years ago in his well-known 'The Path of the Law'. We need, he said, to look at law less from the Judge's Vantage and more from the Lawyer's Vantage. Certainly we need to do this when it comes to legal education, and the unrelenting diet of top appeal court cases students are invariably fed in all but a legal aid-type course here or (possibly) a statutory interpretation course there.

William Twining, and perhaps Bentham himself, would agree that legal education needs to move away from its overwhelming judge-centred focus. However, they might suggest that it is more of the Legislator's Vantage that is needed. Perhaps Jeremy Waldron would agree, not least in the hope that such a shift in focus might produce more lawyers who are comparatively more sympathetic to legislators vis-à-vis judges, and to the dignity of legislation, than at present. It might, as an empirical matter, lessen undue deference to the judiciary.

Yet those calls for a shift in focus in legal education notwithstanding, a century and more on from Holmes, and the gravamen remains with us today. Nor is it one that relates only to legal education. As I noted to start this final chapter, much thinking and writing about law occurs from the explicit or implicit perspective of the judge.

Take any attempt to build a theory of law out of a theory of adjudication – or out of a theory of how best to interpret, which may be narrower. Any plausible effort along those lines will end up adopting the Judge's Vantage much, if not all, of the time. Moreover, it will almost certainly pre-suppose that the law under consideration is the law of a Benevolent Legal System. Asking the reader to understand law in terms of how best to decide hard or difficult or penumbral cases is asking the reader to think of himself or herself as a top judge. And it is asking the reader to do so in a jurisdiction where such judges are independent and free to decide without fear or favour, which amounts to saying they are in a Benevolent Legal System. The attempt to transmogrify a theory of adjudication into a theory of law requires adjudication to be a defining feature – or at the very least an important part – of the legal system in question.

It strikes me as virtually impossible to assert, as an empirical matter, that this is the case in Wicked Legal Systems. It is more arguable in So-So Legal Systems, but only marginally so. Meanwhile in Theocratic Legal Systems adjudication is an important task, perhaps a central task. But I cannot see how, where the text is taken to be divinely inspired, the text itself can ever be questioned. Here, building up from a theory of adjudication will always hit a ceiling that prevents further progress towards an understanding of law without explicit recourse to God and to all the claims and metaphysics that brings with it.

As I said, building a theory of law out of a theory of adjudication is implicitly to assume that you are in a Benevolent Legal System. It is to focus on only a portion of today's legal systems, and a tiny or near-on insignificant portion in historical terms.

Yet even having restricted oneself to the sub-set of legal systems that might be classed as benevolent, there are problems with building a theory of law out of a theory of adjudication. And the gist of the problem relates to the contestability – and desirability – of adopting the Judge's Vantage in understanding law. The difficulty is to explain why that vantage is preferable or superior to that of the Concerned Citizen, or Legislator, or Visiting Martian, or even Bad Man.

One way to make it easier to justify adopting the Judge's Vantage, and doing so in a Benevolent Legal System, is to offer not a theory of law but a theory of the Anglo-Commonwealth common law. The common law, after all, is the label that nowadays stands for judge-made law. At core, this sort of law rests not on laid-down texts, but on a shared practice of decision making with social constraints on that decision making.

Not unrelatedly, Dworkin is at his most comparatively persuasive vis-à-vis Hart when just such a more circumscribed, give-us-a-theory-of-the-common-law-only, offering is advanced. Almost by default, attention turns to Benevolent Legal Systems. And justifying the adoption of the Judge's Vantage becomes markedly easier than when offering a wider and far more encompassing theory of law. Notice, as well, that any jurisdiction that opts to hand final say as to the meaning of an entrenched, justiciable bill of rights (or a statutory near equivalent) to the top judges will – as far as that bill of rights is concerned – produce something that looks not unlike a constitutional common law. Again, this theory of constitutionalized bill of rights interpreting should be (and is) more fertile ground for Dworkin's theories than Hart's. Put differently, and more broadly, the relative attractions and weaknesses of Hartian and Dworkian theories depend to a significant extent on the reader's preferred vantage from which to consider law.

That said, even where adjudication is a defining, or at least an important, feature of some Benevolent Legal System, there are still grounds for insisting on understanding and conceiving of the law of that legal system (in part at least) from vantages other than that of a top appeal court judge. In one sense this book has been an extended argument on why that is so.

In fact, even at the core of that most Dworkinian of issues – how to decide Hard Cases – the Concerned Citizen's Vantage, for example, produces markedly different conclusions from the Judge's. From the Concerned Citizen's Vantage there is little, if any, difference between *a)* the scenario in which the point-of-application interpreter decides a case retrospectively (in the sense that he or she has discretion because no rules, or principles, dictate an outcome) and *b)* the scenario in which the point-of-application interpreter decides a case based on rights the parties did not know existed. And this would be true even if Dworkin or someone else were able to convince you that from the Judge's Vantage scenario *a)* never arises. From the Concerned Citizen's Vantage, and indeed from the Legislator's, Bad Man's, and possibly all non-judicial vantages, scenario *b)* collapses into scenario *a)* in virtually all respects. The sole respect in which it may not is that scenario *b)* leaves some room to blame the parties (and their legal representatives) for their ignorance. Yet the blame in such instances would amount to blame or condemnation for not knowing how the majority of top judges will decide a case where no pre-existing rule clearly applies, where a variety of non-rule standards can be brought to bear in resolving the case but these standards point in different ways to produce competing outcomes, and where the Herculean best background fit that ultimately resolves the case will depend at least in part on the second-order moral and political evaluations, judgments and preferences that the point-of-application judge brings with him to the task. In other words, in most real-life disputed cases that reach the top courts no blame at all can be imputed to the parties for not knowing what rights the judges would say always existed, though no one else – including the 2, or 3, or 4 judges in dissent on the case – knew they existed.

This book, then, can be taken as a plea for more thinking about law to take place from vantages other than the judge's. The desirability of separating law and morality – the old-fashioned Benthamite concern with making law better, tied as it was to a hostility to natural law thinking – is one such area where the vantage adopted matters. From many vantages, even in a Benevolent Legal System, law can be bad even when it is explicitly and implicitly claiming to be good. In fact, this is the case from all vantages, even the judge's. It is just so much more obviously so from the non-Judge's Vantage.

For the Concerned Citizen, the fact that the legislature has passed some statute (with whatever implied claims as to the new law's moral goodness one takes to accompany that enactment) does not automatically or conclusively make it a morally good law. Likewise, the fact that the jurisdiction's top judges – or more accurately put, the fact that the majority of the jurisdiction's top judges – has decided a particular case in a particular way, thereby creating judge-made law (with whatever implied claims as to the moral goodness of that law one takes to accompany it) does not automatically make it a morally good law for the Concerned Citizen. He can separate this outcome, what the law now is, and morality. Even if some group of officials were explicitly to certify some decision or judgment or enactment as moral, that certification in itself does not make it so. It does not make it so in some conclusive sense, or in some mind-independent sense, or for those who disagree (and who do not think what is morally best is always and everywhere determined by that same group of officials).

As discussed in Chapters 1 and 2, the Concerned Citizen's Vantage is one that makes separating law and morality relatively easy. The same is true of the Visiting Martian's Vantage, perhaps to an even greater extent. Meanwhile the Bad Man's Vantage positively requires one to separate them; it makes abundantly clear that law and morality *can* be kept separate.

The same is not true of the Judge's Vantage. Yet even from the Judge's Vantage 'law as it is' *can be* kept separate from 'law as it ought to be'. Indeed a judge in the mould of Lon Fuller's fictional Justice Keen might even go so far as to dispute the holding in *Riggs* v. *Palmer*, arguing that the then existing law entitled the murdering grandson to recover under the murdered grandfather's will, however morally distasteful that result. Such a judge would think it not the job of the judiciary morally to remake the law on a case-by-case basis, with all the democratic illegitimacy and retrospective trappings that would carry with it. The legislature would do so soon enough after such egregious outcomes.

Yet even if many people might prefer their top judges leavened with a greater tendency 'to do the right thing' (by their own lights) than a Justice Keen, that institutional preference does not alter the fact that even from the Judge's Vantage law and morality *can* be kept separate.

It is from the Concerned Citizen's Vantage, however, that it is most obvious that they should be kept separate, that 'law as it is' should be kept distinct from 'law as it ought to be'. And as Chapters 1 and 2 detailed, the basis for this 'should' claim is wider than the one Hart provides in chapter nine of *The Concept of Law*.

The second main area discussed in this book where vantage really matters is bills of rights. These are instruments that explicitly set out to infuse a moral test into what will count as a valid law. They are not alone in doing this. Various statutes can be found that have provisions that make determinative tests such as 'the best interests of the child'. Nevertheless, it is only bills of rights that aim to make a list of vague, amorphous moral standards articulated in the language of rights determinative of whether an otherwise valid law ought to be valid; and if not, to empower the judge to strike it down (as in the United States and Canada) or to re-write it (using the reading down provision as in the United Kingdom and New Zealand). So bills of rights infuse a moral test, but they infuse one whose details are settled from the Judge's Vantage.

I said above that one way to read this book is as an extended argument on why it is often desirable to understand and conceive of law from vantages other than the judge's, even in a Benevolent Legal System. An alternative way to read this book is as an indirect commentary on bills of rights – on how the desirability of having one varies with the vantage adopted in assessing them and how, unsurprisingly, they are generally judged most desirable – even necessary – when the Judge's Vantage (and maybe, for the reasons given above, the Law Professor's Vantage) is taken up. The more you put yourself, implicitly or explicitly, in the shoes of the top appeal court judge deciding this or that contentious case, the more likely it is – in my view – that you will think it a good idea to adopt or retain a bill of rights.

US-style constitutionalized bills of rights create a body of common law, but with the notable difference that the elected legislature cannot gainsay the unelected judges. It is a common law-on-steroids strain of judge-made law. Analogies to tort law, say, or to other ordinary strains of the common law fail because the relative competencies and who has the last word – the judges or the legislators – differ.

Vantage matters, then, both on the question of whether law and morality should be kept separate and on the question of whether a bill of rights is desirable. It is the extent to which bills of rights explicitly set out to blend morality and moral evaluations into what counts as a valid law that links the two questions so closely together. Bills of rights, and for that matter much of the modern natural law edifice that is the post-World War II human rights movement, are built using vague, comparatively indeterminate and amorphous rights entitlements, protections and guarantees which are enunciated up in the Olympian heights of moral abstractions. These rights are not self-defining. For the vast preponderance of cases that reach the highest judicial bodies the language of the right – the moral guarantee – does not determine the outcome. In applying the broad rights guarantee to the specific dispute before the court, the judge's morality and moral sentiments and moral judgments will matter; they will matter a lot. And recalling that the rights in a bill of rights – either implicitly as in the US or explicitly as in Canada and Europe – are rarely, if ever, absolute but are limited and abridged by what is thought reasonable in a free and democratic society changes this not a whit. Here, too, it will be the judge's views of what is reasonable – a moral and political call without doubt – that prevail.

Hence one inescapable question that pervades discussion of bills of rights is whether we want judges' morality to prevail, and irrebuttably so in the case of constitutionalized versions. That question, in some circumstances if not others, will be answered differently by the Legislator, the Bad Man, the Sanctimonious Man, the Law Professor, the Concerned Citizen and the Judge. Yes, we could add the Puzzled Man and the Apathetic Man, and others too, to that list. For the weak-rights consequentialist in a Benevolent Legal System, whether she wants the judges' morality to prevail will depend upon whether that delivers better consequences – after factoring in institutional-competence arguments and balance-of-power considerations and any benefits and drawbacks related to 'who decides' or the perceived legitimacy of the decision making process – than letting the elected legislators' morality prevail. That boils down to saying that the amorphous rights entitlements in a bill of rights only deliver good consequences if the point-of-application judges' interpretations of them in the specific cases that arise deliver better consequences, on average, over time, all things considered, than what would have been the case in the absence of that bill of rights.

Again, vantage will matter in making that calculation.

Let me finish these concluding remarks, and the book, by doing two final things. The first is to answer a question that may well already have struck the reader, namely, what is my preferred vantage. Now I have suggested already that in one sense this book has been an extended argument for understanding and conceiving of law from vantages other than that of a top appeal court judge. But the question here is asking for more than that.

Some might therefore think I am at this point required to commit myself to some Grand Theory or other and expand on how, say, non-cognitivism or moral scepticism is more plausible than moral realism and how utilitarianism – for all its well-documented faults – offers an inter-subjective standard of good and bad that allows escape from Bentham's feared sympathy and antipathy, 'I like it' and 'I don't like it' slough of raw subjectivism. But I think that sort of demand for a Grand Theory in this context, as I made clear at the very start of this book, is misplaced. I say that even though I have offered something more or less in that vein myself in the past.[1] One can urge the benefits of moving away from the Judge's Vantage, at least sometimes, without having to commit oneself to some fully worked-out deontological or consequentialist or any other philosophical theory.

Yet even disavowing the need for some sort of Grand Theory to buttress my arguments about vantage, there is nevertheless a sense in which I do need to tell the reader my own preferred vantage. Of course once you ask that question about my preferred vantage you soon realise the query is ambiguous. It is ambiguous because one can answer on the first-order plane of what is the best vantage point from which to think about law's relation to morality or about bills of rights or about anything else I have discussed in this book by shifting between vantages. Alternatively, the question can be taken on the second-order (or meta) plane of what vantage is best for thinking about how the first-order vantage you choose affects one's preparedness to want to separate law and morality or to forswear a bill of rights or what have you.

The demand to know my preferred vantage on the first-order plane is not terribly interesting. As I have made clear throughout this book, different vantages often produce different outcomes or judgments and there is no reason why one cannot shift between vantages in considering issues such as those discussed in this book. That is true even if, like me, one is disposed to prefer first-order vantages other than the judge's more often than not. There is no reason I can think of for having to stick with just one vantage when thinking about law or the rule of law or moral input at the point-of-application or anything else already discussed in this book.

The far more interesting question is the one on the second-order plane. From which vantage am I writing when I look down, move between, and compare what is likely to be thought from the Bad Man's Vantage and the Judge's and the Visiting Martian's and the Concerned Citizen's and all the others? On the first-order plane, vantage point can simply mean, or be shorthand for, the point of view of the typical sort of person holding that job or that outlook or filling that social role. On the second-order plane, though, vantage refers more to what is being given normative value. And in that sense the answer to this question is that my second-order vantage in this book is clearly that of the consequentialist. It

---

1   See my *A Sceptical Theory of Morality and Law* (New York: Peter Lang, 1998).

is the consequences of citing foreign law or of opting for democratic decision making or of aiming for a diversity of interpretive approaches on the bench or of adopting a bill of rights or of puncturing moral windbags that I aim to discover by shifting between the vantages of the Law Professor, Bad Man, Judge, Visiting Martian, Omniscient Being, Concerned Citizen and Sanctimonious Man. That is what underlies my claims and conclusions in this book, and they will appeal to the extent one likes or condones that second-order vantage.

Of course any underlying version of consequentialism and aiming to hunt out likely best consequences is no straightforward proxy for the Visiting Martian's descriptive, empirical, outside-observer outlook. Yes, there are elements of that. But it meshes well in part, too, with the Bad Man's amoral outlook, provided one restricts the consequences that matter to those valued by that Bad Man. Likewise the Concerned Citizen's Vantage can be a wholly consequentialist one when it comes to normative values. It *can be*, but it does not have to be. Some Concerned Citizens will be consequentialists, some will not. Indeed to some extent all the vantages I have used can adopt this second-order value framework.

Notice, too, that this distinction I have drawn between first-order and second-order vantages makes clear how I can move back and forth between a variety of vantages on the former plane, more or less as mood and circumstances dictate, without being open to criticism that I am picking and choosing and changing my underlying normative framework.

Put slightly differently, I am not here offering an advisory opinion on what is the best legal theory or what has the most beneficial consequences for society. If anything, I am hoping to show that any such claims on behalf of an indivisible construct such as 'society' are implausible. I am forswearing the Grand Theory but nevertheless hoping to offer the reader some thought-provoking insights into the issues I have discussed. Being able to move between vantage points is a tool to help provide those insights.

I mentioned above that before finishing there were two final things I wanted to do, and the second of those is to end with a short dialogue that raises some of the aforementioned issues and concerns in a more abbreviated and possibly accessible way. Imagine an after-dinner conversation between people who personify the vantages employed in this book. After a good dinner and a few drinks, while still sitting around the table, one such conversation might proceed as follows:

Judge (named Judy):

> Trying to keep law separate from morality is near-on impossible in my line of work. When I decide the cases that come before me the source-based, or officially recognized, valid rules leave me with scope to decide for either of the litigating parties. What tilts the balance in the case is some value-based judgment of mine. What's the best interpretation, say, of some rights guarantee? Or is there room for the federal division of powers to allow the central government to pass this particular law? Or is that 30-year-old precedent binding on me? I'm always

bringing a host of ought-judgments – *my* ought-judgments that not infrequently differ from those of my fellow top judges – to bear in coming to a conclusion as to which party will prevail. And so for me, in my line of work, it's quite easy to elide law and morality, 'law as it is' and 'law as it ought to be'.

Visiting Martian (here played by an Overseas Sociologist named Max):

Of course, Judy, you make the mistake commonly made by those in the judiciary of forgetting about selection bias. You sit on the top court in the land. The cases that reach you are those cases in which the parties are prepared to spend considerable amounts of money and huge dollops of time. It's hardly surprising, then, that in the handful of cases you hear each year both sides have an arguable case – that the established body of law leaves you with scope to decide either way. From the fact that there is that sort of uncertainty in the 30, 50 or 100 disputes you help resolve each year nothing at all follows as regards the millions of other disputes that occur each year across the country. These cases you hear are self-selecting. They may well just be failures in the system, in the sense that they raise issues which the laid-down rules do not clearly resolve. It's hardly surprising, in other words, that in your job at the apex of the court system you feed on a steady diet of cases in which the legally mandated outcomes are uncertain.

Concerned Citizen (named Kane):

I suspect, Max, that these cases look like failures in the system to us, but not to Judy. To Judy they are her life's work. I also think, Max, that you understate the causes of why there is uncertainty as to outcome in the cases Judy regularly hears. It's not just because these are cases that throw up fact situations where the legal rules – the language used to enunciate these legal rules – do not clearly apply. Sure, there may sometimes be that sort of uncertainty, and hence discretion for Judy. But there is also moral dissensus. People disagree about values. Even judges disagree. Even Judy and her eight colleagues disagree. And that means that there can also be uncertainty as to outcome any time a legal rule makes reference to an indeterminate moral standard – take the right not be subject to an unreasonable search as an example. In fact take any of the provisions of any bill of rights as an example. The uncertainty as to outcome flows from the fact that human beings disagree about what should and shouldn't count as an unreasonable search, or permissible free speech or unacceptable religious practice.

Bad Man (named Oliver):

I don't have any trouble at all keeping law and morality separate. Or rather, the only morality that interests me in the slightest is Judy's. What I want to know is what the law lays down. Nothing more. I don't care in the slightest what Kane or anyone else thinks is morally acceptable or repugnant. I do care, however, about avoiding legal sanctions. As far as I can tell, Kane's moral evaluations and judgments are wholly irrelevant to that, save that he gets a vote every few years to elect law makers who might, just possibly, enact laws motivated by his sort of moral preferences. Judy, however, has convinced me that her moral sentiments can matter a lot. She's in the unique position as a top judge of being able to bring her moral views to bear to reach outcomes in specific cases. I don't care in the least if what Judy is doing is filling in gaps where the law is silent, or is some more interpretive exercise, like writing the tenth chapter of a chain novel. The simple fact is that her moral sentiments sometimes matter to me in a way that Kane's, and for that matter near-on everybody else's in society, do not. Her 'oughts' count when I think about law, but Kane's don't.

Kane:

I don't have any trouble separating law and morality either, but not for the amoral, immediately self-interested reasons Oliver gives. I'd actually like the laws of my legal system to improve over time. They're not perfect now, that's for sure. It's extremely useful to keep 'what the law is' distinct from 'what I think it ought to be'. That enables me to push for reform. And let's be clear Judy, in a way you often are not, that no non-judges get to infuse their moral judgments and preferences into the task of deciding what the law is. We ordinary citizens have no input into the interpretive task at all. Zero. Our only input occurs at the legislative stage, in voting for legislators and pushing for change. For all of us non-judges, the H.L.A. Hart view of the legal world looks most apt and accurate. There are identifiable legal rules. There may even be a few identifiable standards. Sometimes, though, applying those rules to the facts in dispute will not determine an outcome, even in the sense that most well-informed people would agree what it should be. In those cases, Judy, you and your colleagues can do whatever you can get away with. All that succeeds is success, though there may be good pragmatic grounds for you to pretend that the answer you give was always the indisputable one.

Judy:

It never feels that way to me. I never feel that law is whatever I say it is, even in what Max calls the self-selecting 'failures in the system' cases I hear each year.

Legislator (named Jeremy):

I wonder if there's not, perhaps, a tad too much deference to the judiciary these days. Certainly Judy has no more moral expertise than I do or Kane does. Her moral antennae are no better than ours. You could hardly suppose that a few years of law school and a decade or two of legal practice before becoming a judge makes someone more morally attuned – gives them a pipeline to God about where to draw highly debated and contentious lines pertaining to social issues such as who can marry, when speech can be curtailed, whether girls can cover their faces at school because of some religious precept, how to treat would-be immigrants, and so on and so on.

Judy:

It's an institutional thing, Jeremy, not a personal thing. I don't have to cater to voters every few years the way you do.

Jeremy:

It's those voters you say I'm catering to who are the ones who come up big in moral crises Judy. They're the ones whose actions (as opposed to speechifying words only) tend to look good in hindsight. It's not the likes of you and me Judy. Anyway, what makes you think the plumbers and secretaries who elect me are any less morally attuned than a lawyer or judge? That whole institutional argument rests on implicit assumptions of fact. But those assumptions are never cashed in. We never get any empirical data backing them up and showing that the costs of bill of rights judicial review are worth it because judges with life tenure both *a)* do stand up to the majority in times of moral panic and *b)* do not over-reach themselves in normal times.

Max:

If the judiciary's role really were best justified on some institutional, or checks-and-balances, basis, then I can't see why there shouldn't be a need for a qualified majority before striking down a statute. You could have a rule that required 7 of 9, or even 8 of 9, judges to think a statute unconstitutional before it would be held invalid or struck down or re-written. The idea would be that it's much easier to justify the counter-majoritarian aspect of striking down the elected legislature's enactment when you can't get even 2 or 3 judges out of 9 to uphold it. If we really do want some sort of institutionalized check on the majority – something in addition to federalism and bicameralism – then it strikes me it will amount to some version or other of the 'puke test'. This law is so egregious it makes me want to puke! And if that's what we want from a few ex-lawyers not accountable to the voters, nothing more, then let's require that a supermajority of them feel that way.

Law Professor (name Ronnie):

I don't agree at all. People know that slavery is wrong or bear-baiting is wrong not simply because they happen to feel that it is. It would be wrong even if every other person on earth thought it was okay.

Max:

But not, Ronnie, if that person making the evaluation herself thought it was okay. Surely that would just be plain out weird. 'I think or feel that bear-baiting is morally okay – but it's actually not okay.' There's a bit of sleight of hand at work here with these transcendent claims once they're disconnected from a theistic God or from the whole natural law edifice.

Ronnie:

No, there isn't any sleight of hand. But let me finish. In the kind of moral world I think exists, a deontological moral world where there are mind-independently right moral answers and choices, the post-World War II renaissance of natural law thinking in the shape of human rights law is only to be welcomed.

Kane:

Personally, I'd be inclined to say that this natural law edifice delivers good consequences if and only if the judges do. And that is in no way a foregone conclusion. Moreover, there are consequences other than the direct 'what's achieving the best outcome in this case' ones that need to be considered. There are the consequences related to how a decision was made, those tied to the legitimacy of the process used, that also must be factored in. I'm sure that Jeremy and I (and maybe even you too Ronnie if you thought about decision making in your law school and thought of the dean as a proxy for the judiciary) could point to a variety of potential bad consequences flowing from abdicating final decision making to an unelected judiciary – consequences that are the effects of this sort of process, regardless of whether judges are thought to get the outcomes right more than anyone else would. Jeremy and I could point to voter apathy, growing cynicism about democratic politics, the temptation for politicians to take irresponsible positions (think of flag-burning in the US) knowing the judges are standing behind them to overrule them, the inevitably huge focus that will come about on how judges are selected, the even more elevated position in society that lawyers, judges and even law professors will win, all the various lost republican virtues associated with an involved citizenry, the plausible claim that on many issues there is wisdom in numbers, and more. Once we start talking consequences, then these ones need to be counted too. And that's what most bill of rights proponents signally fail to do.

Jeremy:

Well, I certainly think that a bill of rights, any sort really, looks better from Judy's vantage than from mine.

Max:

Really? It's you legislators Jeremy who enacted statutory versions in the UK and New Zealand. In fact judges are never the ones who bring these instruments into being. They just operate them. It's not their fault one happens to be in place.

Kane:

Okay. But they are the ones who decide how they will operate it – how they will interpret its provisions. And some choices are notably more deferential to democratic decision making than others.

Oliver:

From my perspective, I like the idea of a bill of rights making it easier for me to avoid the sanctions of the law. But I don't like the prospect of it doing so for others.

Max:

Well, I've got to leave in a moment. And all this bill of rights talk really does get tiresome. They have become the flavour of the day, bills of rights. Every well-off democratic country has one, except Australia. I agree that the standards such instruments enunciate in the language of rights are indeterminate and vague. I agree they cannot be taken literally or absolutely. And I agree that they hand considerable line-drawing social policy-making power to the point-of-application judges. But outside of Australia, all of this is quite moot. Or does one of you actually foresee the possibility of a bill of rights being repealed somewhere in the democratic world? No, I didn't think so. The only practical issue, at least for the present, is how best to interpret them. Some approaches will limit what the judges can do, and the scope the judges have to make determinative their own second-order moral input, more than others. But that's a debate that takes it for granted that Judy's 'oughts' will count for more than Kane's, whatever its resolution.

Selected Bibliography

Alexander, L. (ed.), *Constitutionalism, Philosophical Foundations* (Cambridge: Cambridge University Press, 1998).

Alexander, L. and Schauer, F., 'Is Policy within Law's Limited Domain?' (2007) 26 *University of Queensland Law Journal*.

Alexander, L. and Sherwin, E., *The Rule of Rules* (Durham, NC: Duke University Press, 2001).

Allan, T.R.S., *Constitutional Justice, A Liberal Theory of the Rule of Law* (Oxford: Oxford University Press, 2001).

Bentham, J., *An Introduction to the Principles of Morals and Legislation,* edited by J.H. Burns and H.L.A. Hart (London: Athlone Press, 1970).

——, 'Anarchical Fallacies', in J. Waldron (ed.), *Nonsense upon Stilts* (London: Methuen, 1987).

——, *A Fragment on Government*, edited by J.H. Burns and H.L.A. Hart (Cambridge: Cambridge University Press, 1988).

Bix, B. (ed.), *Analyzing Law* (Oxford: Clarendon Press, 1998).

Campbell, T., *The Legal Theory of Ethical Positivism* (Aldershot: Dartmouth, 1996).

——, *Prescriptive Legal Positivism* (London: UCL Press, 2004).

Coleman, J. (ed.), 'Incorporationism, Conventionality, and the Practical Difference Thesis' (1998) 4 *Legal Theory*.

——, *Hart's Postscript* (Oxford: Oxford University Press, 2001).

Dworkin, R., *Taking Rights Seriously* (London: Duckworth, second impression, 1978).

——, *Law's Empire* (Cambridge, MA: Belknap Press, 1986).

——, 'Objectivity and Truth: You'd Better Believe It' (1996) 25 *Philosophy and Public Affairs*.

——, *Freedom's Law* (Cambridge, MA: Harvard University Press, 1996).

Dyzenhaus, D., 'Positivism's Stagnant Research Programme' (2000) 20 *Oxford Journal of Legal Studies*.

Finnis, J., *Natural Law and Natural Rights* (Oxford: Clarendon Press, 1980).

Fuller, L., 'The Case of the Speluncean Explorers' (1949) 62 *Harvard Law Review*.

——, 'Positivism and the Separation of Law and Morals – A Reply to Professor Hart' (1958) 71 *Harvard Law Review*.

——, *The Morality of Law* (New Haven, CT: Yale University Press, 1969).

Gallie, W.B., 'Essentially Contested Concepts' (1965) 56 *Proceedings of the Aristotelian Society*.

George, R. (ed.), *Natural Law Theory* (Oxford: Clarendon Press, 1992).

Goldsworthy, J., *The Sovereignty of Parliament* (Oxford: Clarendon Press, 1999).
——, 'Legislative Sovereignty and the Rule of Law', in T. Campbell et al. (eds), *Sceptical Essays on Human Rights* (Oxford: Oxford University Press, 2001).
Hart, H.L.A., 'Positivism and the Separation of Law and Morals' (1958) 71 *Harvard Law Review*.
——, *Essays on Bentham* (Oxford: Clarendon Press, 1982).
——, *Essays in Jurisprudence and Philosophy* (Oxford: Clarendon Press, 1983).
——, *The Concept of Law* (Oxford: Clarendon Press, 1961; 2nd edn with a Postscript 1994).
Holmes, O.W., 'The Path of the Law' (1897) 10 *Harvard Law Review*.
Honderich, T. (ed.), *Morality and Objectivity* (London: Routledge and Kegan Paul, 1985).
Huscroft, G., 'Thank God We're Here: Judicial Exclusivity and Its Consequences' (2004) 25 *Supreme Court Law Review*.
——, 'The Trouble with Living Tree Interpretation' (2006) 25 *University of Queensland Law Journal*.
Huscroft, G. and Brodie, I. (eds), *Constitutionalism in the Charter Era* (Markham: LexisNexis, 2004).
Kay, R., 'Adherence to the Original Intentions in Constitutional Adjudication: Three Objections and Responses' (1988) 82 *Northwestern Law Review*.
——, 'Judicial Policy-Making and the Peculiar Function of Law' (2007) 26 *University of Queensland Law Journal*.
Klug, F. and Starmer, K., 'Standing Back from the *Human Rights Act:* How Effective Is It Five Years On?' [2005] *Public Law*.
Kramer, M., 'Also among the Prophets: Some Rejoinders to Ronald Dworkin's Attacks on Legal Positivism' (1999) 12 *Canadian Journal of Law and Jurisprudence*.
——, 'Dogmas and Distortions: Legal Positivism Defended – A Reply to David Dyzenhaus' (2001) 21 *Oxford Journal of Legal Studies*.
Lacey, N., *A Life of H.L.A. Hart* (Oxford: Oxford University Press, 2004).
Leiter, B., 'Legal Realism and Legal Positivism Reconsidered' (2001) 111 *Ethics*.
Lyons, D., 'Utility and Rights', in J. Waldron (ed.), *Theories of Rights* (Oxford: Oxford University Press, 1984).
Mackie, J.L., 'The Third Theory of Law', in J. Mackie and P. Mackie (eds), *Persons and Values* (Oxford: Clarendon Press, 1985).
McGinnis, J. and Somin, I., 'Should International Law be Part of our Law?' (2007) 59 *Stanford Law Review*.
Paulson, S., 'Formalism, "Free Law", and the "Cognition" Quandary: Hans Kelsen's Approaches to Legal Interpretation' (2008) 27 *University of Queensland Law Journal*.
Posner, R., 'The Problematics of Moral and Legal Theory' (1997) *Harvard Law Review*.
——, '2004 Term Foreword: A Political Court' (2005) 119 *Harvard Law Review*.

Postema, G., *Bentham and the Common Law Tradition* (Oxford: Oxford University Press, 1986).

Raz, J., 'Incorporation by Law' (2004) 10 *Legal Theory.*

Sen, A., 'Democracy as a Universal Value' (1999) 10 *Journal of Democracy.*

Schauer, F., *Playing by the Rules* (Oxford: Clarendon Press, 1991).

——, 'Judicial Supremacy and the Modest Constitution' (2004) 92 *California Law Review.*

——, 'Book Review – (Re) Taking Hart' (2006) 119 *Harvard Law Review.*

Simmonds, N.E., 'Law as a Moral Idea' (2005) 55 *University of Toronto Law Journal.*

Sinnott-Armstrong, W., 'A Perspectival Theory of Law', in Tom D. Campbell and Jeffrey Goldsworthy, *Judicial Power, Democracy and Legal Positivism*, (Aldershot: Ashgate Publishing, 2000).

Smith, S., *Law's Quandary* (Cambridge, MA: Harvard University Press, 2004).

Tamanaha, B., 'The Contemporary Relevance of Legal Positivism' (2007) 32 *Australian Journal of Legal Philosophy.*

Tushnet, M., 'Scepticism about Judicial Review: A Perspective from the United States' in T. Campbell et. al. (eds), *Sceptical Essays on Human Rights* (Oxford: Oxford University Press, 2001).

Twining, W., 'The Bad Man Revisited' (1973) 58 *Cornell Law Review.*

——, 'The Great Juristic Bazaar' (1978) 14 *Journal of the Society of Public Teachers of Law.*

Waldron, J., 'The Irrelevance of Moral Objectivity', in R. George (ed.), *Natural Law Theory* (Oxford: Clarendon Press, 1992).

——, 'A Right-Based Critique of Constitutional Rights' (1993) 13 *Oxford Journal of Legal Studies.*

——, *Law and Disagreement* (Oxford: Clarendon Press, 1999).

——, 'Ego-Bloated Hovel' (2000) 94 *Northwestern University Law Review.*

——, 'Eisgruber's House of Lords' (2002) 37 *University of San Francisco Law Review.*

——, 'Foreign Law and the Modern *Ius Gentium*' (2005) 119 *Harvard Law Review.*

——, 'The Core of the Case against Judicial Review' (2006) 115 *Yale Law Journal.*

Whittington, K., 'The New Originalism' (2004) 2 *Georgetown Journal of Law and Public Policy.*

Index

www.ingramcontent.com/pod-product-compliance
Ingram Content Group UK Ltd.
Pitfield, Milton Keynes, MK11 3LW, UK
UKHW020352010325
455677UK00021B/424